And be home before dark

And be home before dark

A childhood on the edge of nowhere

ROLAND ROCCHICCIOLI

Hardie Grant Books

Published in Australia in 2008 by
Hardie Grant Books
85 High Street
Prahran, Victoria 3181, Australia
www.hardiegrant.com.au

All rights reserved. No part of this publication may be reproduced, stored in a retrieval system or transmitted in any form by any means, electronic, mechanical, photocopying, recording or otherwise, without the prior written permission of the publishers and copyright holders.

Copyright © Roland Rocchiccioli 2008

The moral rights of the author have been asserted.

National Library of Australia Cataloguing-in-Publication Data:

Rocchiccioli, Roland.
   And be home before dark: a childhood on the
   edge of nowhere/Roland Rocchiccioli.
   Edition: 1st ed.
   ISBN 9781740665513 (pbk.)
   Subjects: Rocchiccioli, Roland.
   Entertainers – Australia – Biography.
   Boys – Western Australia – North-eastern Goldfields
   – Biography.
   North-eastern Goldfields (W.A.) – Biography.
791.092

Jacket and internal design by Luke Causby/Blue Cork
Typeset by Kirby Jones
Printed and bound in Australia by McPherson's Printing Group

10 9 8 7 6 5 4 3

This book is dedicated to the memories of
Beria and Ginger, and my brother Lewie.

Beria May Stammers
Born in Beria, Western Australia, 6 May 1911,
died in Melbourne, 25 May 2007.

Nello Giuseppe (Ginger) Rocchiccioli
Born in Magliano, Italy, 10 February 1909,
died in Kalgoorlie, 15 October 1972.

Lewie Roccheccioli
Born in Wiluna, Western Australia, 4 November 1933,
died in Perth, 18 January 2006.

'Each has his past shut in him, like the leaves of a book known to him by heart; and his friends can only read the title.'
VIRGINIA WOOLF

From wherever you were in Gwalia you could see, in the cloudless blue sky, the trail of black, sometimes white, smoke from the tall black chimneystack of the Sons of Gwalia goldmine. For the ten years before I was sent away to boarding school it was the epicentre of my childhood universe. The regular roar of the gold-bearing ore spilling into the crusher was as comforting as the heartbeat of a mother.

The open cut on the mine was a hole in the ground almost a mile across and hundreds of feet deep. It was so big feral goats and pigeons lived on the slopes and in the caves. The first time I saw it I was with my mother, Beria. We were walking down the block to the store. I was holding her hand and my grip tightened. 'It's alright,' she told me. 'It's nothing to be scared of. Just don't let me catch you going anywhere near it, because if you do, and I find out, you'll get a bloody good hiding.'

The kids were always being told to stay away from the open cut – not that they took any notice. I don't know exactly how deep it was because I was never game enough to look, but the other kids did. It was surrounded by a three-strand wire fence and in the school holidays we played there all the time; some kids sat on the edge of the pit with their legs hanging over the side. The miners kept a look out and chased them. 'Hey, you little bastards, get the hell out of here; and if we catch you again you'll get a bloody good kick in the arse!'

When two of the big kids climbed down the ropes and followed the tunnels to the number one and four levels of the main shaft where the men were working – digging and blasting for gold – the miners were waiting for them. They waited until the kids had gone past and then made a bang which frightened the hell out of them. The kids came racing out of the tunnel and climbed up the ropes like hairy-arsed mountain goats. It didn't stop them. The next week they were back doing the same thing. They reckoned I was a sissy because I stayed back near the fence, well away from the edge, and ran home when they threatened to dive into the open cut and kill themselves. I didn't care about their threat. I was worried what Beria would do if it came to light I was there when they jumped.

Every weekday at lunchtime, Ante (Tony) Baletich set off the blasting in the open cut, shattering the silence of the town. Our dog, Puppy, hated it. But he wasn't the only one. So did every other dog in the town. As soon as they heard it they all started barking. The fur on Puppy's back would stand on end and he would charge down to the corner of the yard near the 44-gallon drum rubbish bin. He wouldn't stop barking, no matter what. Some kids tried to see how close they could get as the dynamite was going off but I wasn't game enough. I knew if Beria found out, I'd be in trouble. Having been warned once, I'd get a belting.

Tony Baletich worked in the open cut for years and was a friend of both Beria and her de facto, and later husband, Steve Salinovich. Like a number of men on the goldfields, Baletich left a wife and children in Yugoslavia, and never contacted them again. From where we lived, and no matter where I was headed, I usually had to walk past his place. It was down behind the Co-Op store amongst a cluster of two-room camps a short distance from Grinning Joe's house, where we lived. If he saw me passing, Baletich called out, persuading me to come inside. In the summer he slept on his central verandah with both doors open. His bed was the only place on which to sit, and no matter how far away I positioned myself he soon started rubbing my groin and masturbating himself, coercing me to do it for him. Before I left, Baletich always gave me money and told me not to tell anyone or I would be in trouble. This went on until I was old enough to threaten him with telling my father. When I did pluck up the courage my father spat in my face. 'You're bloody rubbish,' he said, 'nothing but a mobile brothel.' It was never mentioned again.

The Sons of Gwalia mine was one of the few incline workings in the world. At a 40 degree angle, the main shaft drove 3778 feet into the earth's crust. The men worked from twenty-eight levels, 100 to 200 feet apart. From the edge of the landing platform where they clambered in and out of the steel underground skips, you could peer into the inky-black nothingness. The constant flow of fusty hot air brushing your face was heavy with the caustic lime residue from the miners' carbide lamps.

The other kids, boys and girls, fell over each other trying to get to the edge of the shaft. Not me. My legs remained stiff as I shuffled forward, my feet heavy and glued to the ground. The straddling base of the sinister wooden poppet head stood like a giant four-legged colossus – a looming monster – guarding the entrance to Hades. Topped by two eight-foot spoked steel wheels, over the top of which ran the two-inch wire rope which pulled and lowered the skips and ore trucks, it was the tallest structure in my life. The single safety rail, the fragile barrier between me and the centre of the earth, was worn smooth and shiny over the years from the touch of hundreds of miners. Feet away from the gaping hole, I shuddered and backed away in exactly the same fashion I had approached. The other kids couldn't understand why I didn't want to go underground, and on the rare occasions of a tour I went missing without a word of explanation, or a moment of regret. Bob Tagliaferri was an underground machine miner for fourteen years. My father taught him, and Bob considered the Sons of Gwalia one of the worst mines in Australia. 'It was hot, humid and dangerous.'

The shaft had a fresh-air ventilation system but the men worked without any form of dust protection. When they came up from underground at changeover time, their faces, necks and arms were black. A lot of them ended up with silicosis or miners' complaint – 'dust on the lungs'. A few, like my father, also developed tuberculosis, which they sometimes passed on to their families. I was told you could catch it if you shared a cracked teacup or drank from the same waterbag.

In order to catch the slightest breeze, the one-gallon reinforced heavy-duty duck-canvas waterbag hung from a steel butcher's hook just inside the verandah back door. In the summer my father filled it every morning before leaving for work and the cold water lasted for the day. The waterbag was fitted with a cork on a string and had a round glass pouring spout in one corner. The taste of the water was pleasantly tainted by the canvas. My father always drank straight from the bag. He held the spout several inches away from his mouth, pouring and swallowing with a gurgle. I was so perturbed by his cough I couldn't bring myself to drink from the bag, preferring the garden hose or the brass tap in the washhouse. The other kids put their mouths over the tap, but I never did in case there was a red-back spider inside the tap and I swallowed it.

When my father coughed, it came from the soles of his feet. The debilitating coughing fits were exacerbated by years of smoking roll-your-own cigarettes, which he made from blocks of Log Cabin fine-cut tobacco and Riz La cigarette papers. Every night after tea he sat and filled his tobacco tin, breaking the strips of tobacco from the block and rolling them in his palms, one hand on top of the other. With the first intake of smoke he coughed, frenziedly. His face turned puce, his eyes streamed, and he battled to catch his breath; the veins on his neck stood out. He coughed so hard I thought his lungs would burst. He brought up solid lumps of thick, bright green phlegm which he spat into the burning wood fire. The sound of it sizzling on the coals turned my stomach. When the coughing stopped it took him some minutes to regain his strength and catch his breath.

When I was four, by which time my parents were living apart, I sat on the kitchen floor, listening in as Beria recounted every detail of the underground accident. At about eleven o'clock on Friday, 1 June 1951, three men were killed and one had his foot crushed by the trailing skip when the connecting toughened steel chains snapped at the twenty-fourth level. Bob Tagliaferri remembered it well. 'I was working on the twenty-sixth level and I heard the roar as the skip went careering past, crashing into the wall at the bottom of the shaft on the twenty-eighth level.'

Ettore Zanni, twenty-five, and Angelo Grazioili, fifty-eight, were working at the bottom of the shaft. Caught between the wall and the runaway skip, they took its full force and their bodies exploded on impact. The other men picked up their remains by hand and brought them to the surface in six or seven chaff bags. They managed to identify Zanni from part of his hand and a signet ring he was wearing, and Grazioili from his grey hair on a small piece of scalp. The two men were buried three days later by Father Spain from the St Francis of Assisi Catholic Church, Gwalia. The mine was closed for the day and all the men of the town marched behind the hearse on the three-mile journey to the cemetery.

The third man killed, Ivan Kouzmin, was from Belarus, married with four children. Standing well over six feet tall, the impact of the skip compressed his chest and he died instantly. Mrs Kouzmin was at the shaft when they brought his body to the surface. She was wearing a brightly embroidered Russian peasant blouse which became stained with his blood when she cradled his head in her arms. She took the blouse off and used it to cover his face. Mrs Kouzmin prepared her husband's body for burial and wouldn't allow anyone else in the morgue to touch him. She dressed him in his best suit and took him back to their house, laying him out in the front room, his coffin surrounded by lighted candles. For four days she held a prayer vigil until he was taken by train to Perth and buried in the Karrakatta cemetery. Mrs Kouzmin travelled in the guard's van with the coffin. Soon after that the Kouzmins left the town.

The survivor, Michael Januzkiewcz, together with his wife Anna and their three children, only arrived in Gwalia in 1951, from their native Belarus, via India and Rhodesia. When the Russians occupied Belarus, Anna and her family were transported for three years to Siberia. Mr Januzkiewcz had been working underground on the Sons of Gwalia mine for two weeks and was sitting with one leg stretched over the rail track when the skip hurtled past, running over his foot.

The underground was fitted with an alarm system which ran from the winder room and was attached to the wooden supports running down the shaft. When the supports were knocked out, the alarm went off, allowing the winder driver to stop the skip and blow twelve blasts on the steam whistle to alert workers and everyone in the town to an accident. The skip travelled at such speed it sometimes derailed, and the men had to physically lift it back onto the narrow gauge rail track.

News of the accident spread fast. Dr Harry Moore, the resident physician and surgeon, went underground to bring the patient to the surface. Mr Januzkiewcz's foot was crushed to a pulp inside his boot and the leg bones were cracked. In a state of shock, he was taken by ambulance to Leonora District Hospital, two miles away.

Dr Moore and his nursing-sister wife Helen were a popular couple and he was much admired for his skill in the operating theatre. For six months of the year Helen was acting matron and the hospital's only theatre sister. When Dr Moore arrived in Leonora there was no blood bank and he set about establishing a revolutionary donor list. He located and listed a number of universal donors – blood group O negative. Mr Januzkiewcz had lost a third of his blood supply, and before he could operate the doctor called in four donors to each give the patient a pint of blood. It was a basic procedure. The mixed blood of the donor and the patient was examined under a microscope. If it didn't clot he went ahead with the transfusion.

For eight hours the doctor and matron worked to save Mr Januzkiewcz; several times they thought he was going to die. It was early evening before the patient was transfused, stabilised, and ready to be wheeled into theatre. Dr Moore admitted to being nervous. He had never done an amputation and had to read up on the procedure in a medical book.

The operation took two hours, during which time he monitored the patient's condition by checking the pupils of his eyes. Assisted by the matron and a fifteen-year-old nursing aide who stayed outside the sterile area, Dr Moore amputated the leg below mid-calf, using his father's surgical instruments from the Boer War. Mr Januzkiewcz remained in hospital for two years, going home on the weekends. His wife came to see him in hospital every second day. Eventually he was fitted with an artificial leg and returned to a surface job on the mine, his limp barely discernible.

I was friends with the Januzkiewcz boys, John and Stanley, but I was wary of their father. He was surly, short and stocky, and brutal.

The family did as he said, without a word of argument. He hit his wife – 'he was a very hard man' – and belted both his sons. One of John's minor indiscretions resulted in a violent thrashing using a length of rubber hosing. John was about twelve at the time, tall and solid for his age, but he stood, doubled over, crying and screaming out in agony. He was too frightened to run away.

Mrs Januzkiewcz spoke little English and her only outing was walking to the shop. She was kept busy in the house coping with her children, ducks and chooks, sweeping the enormous yard, and tending the large vegetable garden and the grape and passionfruit vines. For two years, Tommy and Eric, a couple of Dutchmen, boarded with them. Mrs Januzkiewcz did all their cooking, cleaning, washing and ironing, including their work clothes from the mine. She didn't have a washing machine and everything had to be boiled or hand-washed.

Sometimes during the school holidays I went to play at their place. It was mostly cowboys and Indians; running around and pretending to control a sixteen-hand stallion and shooting Indians. Somebody always had to be the girl and, since I was blonde and small and not interested in shooting the redskins, it was always me.

We galloped over the top and around the base of the purple dumps – two sunbaked, cracked slagheaps down by the gravel football oval. Behind them was the Co-Op store rubbish tip, a shallow hole in the ground where they burnt jarrah and cardboard packing boxes, and damaged tins of food which expanded in the heat of the fire. We rummaged around in the ashes, looking for the apricot, dark plum and raspberry jam, and the condensed milk, which we opened with a screwdriver and a rock. We ate the jam with our fingers and sucked the thick condensed milk from the tin through a small hole.

Mr Januzkiewcz's 'wooden leg' was stored under the double bed on the front verandah. Moulded from flesh-coloured plastic with leather straps and numerous metal attachments, the sight of it sticking out of the shadows, permanently fitted with a sock and shoe, gave me the creeps. Mr Januzkiewcz also walked using two crutches and, when he was not around, John and Stanley would chase me across the yard and out into the road, waving their father's leg in the air. They laughed and teased me. 'Look out, you sissy,' they shouted. 'We're going to get you with the wooden leg!'

The sons of Gwalia mine employed about 160 men, with about seventy working underground on the day shift. Before he got a surface job, my father was one of the best machine miners; the rest were pick-and-shovel men, who cleared the rubbish, or mullockers, whose job it was to fill in the stope which stopped it from collapsing after the gold-bearing ore had been carted away. In some spots the tunnels were so narrow the men crawled to the rock face. In the late 1950s it was decided to mine using the 'room and pillar' system. Two tunnels were constructed a distance apart and connected by a series of independent dugout rooms. Pillars, the same size as the rooms, were left between to support the roof. In the second stage, the rooms were filled in with carted ore and the pillars were mined. This was the most dangerous period as the filling ore was not as tightly compressed and rock falls were common.

The miners worked eight-hour shifts, and depending on the size of the stope they worked alone or in pairs. Each miner carried a two-gallon waterbag. The men out on the wood line cutting the mulga filled their bags with three parts water and one part red wine, as a thirst quencher. The miners lost so much fluid in the underground heat the management provided salt tablets. On every second or third underground level, the men had a crib room cut into the shaft wall with electricity connected for light and hot water. One day Jacky Prince brought saveloys for his crib and boiled them in the urn. When the other men went to make a cup of tea, the water ran red. Some men carried their crib packed in a tin lunchbox which looked like a child's small school-case; others used one of the discarded black cloth dynamite bags. To keep it away from the cockroaches and mice, they tied the cloth bag with a length of greased wire and hung it in the air from an exposed pipe.

Up until 1955 the Sons of Gwalia used horses underground to pull the ore trucks. Their stables were cut into the walls of the shaft. The abundance of chaff and manure provided a perfect breeding ground for cockroaches. One first-time miner reeled when a workmate kicked a solid-looking twenty-foot post and it shrank three inches in diameter as thousands of resting cockroaches darted for cover. Entire rock faces were carpeted in cockroaches and millions of them had to be poisoned with a spray of one part DDT and five parts kerosene. The poisoned cockroaches headed for water and blocked all the underground pumps; the water storage dam was coated one foot thick with dead cockroaches.

There were about thirty horses underground at any one time. They were a mixture of broken-down racehorses, draughthorses and ponies, which were bought from a knackery in Perth and transported by train to Gwalia. Until they were ready to be taken underground they lived in stables on the side of Staff Hill. A couple of times a week while Beria was ironing in one of the staff houses, I walked to the stables and stood at the railings, watching. It took only a minute for the horses to come foraging for food.

To move them underground took up to twelve men. The horse's legs were tied with ropes, which the men pulled until the animal toppled sideways onto a tarpaulin, which they used as a sling to lift it onto the wooden trolley. The trussed horse was then secured and taken underground. Often, by the time they arrived at the designated level, the men would have to help the horse to its feet because its legs would have cramped from tethering. The horses were well cared for but doomed to a life of darkness and hard work, sometimes for as long as two or three years. One miner, George Stokes, worked with the same horse for eleven years.

A horse's life expectancy was determined by its continuing strength to haul an ore-filled truck. They were worked hard, performing the heavy tasks which otherwise would fall to the miners. There was no protection and a few were crushed by falling rocks or runaway trucks. Living in the damp heat, they developed respiratory problems. On being brought to the surface their nervous systems reacted violently to the fresh air and sunlight, blinding them and bringing on a slough which caused their fur and several layers of skin to fall away. In most cases their sight returned in a few days and the horses were fattened up and sent back to work underground. Those beyond treatment were killed, usually with a bullet to the head.

It was hard to recognise one man from another as they came up from underground. They wore identical helmets, dungaree trousers and collarless short-sleeved thick grey flannel shirts to absorb the perspiration. Some of the men's working clothes were so patched, little of the original fabric remained. Beria spent part of every Sunday darning Steve's working clothes in readiness for Monday morning. In the damp underground they used waxed matches to light their hand-held carbide lamps, which gave off a cloying acrid smell that caught in the back of your nose and throat, and no matter how much you hawked and spat, the metallic taste contaminated your mouth. The lamps were dangerous, causing fires and sometimes burning the men – seriously. Each lamp had a reflector behind the bare flame to help project the light forward. The residue from the reacted carbide, a wet paste of caustic lime, was toxic to animals. In the mid-1950s the carbide lamps were replaced by battery-operated helmet lights.

My ears pricked up if I heard Beria say: 'Someone had an accident on the mine today.' Danger was an everyday part of our lives. Some wives developed a sixth sense and knew of an accident before they were told. The eight-inch sticks of dynamite were protected in black cloth bags and tightly packed in sawdust. The purpose-built nail-free pine crates, black stencilled *HIGHLY EXPLOSIVE – HANDLE WITH CARE*, were held together by dovetail joints. The mine's armoury and chemicals were stored in a 200-yard tunnel driven into the base of a rise on the far side of the mine, away from the town, and protected by a chained and padlocked galvanised-iron and cyclone-wire gate.

The rounds of 100 detonators came in black glossy three-inch tins. The lids were difficult to remove, intentionally. My brother Lewie was about eleven or twelve when he, Ken Winter, and a couple of others kids pinched some detonators from the mine in Agnew. Nita was only about four at the time. They lined the detonators up on the railway track, then told Nita to hit them with a hammer to detonate them. Beria heard about it when the policeman came knocking on the door. 'I nearly died when he told me what they'd been up to. Nita could have killed herself, or anything. She's lucky it didn't blow her hand off. God, did I give Lewie a hiding; I took to him. I don't think he could sit down for a week when I'd finished with him.'

I was not allowed to touch anything on the mine, and although my curiosity almost got the better of me, I didn't dare. One day somebody spotted me eying a pile of discarded tins and asked, 'Hey, Snowy. Do you want one of these tins?' It was what I had been waiting for. 'Oh, yes please.' He threw me one. The lid was covered in fine white print. I sat and read the story of the Swedish scientist Alfred Nobel, who discovered dynamite, his lifelong regret at the devastation it caused, and the establishment of the Nobel Prize. Just as I finished reading my father arrived. I jumped up, and holding his big rough hand, and clutching my treasured tin, we set off for home.

My mother, Beria May Stammers, was born on 6 May 1911, in Beria, a goldmining town just outside of Laverton, 250 miles north of Kalgoorlie – the richest mile of gold-bearing dirt in the world.

Laverton had the reputation of being the wildest town in the west. At one time it was claimed the only person in the cemetery who died of natural causes was a six-week-old baby. Beria was named after the mine, an Aboriginal word meaning 'large open field'. My grandfather, Charles Lochfyne Stammers, was a miner who died in the Laverton hospital from hepatitis when Beria was six weeks old. He was thirty-four and came from Matlock, Victoria. Beria always believed he died on the mine: 'Les Mead was the publican at the Murrin-Murrin hotel, and he told me he saw them bringing Dad's dead body up from underground. So I'm buggered if I know.'

My mother's family origins are clouded and involve an extravagant tale of aristocrats, sexual tomfoolery, distant sea voyages and an identity swap. My great-great-grandfather Kelly was supposed to have committed a serious social faux pas with a servant girl in the late 1800s. In disgrace, he was bundled onto a ship and banished to the colonies. On the journey he befriended a young man who died and was buried at sea. With a beer or two under his belt, my garrulous great-great-grandfather delighted in regaling his family with details of how he swapped his papers with those of his dead friend, changing his name from Fitzroy-Harvey to Kelly. He landed in South Australia and, with his new identity, established a life for himself. The Fitzroy-Harvey family had an estate in Scotland which shared a boundary with Glamis, the childhood home of Queen Elizabeth, The Queen Mother. Great-great-grandfather Kelly said he was born in Clapham, London, and never bothered to explain his heavy Scottish brogue.

At the time Grandfather Stammers died there was no insurance or compensation so the miners passed the hat around and collected £100. My grandmother, Sarah Stammers, packed up her five children and moved to Kalgoorlie, where she worked for her mother, Mary Anne Coveney, who ran a boarding house, Whitlow House, located behind the Halfway Hotel on the Boulder Road.

My great-grandmother Mary-Anne was born in South Australia in 1858. A tall, thin, dour woman with a strident personality, she spoke her mind. My great-grandfather James was convinced of her numerous infidelities, and spent much of his time spying on her. A devout Christian woman, she grew tired of his baloney and after a couple of years sent him packing with a hefty divorce settlement.

Without fail on Saturday morning, great-grandma Coveney gave my aunt Silvia sixpence and sent her to collect her weekly supply of beer, which the barman poured into a crudely made billycan fitted with a wire handle. On the way back one time, Silvia was swinging the can in a full circle without spilling a drop when the flimsy wire handle gave way. She stared in disbelief as the billycan flew through the air, landed with a splat, and the amber liquid soaked into the thirsty red earth. Great-grandma was livid that she had to go the whole week without.

Great-Grandma Coveney wore the uniform of a woman in service – a long black skirt, a long-sleeved blouse with a lace high collar and cuffs, and an enormous cameo at her throat. Until the end of her life she dressed in black, raising her hemline only slightly. She died from cancer, nursed by her daughter – my great-aunt Gladys – in the front room of her house in Boulder, the twin town of Kalgoorlie. She had an open wound and the doctor was summoned when the pain became too acute. He spoke to the family before asking them to leave the room. Doctor and patient spent some time alone and her death came soon after.

My grandmother, Sarah Stammers, was a secretive woman who kept her personal business private. Not even her sister Gladys was privy to the detail. Grandma never remarried but she had two more children after my grandfather died. My Uncle George – who was known as Billy – was born in November 1914. Sarah never revealed the identity of the father, and in court documents she nominated my grandfather, who had been dead for three years, and not William Crook, who is whispered to have been Billy's father. My aunt Edith was born in 1917. Her father was an Italian soldier stationed in Kalgoorlie for a couple of months during the Great War.

For a time before the Stammers children were removed by the court, they were cared for by Bessie Jordan, who owned a sweet shop on the Boulder block. However, they were deemed to be neglected and on 26 May 1916, at the Children's Court in Kalgoorlie, three weeks after Beria's fifth birthday, she and my aunts Dorothy Olive Elizabeth, Silvia Thelma, Mary-Anne Annie and Linda May, along with uncle James Robert Charles and baby Billy, were declared wards of the state and placed under a term of detention until the age of eighteen. They were declared to be in moral danger even though the magistrate made a point of declaring Grandma Stammers to be a woman of sober habits. My grandmother believed her mother was to blame for the children being taken away from her.

Beria and Billy went first to a receiving home in Subiaco, while my four aunts were sent to the Salvation Army homes. The Great War in Europe had been raging for two years, and as a wartime precaution the girls were housed in Collie, a coalmining town 125 miles from Perth. My uncle James was sent to the Swan Boys' Home on the banks of the Swan River and soon lost contact with his family. Beria never saw or heard from him again. What became of Billy also remains a mystery, although it is thought he was adopted. After an unsuccessful fostering, Beria was sent to join my aunts – rejected, she thinks, because she wet the bed.

At the end of the Great War, in November 1918, three of the girls were transferred to the Salvation Army home in Broome Street, Cottesloe. My Aunt Dorothy – who was known as Ollie – was put into service, while Linda was sent to a home in Gosnells. Over the years the sisters lost contact, and I never met my aunts Ollie and Linda. Beria was under the control of the Salvation Army home for thirteen years, and during that time no one ever hugged her. 'There were about 100 girls and six officers at Cottesloe. They used to wear big white starched aprons, and across the front was embroidered "All For Jesus". We lived in two houses; the front one was called Kia Ora. It had a ballroom and a tower, which was out of bounds. We used to sneak up there and look over the side, watching the other girls running around looking for us.'

The officers at the home considered the name Beria unsuitable and changed it to Beryl. It was 1954 before she learned her name was Beria. Grandma Stammers came to visit twice while her girls were in the home. When she was leaving at the end of one visit an officer told Annie to kiss her goodbye. 'No, why should I?' she said. 'I don't know her; she's not my mother.'

Beria remembers a couple of the officers as being vicious. 'Agnes was a teenager who ran away, and when the police brought her back a couple days later they were waiting for her. Boy, did she cop a hiding. Captain Thorne was a big fat thing, and she and her mate took Agnes down to the laundry. One of them held her mouth shut so she couldn't scream, while the other one thrashed her with a piece of harness.'

When Beria was accused of breaking another girl's bottle of lavender water, she was ordered to see Matron Rubina Pratt. She was a tall, thin woman – a real sourpuss – and the kids were scared of her. Beria was only about seven or eight and she was so frightened that she wet herself while she was waiting in the hall. 'Matron Pratt called me a thief and a liar, and as a punishment they locked me in the officers' bathroom for a week, except for school. I had my mattress on the floor and they brought my meals on a tray. No one ever owned up, but I just hope the little bitch who *did* break it rots in hell.'

They had their own school in the grounds and Beria loved singing and poetry. 'I always wanted to be a hairdresser, but they weren't interested. The only thing they taught us was needlework and housework. The day you turned fourteen was the day you left school. Then for two years you worked full-time on a three-monthly roster, without pay, in the laundry, the kitchen or the sewing room.'

Soon after her sixteenth birthday Beria was sent to work for Mrs Cotter, just around the corner from the home. 'I was the live-in housemaid. She paid me seven shillings and sixpence a week. She kept five shillings to pay for my clothes and board and gave me two and six. I used to get a half day a week off, and I'd go back to the home to see my friends and have a meal.'

Beria worked for Mrs Cotter for two years without a holiday: 'I suppose I must have, but do you know, for the life of me I can't remember having a bath in that time.' She shared a bedroom with Mrs Cotter's daughter, sleeping in the corner behind a curtain. Mrs Cotter's widowed brother-in-law and his two kids were living with her at the time. He was about thirty and a labourer on the Fremantle wharf. 'Mrs Cotter didn't know, but he used to give me a shilling a week if I let him touch me. I had no idea what was going on, and to tell you the truth I'm not sure he got his money's worth. They never told us anything about the facts of life in the Salvation Army home. We were innocents when they sent us out into the world.'

In May 1929 Beria turned eighteen. She gave Mrs Cotter a week's notice, and when she asked for any money owing to her, Mrs Cotter said, 'There isn't any, it's all been accounted for – to the penny.'

My aunt Annie was a quiet little thing, who rarely spoke out of turn. When the Salvation Army put her out to work she was sent to a family with two teenage sons. She wasn't even seventeen when she got pregnant. One of the sons – they're not sure which one – was the father. She was five months gone when they sent her to Hillcrest to wait for the baby. Her best friend from the home, Bella, was there in the same condition. The husband from the house where she was sent got her pregnant. The Salvation Army tried to force Annie to give the baby away but she refused. 'No,' she said. 'He's mine, and I'm keeping him.' She called him Ivan, and for years she paid a foster family to look after him while she worked.

In 1931 Beria went to live with her mother in a house in Egan Street, Kalgoorlie, and met her sister Edith for the first time. Beria had a couple of jobs but she really wasn't all that interested. She worked for a time in a sweet shop but got her nose out of joint when the owner chipped her for eating the stock. 'If that's how you feel you can make up my pay right now,' Beria said. 'I'm leaving.'

Taken aback, the owner said, 'It's busy, you can't leave now.'

However, Beria had made up her mind. 'Who says I can't? I'll do what I bloody well like, and you can stick your job up your arse.'

It was a stormy relationship between Beria and her mother. They argued about Beria's wild lifestyle. After years of being locked up she was enjoying her first taste of freedom and the companionship of men her own age, who found her irresistible. For a while in Kalgoorlie she went out with Slom Sunter, a good-looking policeman with a lady-killer reputation. 'He wanted me to go with him all the time, and he got really wild one night when I said no.' Early in 1932, Beria and her mother had another serious falling-out. When two men offered her a lift to Wiluna she accepted. As she walked out the front door she said, 'Goodbye, Mrs Stammers.' Wiluna was 200 miles north of Kalgoorlie, and within days of arriving she found work as a housemaid in a boarding house. It was Beria's job to make the beds, clean and help with the cooking. Josie, a half-caste Aborigine, did all the washing and ironing.

Beria met her sister Ollie in Wiluna. She was married to Jack Mowlan, the blacksmith on the mine. He was an alcoholic. One day Beria went into the local haberdashery to buy some dressmaking material. A woman followed and asked her name. When Beria wanted to know why, the other woman said, 'I'll tell you why. My name's Ollie, and if your surname is Stammers I reckon there's a bloody good chance we're sisters.' Ollie told Beria later, 'I recognised you straight away. You look exactly like Mum.' Beria was twenty-one and it was the first time they'd met since they were separated sixteen years earlier.

They had a wind-up gramophone in the dining room of the boarding house and Beria used to play a song called 'She's Everybody's Sweetheart and Nobody's Gal'. Sergio Gherardi, who lived at the boarding house, hated it. Whenever she put it on, he would come and turn it off. 'Eh, who the hell do you think you are?'

Beria told him, 'Just mind your own business and leave it alone. If you don't like it, don't listen. No one's forcing you.' And she'd put it back on again just to annoy him. Sergio was nice-looking, not very tall, with dark wavy hair. Beria didn't like him much to begin with, but eventually they started talking: 'I don't know how but one thing sort of led to another and I took up with him in the end. We were together for seven years.'

My brother Lewie was born at the Wiluna hospital in November 1933. They named him Luigi after Sergio's father back in the old country. Beria didn't know at the time, but Sergio had a wife back in Italy and another son, also called Luigi, who was born a few months after Sergio arrived in Australia in 1926. He never talked about them, and to the best of Beria's knowledge he never sent them any money or saw them again.

My father, Nello Giuseppe Rocchiccioli, was born in February 1909 in Magliano, a small Tuscan village where his family had been shepherds and subsistence market farmers for nearly 400 years. My grandparents and my seven aunts and uncles lived in a two-storey, five-room stone cottage with an outside bathroom and lavatory. During the summer my father tended the milking sheep and worked as a field labourer in the surrounding market gardens. The harsh winters came early and the days were short. The sheep were kept sheltered in an area under the house. The warm air rising from them provided a form of household heating.

My grandfather Pellegrino's first wife died, leaving behind four children – my aunt Caterina and uncles Angelino, Pietro and Antonio. Pellegrino began a relationship with Giovanna Pedrini, who was seventeen years his junior. They never married but had two children – my father Nello and my uncle Flavio. In accordance with Italian law,

Grandfather Pellegrino adopted both boys. He also adopted Maria Pedrini, the daughter of his unmarried sister-in-law, Genoeffa. My sister Nita looks exactly like Maria.

My father and two of his village friends sailed from Genoa on the *Palermo* and disembarked at Fremantle on 28 December 1926. The trio planned to work for six months, save their money and return home. My father had left behind a fiancée in the village. To pay for the trip, Nello borrowed £40 from my maternal great-grandfather, Giuseppe Pedrini, with a promise to repay it on his return.

As fare-paying passengers, my father and his friends weren't bound to work as indentured labourers on one of the Australian government building and construction projects. Experienced market gardeners, they soon found work in Wandering and at York, south-east of Perth. As employment became more scarce my father decided to try his luck in the goldfields. Leaving his two friends, he headed for Kalgoorlie, and then further inland to the North-eastern Goldfields. The three men lost contact. Unlike his two friends, my father never returned to Italy.

My father's nickname, Ginger, came from the colour of his hair. He was five foot seven and a half inches tall with grey eyes, a scar on his right forearm and a skin tag on his upper left eyelid. He was muscular and well shaped and walked with a distinctive gait – flick-kicking his knees. His hands were enormous and rough, and his fingernails were circular in shape. Three-quarters of his arms, his face and his neck were deeply suntanned; the rest of his body was milky white. He only wore his false teeth on special occasions.

Nello Rocchiccioli had been living in Kalgoorlie for several years when the Australia Day riots broke out in 1934. He had a room at the All Nations boarding house, not far from the Home From Home Hotel, where it all began. 'It was the only time I have ever been scared that something was going to happen to me,' he said later. 'I thought I was going to die. It's why we took off and hid in the bush.' It was more than a week before it was considered safe for my father and other Europeans to return. He lost all his belongings in the fires that accompanied the riots. From there he moved to the Boulder Hotel as a permanent boarder.

My parents met at the Duke of Cornwall Hotel, Boulder, at Christmas 1937. Beria, Sergio and Lewie were there on holiday. At the time, they were living in Riverina, a small mining settlement just outside of Menzies. A few months after Beria and Sergio went back to Riverina, my father arrived and asked Beria to live with him. They seemed to get along okay so Beria said yes. They left by train. Sergio was on the day shift, and by the time he arrived home Beria and Ginger were gone. She took Lewie, and didn't even bother to leave a note.

They went first to Laverton, and then moved on to nearby Lancefield, where my father found a job on the mine. My sister Nita was born at the Laverton hospital on 1 August 1939. Four months later my parents were married at the Beria state school, according to the rites of the Roman Catholic Church. Before meeting my mother, my father had had a long-term relationship with a part-Aboriginal woman, Tessa, who worked as a prostitute at one of the brothels in Kalgoorlie. He proposed a couple of times but she said no.

I was born at 9.03 pm on 20 February 1947 in Agnew, a goldmining shanty town with a population of about 200, located 600 miles north-east of Perth, on the south-west edge of the desert named after the British monarch Victoria, who according to one of my royal books, 'Wrought Her People Lasting Good'.

An arid and sparsely populated region of sandhills, spinifex, mulga and salt lakes, the Great Victoria Desert covered 265,000 square miles.

With an average rainfall of eight to ten inches, and fifteen to twenty spectacular thunderstorms each year, the winters were brief, and by September the summer temperatures and scorching north winds arrived. The summers of my childhood lasted for eight months. According to Beria you put your shorts on in October, and you wore them until the following May. Like all desert regions, the nights were cold and in winter it was freezing. First thing in the morning, it was not unusual to find ice on top of the water in the fowl house. I had to crack it so the chooks could drink. 'How many times do I have to tell you? Don't eat the ice off the chooks' water. It'll make you sick,' Beria said.

I was born at home in a typical goldfields miner's camp – galvanised iron lined with hessian, sitting close to the ground on mulga stumps with tin caps to stop the advancing white ants, which ate everything – even the grapevines and the fig trees. The two-room camp had a latticed back verandah with a bathroom at one end, and a bedroom at the other for Lewie and Nita. The kitchen had a wood stove and there was running cold water in the bathroom; the washhouse and pan lavatory were a short distance from the back door. Wherever she lived, Beria always had chooks.

I was due on 27 February, and arrived a week early on the hottest day of a month-long heatwave. It was 115 degrees Fahrenheit. Beria intended to take the Dove aircraft to Leonora the following Saturday and had already sent our suitcase ahead on the mail truck. Fortuitously, she kept a couple of nappies behind. That evening she noticed the sun was a spectacular red ball as it dipped towards the horizon, turning the sky a brilliant magenta. It was about six o'clock when her waters burst and she went into labour. She was thirty-six. Beria sent fourteen-year-old Lewie racing across the flat, howling his eyes out, to call Mrs Hooker, the unqualified midwife and self-appointed bush nurse. Three hours later I made my entrance into the world, a long thin baby tipping the scales at eight pounds. My father was working underground on the Emu mine, and by the time he arrived home at midnight I was sleeping soundly.

The heatwave in Agnew continued, and by ten o'clock the following morning the temperature was already well into the nineties. Our house was on the edge of the town, out on the flat, and a fifteen-minute walk from the shops. I was thirteen hours old when my mother's friend, Mrs Saunders, insisted on taking me to the butcher's shop to be weighed. She wrapped me in a bunny rug and carried me outside into the sun. I sweated like a pig. The back of my neck was burnt and I got heatstroke. By the time we arrived back home I was screaming and couldn't be pacified. After a couple of hours they sent for Mrs Hooker. She spent the day and most of the night walking the floor, nursing and trying to soothe me. When my condition didn't improve it was decided early on Saturday morning that Beria and Mrs Hooker should take me to the Leonora District Hospital, ninety miles down the rough unsealed dirt track. One of the Lambert boys, whose father owned the general store, drove us there in the family's canvas-canopied car. As we came around the hill at Doyle's Well the heavens opened and the flash-flooding turned the road and creeks into a raging torrent, with water lapping at the running boards. Beria didn't think we'd get through.

I was still screaming when we arrived at the hospital. Dr Kristian Wilson took one look at me before turning his attention to Beria: 'You're a bloody fool, Rocky. Letting that stupid woman take your baby out in the heat at that time of day.'

'It's not my fault,' Beria protested. 'She's old. What could I do?'

'Of course it's your fault. You should have stopped her. He's your baby, Rocky, and now there's a bloody good chance he might die!'

We spent eleven days in the Leonora hospital. My survival is due entirely to the dedication of Dr Wilson and Matron Embling. The pair barely left my side in the first week, feeding me boiled water with an eyedropper and putting me in and out of a tepid bath. It was a week before Dr Wilson could confidently tell Beria I was in the clear. Beria couldn't stop crying and the doctor had tears in his eyes. 'Just don't do it again, Rocky,' he said, 'because next time we might not be so bloody lucky.'

My father brought Lewie and Nita when he came to collect us from the hospital. So he could keep an eye on me, Dr Wilson insisted we all stay for a week at May Hill's Central Hotel. On 13 March, at age three weeks, I was baptised by Father Keith Spain at the Sacred Heart Church, Leonora. He named me Ronald Arthur, which are not the names recorded on my birth certificate. Beria would have none of it when I told her years later. 'What are you talking about? Arthur! Of course I didn't christen you Arthur. It's a bloody awful name. I wouldn't dream of calling you that.' My name was Roland but Beria, and everyone else, called me Ronnie.

My godparents were the State Member of Parliament, Peter Coyne, and his wife Nancy. They took my parents and Father Spain for a meal at the White House Hotel, where they presented me with an EPNS spoon and fork set with Puss in Boots pressed on the end of the handle.

My father was not a naturalised Australian when Italy declared war on Britain and France in 1940. Following the lead of England's xenophobic prime minister, Winston Churchill, the Australian government rounded up all the resident aliens. On 23 June my father became an official Australian Prisoner of War, Number 12645, and was interned on Rottnest Island. The policeman who brought the news of my father's impending internment was a friend, who tried unsuccessfully to delay the inevitable. In the days leading up to his departure, my father had to sleep in the local hall with the other enemy alien men. Beria was legally required to report to the police once a week and not allowed to move between towns without permission. She was incensed by her treatment. 'They even came and took my fingerprints like I was a common criminal.'

When the government interned my father, Beria was left alone with no money and two children to feed. Nita was ten months old and Lewie was nearly seven. Beria took in washing and ironing and did what she could to make ends meet. Even though she was born in Australia and was a British subject, the federal and state governments refused to provide any financial support. 'Eventually they gave us a lousy pound a week. I'd like to see the politicians feed themselves and two kids on a pound a week.' The stores came out from town once a week by horse and cart. When she asked one time if she could pay next week the shopkeeper refused and told her to put everything back on the cart. She had no food that week.

While my father was interned, Beria began a casual relationship with a local man, Jack. He helped her with extra food and money, and handed over his food and clothing coupons and his ration card. Jack was not eligible for military call-up, having lost part of a leg in a mining accident. During the day he worked, driving his delivery utility, and came back to stay at night. Beria said: 'I can't remember his last name. And to tell you the truth, I don't think I ever knew.' When Lewie told Beria about the silver threepenny and sixpenny pieces he found on her bedroom floor, she demanded he hand them over. Lewie refused. 'If you take them I'll tell Ginger what I saw.' Tipping he had been peeping through her bedroom window, she grabbed a hold of one arm, belted him and took the coins as punishment.

For the duration of the war, Rottnest Island was an internment camp and declared off-limits. Eventually, the government provided some basic assisted accommodation in Fremantle, enabling wives and children to visit. For Beria it was impossible; she had no money and it was 600 miles away. Instead, she sent a fortnightly supply of Log Cabin tobacco, a packet of Craven A cigarettes – which my father smoked only on weekends and whose advertising slogan was 'For your throat's sake, smoke Craven A – they never vary' – and any spare food she could scrounge. Wartime rationing in the remote goldfields made it tricky to get hold of some goods, and shopkeepers kept luxury items out of sight, hoarding them for friends. Beria would have none of that, and insisted on being supplied.

When my father returned from the Rottnest POW camp the war was still in progress and he found it impossible to find work, even on the mine where he had been a top underground machine miner. It was policy to refuse employment to resident aliens, despite the shortage of manpower. Even those who had been friends before the war wouldn't help him and Ginger was forced to take whatever menial work came his way. Chic Cowan, a successful prospector, offered him a job processing the tailing sands from old Potosi goldmine in Yundamindera. Ginger worked on his own for eight hours a day, filling and emptying the sluice vats. He wore rubber boots and waded knee-deep in a water, cyanide and strychnine solution, not realising the constant exposure to the toxic fumes was damaging the delicate lining of his lungs.

Not much remained of Yundamindera, just two houses and the former hotel which was built from mud bricks and collapsed when damp leached through the walls. Chic Cowan, his wife and two daughters lived in the hotel, and the Crocker family in the other house. My parents moved into a basic two-room camp and slept in a separate flat-roof bough shed which my father built from mulga branches cut by hand and dragged from the surrounding bush. The thatched branches were wired to an iron frame he constructed from discarded half-inch water pipe. The kitchen had a dirt floor, and the second room, where Lewie and Nita slept, was covered in hessian and chaff bags. It had no running water or electricity, the lavatory was a hole in the ground with a board across the top, and Beria cooked outside on an open fire. 'I once spent three days making a batch of marmalade. When Ginger and the two kids didn't like it, I gave it to a couple of gins who came wandering by. The next day they came back and gave me a bunch of pink and white everlastings. They didn't speak any English, they just smiled at me. I kept those everlastings for years. It was the first time anyone ever gave me a bunch of flowers.'

Every second day my father walked a two-mile round trip to fetch a supply of fresh water, carrying it in two kerosene tins attached to a wooden yoke. He tied the tin to a rope which he lowered into a deep-crevice freshwater spring. Sometimes Beria went with him for a walk, taking Lewie and Nita along.

There were only nine school-age children in Yundamindera, leaving them one short of the required number for a permanent Education Department teacher. To satisfy the rules for an assisted school, Nita started school at three and a half. In February 1942, sixteen-year-old Gladys 'Trixie' Crocker, who had passed her Junior Certificate, was appointed a school monitor. To begin with, they used a room in the old hotel until Mr Crocker built a tin and mulga schoolroom next door to their house. Beryl Crocker regularly walked over to visit Beria, and the pair of them sat together, talking and laughing, and eating Milk Arrowroot biscuits which they dunked into a mug of cold water.

When the Potosi tailings ran out my parents had police permission to move to Murrin-Murrin, where my father found a job on the mine. Apart from the wood stove there was no form of heating inside their camp and the unlined tin kitchen was freezing. When Ginger was on afternoon shift, Beria and the kids were in bed by sunset to keep warm. The *Kalgoorlie Miner* serialised her favourite story, *Anne of Green Gables*, which she read by the light of a kerosene lamp. At night she had to cover the beds with chaff bags. Sometimes the frost was so heavy, when you woke up in the morning the top of the bed was coated with a thin layer of ice.

In December 1943, Ginger and Beria moved to Agnew. With a critical shortage of available men to work underground, my father finally secured a job as a machine miner. By the time they arrived in Agnew their marriage was in trouble. Unlike my father, Beria had a keen sense of humour. They stayed in Agnew for five years, during which time I was born. The war ended in August 1945 and my parents were now free to move around Western Australia and the compulsory weekly visits to the police station ended. The Italians in Agnew celebrated the end of the war with a dance on the salt pan. There was a shortage of men, so the women danced with each other. Beria had no interest in celebrating. 'Why would I?' she said later. 'Of course I was glad the war was over, but I had nothing to celebrate about. It was the hardest time of my life.'

A couple of ladies from the Country Women's Association persuaded Beria to join the local branch. My father resented her being away from the house and they argued. 'For God's sake, Ginger, give over, it went a bit longer than they expected,' Beria retorted. 'Anyway, it's once a month. What do you want me to do? Stay here all day, every day, on my own, out in the middle of the bush, with no one to talk to?' When he started to remove his leather working belt to give her a belting, Beria saw red. 'Don't you start that bloody nonsense with me. I'm telling you right now, Ginger. You try and hit me with that belt and I'll kick you in the balls so bloody hard. And don't think I won't.' It was the first and last time he tried that, but Beria stopped going to the Country Women's meetings. 'It wasn't worth the aggravation.'

In 1946, the year before I was born, my mother started an affair with Steve Salinovich, a Croatian miner eleven years her junior. Steve was seventeen when he arrived in Fremantle from Yugoslavia early in 1939, to join his father Mirko. Steve was born and raised in a Spartan mountain village outside of Split where the industrial and agrarian revolutions came to a standstill in the previous century. Subsistence farmers, they shared a village water pump and struggled to live off the land. Steve was six foot tall, slim and conspicuously handsome, with dark wavy hair which he oiled and parted in the centre. His father took him by train to Kalgoorlie, boarded with a Slav family and enrolled him at the Christian Brothers' college, with its reputation for strictness. He stayed for only two months. He spoke no English and the other boys lost no time in getting him to do the wrong thing, mostly ringing the school bell at odd times. The brothers were unaware of the pranks and, confused by the daily canings, Steve took his revenge. He gave the culprits a hiding and took off to join his father in Linden, a remote shanty settlement east of Leonora on the way to Laverton.

Mirko was working on his own, prospecting for gold, and he took full advantage of Steve's youth and strength. He worked his son like a slave, leaving him alone in the bush for weeks on end living in a one-room rusting tin shelter. Steve had no money, and were it not for his Uncle Vince he never would have survived. Steve soon found himself a girlfriend – a full-blood Aboriginal. When they had sex he put a bag over her head. Mirko had a hand-made shotgun which backfired in Steve's face, damaging his eyesight.

The affair between Beria and Steve began when he spotted her walking in the main street. Taken by her trim figure and her sassiness, he wolf-whistled. Beria responded with a barrage of verbal abuse and encouragement. As the weeks passed and the flirtation developed, she began looking out for him in the street. One day he called unannounced at the house while my father was at work and she could not resist his dark curly hair.

Their association soon became public, and when my father heard about it he and Beria argued. Beria took no notice and refused to stop seeing Steve. One time he called at the house when my father was at home, but he was not invited inside. He also visited while my father was on afternoon shift and Nita, who was seven, watched as he sat in my father's chair in front of the wood fire. Steve once brought me a bag of sweets. My parents' domestic problems were exacerbated by persistent rumours the Emu mine was about to close. Uncertain of the future, and unhappy at home, my father decided it was time for us to leave Agnew.

I was about eighteen months old when, in the middle of 1948, my father packed our belongings, including a dozen laying hens and a rooster, onto the back of the old Ford truck and headed for Leonora. He was driving on the wrong side of the road, and Nita, whose head was hanging outside, was almost decapitated when a truck passed on the inside. Beria pulled her back with less than a second to spare. 'It would have taken her head clean off,' she said.

Before we left Agnew, Beria told Steve of our plans and a few days later he followed, moving into the nearby boarding house run by Beria's friend, Mrs Saunders. Mr Saunders had been killed during the war. Although they were never married, Mrs Saunders went under his name and received a war widow's pension.

Leonora was built on the long gradient of Tank Hill, from the top of which you looked out across the town. My parents rented a house from their friend, May Hill, the licensee of the Central Hotel. The house was over the quartz rise behind the post office and on the open flat halfway to the railway station, and, conveniently for Beria, a two-minute walk from the back gate of Steve's boarding house.

The house was built from a combination of galvanised iron and asbestos cement sheeting. It had two bedrooms, a dining room and a kitchen. The top third of the walls and ceiling of the kitchen and dining room were blackened from a badly smoking chimney, which smoked out the house if the wind was blowing in the wrong direction. A bare light bulb, spotted with fly droppings, hung in the centre of each room. The burgundy cotton protection of the cords had begun to fray, exposing the rubber-coated electric wires.

The back verandah was partitioned into a kitchen at one end and a bathroom at the other. The kitchen measured eight by four feet, big enough for a small wooden table and two chairs, a kitchenette in the corner and an armchair in front of the stove which was set into the wall. The stove sat outside the footprint of the house and, because of the land's gradient, was raised about two feet in the air on the side of the building.

The hand-made bath was poured concrete and so deep the water came up to my chin. The central landing between the kitchen and the bathroom had a flight of wooden steps leading down to the washhouse, an open-fronted tin structure with two cement troughs and a corrugated-glass scrubbing board. The copper was at the bottom of the back-door steps and in the winter my father ran a bucket supply of hot water to the bathroom.

There was no plumbing and the water from the bath ran onto the flat, watering a clump of delicious wild berry bushes. The dark purple shiny fruit had a sweet yellow juicy pulp with tiny black seeds. I picked and ate them by the handful. The house had no fence and the ground was overgrown with weeds and littered with household refuse and general rubbish. After lunch, Nita and I lifted rocks looking for centipedes and spiders, tormenting and killing them with a stick. The front verandah was enclosed by a half-wall constructed from asbestos sheeting panels, several of which remained broken for years.

The large rectangular chookhouse was about fifty yards from the back door. Its gate had fallen away from the rotted supporting posts. The rusted and corroded shelters were made from cut-down rainwater tanks and cyanide drums. My father killed and ate the chooks when my mother left and the ground in the chookhouse became overrun with pig melon vines, which popped under your feet. The melons weren't poisonous but made you vomit if you ate them; even the chooks didn't peck at them.

At the far end of the chookhouse, in the corner, was the lavatory. The gap between the top of the curved roof and the top of the front and back walls was left open to provide an airflow. It also meant you got wet in the winter if the wind blew the rain in the wrong direction. A section of the pine timber floor had decayed and collapsed and the dark red paint on the door had faded to a pastel shade. For nine months of the year the unlined tin interior, warmed by the sun, acted as an incubator for the thousands of prickly, chirping brown crickets which covered the walls and roof. With their waving antennae, the highly sound-sensitive scourge jumped in every direction the moment you touched the door. Perfectly harmless, they jumped in your hair and on your arms. No sooner had they settled than they jumped around again when you got up to leave. They didn't seem to bother my father. I went inside, once, and fled in terror, covered in crickets and screaming and flailing about, trying to brush them away. It was the only time I saw my father laugh out loud. From that day I peed on the open flat, or squatted in the corner of the chookhouse to do my 'bigs', in full view of the kitchen window.

A few months after we arrived in Leonora my father bought a share in a small goldmining lease. The show was too far out of town to make a daily round trip so he and the five other prospectors camped in the bush, leaving us in town during the week and coming home for the weekend. While my father was in the bush Beria and Steve continued their affair. Lewie was fifteen and working at Sullivan's garage. One day he arrived home about five o'clock and went looking for Beria. From the kitchen he saw her with Steve down behind the woodheap, having sex. In the first half of 1949 Ginger's mining consortium was forced to sell to a man named Johnson. They had no way of knowing they were only feet and days away from a strike, and a lifetime of financial security. My father was philosophical. 'It didn't have my name on it.'

Following the sale my father moved back into town and went to work underground on the Sons of Gwalia mine. Everyone knew that Beria was on with Steve, but despite my father's objections she wouldn't end her association, denying it was a sexual relationship. 'You know what's wrong with you? You've got a dirty mind.'

Beria and Steve had an arrangement to meet outside the picture theatre every Saturday night. She became suspicious when Steve started making last-minute excuses. From the other side of the road Beria saw him arrive at the pictures with another woman. She waited and followed them, and from the shadows of the oleander trees at the corner of the state school yard she had a clear view of them having sex up against the wall of the Registry Office. Several weeks later Beria confronted Steve. He promised it was all over with the other woman because she refused to do his washing and ironing.

Beria held down three or four jobs at the same time. She worked five days a week as housemaid at the Central Hotel, polishing the linoleum-covered floors on her hands and knees. She started at 5 am and earned £2 a week. She hesitated when a church minister, a single man, offered her a cleaning job, but she accepted after a girlfriend explained: 'It's alright; he's one of those who goes with other men.' Beria was totally smitten with Steve and, while my father was away prospecting, she paid Steve a pound to stay home from work to spend the day with her.

Once a week I went with Beria while she did the ironing at Clover Downs sheep station. The owner, Jack Bell, sent a station hand into town in a utility to collect us. At the back of the homestead was a large lawn and a small flight of wooden steps leading onto a verandah. While Beria ironed I played outside with another boy who smelt of stale urine. I recognised him when I saw him a couple of years later. 'Ronnie, stop your staring,' Beria said when she saw me watching him. 'He can't help it; the poor bugger's simple.'

I was going on three years old when Beria took me into Maude Willis's small overstocked haberdashery and dress shop in Leonora. I was told to stand in the corner, wait quietly, and I was not to touch anything. A dress on a nearby rack caught my attention. Oblivious to a shop assistant watching, I reached out to feel the fabric: 'Hey,' she shouted, waving the yard-long wooden dressmaking ruler. 'You behave yourself, young man, otherwise I'll have to give you a big smack.' I pulled my hand back, stood still, and hardly dared breathe until Beria came for me. From that day on, the moment I realised we were going back into the shop I grabbed Beria by the hand, promising, 'I'll be good, Mum! I'll be good!'

※

In October 1949 Beria and Steve took Lewie and went to Kalgoorlie for three weeks, leaving me and Nita with our father. I was two and a half and Nita was eight. The three of them stayed with a Slav couple who ran a boarding house in Hannan Street. By chance, as it happened, Beria met with Prince, an Italian bloke who was her boyfriend for a year when she lived in Kalgoorlie in 1931. She had not bothered to tell Prince she was going to Wiluna and he spent several months trying to find her, not realising she was working as a housemaid in another town several hundred miles away. Prince told Beria he had been serious about her, and would have married her.

Beria didn't tell my father she was going to Kalgoorlie. Nita was at school and she left me for the day with Mrs Saunders, who broke the news to Ginger when he came home from work. The following day my father went see Father Spain, who made arrangements for the two of us to board with Elizabeth Ansley, a devout Catholic widow who was much lauded for her devotion to the church – especially for providing meals to the priest. To earn some extra money, she ran a boarding house for the boys attending the convent and whose parents lived outside Leonora.

Mrs Ansley was a large woman who lived in the old doctor's house at the bottom of Tower Street. Adjoining it was a disused grain shed, which was connected to the back of the house by a cement slab path and a trellis covered in grapevines. The distance from the floor to the ceiling of the unlined galvanised-iron shed was almost that of a two-storey house. Mrs Ansley had crudely converted this gloomy area into a dormitory by clearing a space and adding a number of beds, and this is where Nita and I slept. There were no other children staying and every night we were in bed before sunset. The grain store was also Mrs Ansley's storage area, and from my bed I could see into the open ceiling. She had a sizeable collection of dusty flags, bicycles, cane chairs and other paraphernalia, all suspended from ropes in the shadows overhead. In the gathering darkness I was sure the grotesque shapes came to life, moving and dancing about the ceiling and tormenting me. I slept with my head under the blankets.

Every morning we had a hard-boiled egg for breakfast. It was dry and difficult to swallow and, even though I gagged, Mrs Ansley wouldn't let us get down from the table until we had finished. At night, Nita and I had a bath together in a minimal amount of water. By the end of the first week I was fretting for my mother. My father visited us every day, and noticing my condition he took me to Dr Wilson, who insisted Nita and I be removed from Mrs Ansley's care.

Nita went to stay at the Dominican convent boarding facility and was the only girl who stayed over the weekend. Every Saturday afternoon Sister Mary Clement baked a sponge cake, which she filled with cream and jam, and gave Nita a huge slice. The cake was so light the other sisters called it 'fly-away sponge'.

I was taken to Gwalia, two miles away, and left in the care of Mrs Winter, or Wint as we affectionately called her, until Beria returned.

The situation at home was tense when Beria returned from Kalgoorlie. She and my father constantly hurled abuse at each other. Although they still slept in the same bed they were leading separate lives, with Beria coming and going as she wanted.

My father was friendly with an Italian couple, Mr and Mrs Fanetti, who called around to see him and discuss Beria's behaviour after watching her at the pictures with Steve. The simmering situation was resolved on a Saturday night in November 1949, when Beria left me at home with my father while she, Nita and Lewie went to meet with Steve at the open-air picture theatre. Unbeknownst to Beria, my father followed her. Having satisfied himself about the affair he went home. When the three of them returned he was waiting at the front door and refused to let them inside. His tirade of personal abuse was on the brink of turning violent and sixteen-year-old Lewie had to step between them. It was the first conflict between the two of them. My father agreed to let Nita into the house, but not Beria and Lewie, and flatly refused to hand me over. Beria was determined and became impatient. 'Now listen, Ginger. I'm not standing here arguing with you all night. I'm taking Ronnie with me, and there's nothing you can bloody well do about it. Either you hand him over or I'll knock you down. Now make up your mind.' My father knew Beria was not one to shy away from a physical confrontation and he offered no resistance as Beria and Lewie pushed past. It was well after midnight when we arrived at Mrs Saunders' boarding house. The next morning Steve took us to Wint in Gwalia. A few days later while my father was at work, Beria went back to the house and collected our belongings, including her Singer sewing machine.

We stayed with Wint until Steve found us a house on the edge of the town, almost to Halfway Creek, which marked the unofficial border between Leonora and Gwalia. Halfway Creek was dry except for about a month every winter when the rains turned it into a knee-deep waterway, spawning thousands of tadpoles.

While there was some ongoing acrimony, it took only a few months for my parents to resolve their major differences. Beria never denied my father access to me and Nita, and I saw him on a regular basis. When Beria asked for maintenance, they agreed on £1 a week for each child, which he paid fortnightly, without fail, bringing the money to the house on payday. He paid even when he was off work on compo. He also bought us clothes and never hesitated if we needed money.

Gwalia is the ancient Gaelic for Wales – a land famous for its dragons and its music. In Gwalia (pronounced Gall-ya), Western Australia, the air was awash with the constant drone of the mine's engines.

Washed by clear blue skies and nestled in the rocky ridges and the outcrops of Mount Leonora, Gwalia was a magical place – an isolated outpost where the passing of time and the beat of the town were determined by the rising and the setting of the sun and interrupted by the regular blowing of the mine's steam whistle and the blasting in the open cut. From the summit of Mount Leonora, the town site was a picturesque shanty settlement surrounded by an uninterrupted 360-degree horizon. There was something spiritual about the clear blinding light and the eerily silent bush. The sun rose over Mount Leonora and disappeared into the flat distant horizon, which stretched far away to the beyond. Whenever I went out to play, Beria warned, without fail: 'You behave yourself, and don't go getting up to any mischief. And be home before dark.'

I never did, and I was, always.

Needing to keep an eye on the sun, it was impossible to miss the brilliance of the sunset as the golden globe sank into the blazing red horizon, which was how I imagined the flames from the fires of hell to be.

The summer full moon was huge and sat high in the inky sky. It was so bright you didn't need a torch, which provided me with a sense of security. The stars were dazzling, and the Milky Way a constant source of wonderment. Its path streamed across the heavens and I marvelled at where it might lead. When I asked Beria, she said: 'Ronnie, how would I know?' The evening star, Venus, and the saucepan constellation, Pavo, were the only ones Beria knew, and she always pointed them out to me.

Gwalia is on the edge of the North-eastern Goldfields, 147 miles due north from the Kalgoorlie Golden Mile. The explorer John Forrest named Mount Leonora in 1869 while leading an unsuccessful search for the remains of the German explorer Ludwig Leichhardt and his lost expedition of 1848. In 1896 three prospectors discovered gold near the base of Mount Leonora and named the claim Sons of Gwalia in honour of the Welsh Tobias brothers – the Coolgardie merchants who funded them. They sold their claim to George Hall for £5000 and he recouped his investment in about one month.

The workers had no transport to take them to the diggings and, as the mine developed, the town was settled by squatters. It started as an assortment of tents, tin shelters, miners' huts and staff houses built around the lease. Even though the town was not officially gazetted, it had two government buildings – the post office and police station. It also had two firsts: a public swimming pool and a state hotel.

Throughout the 1950s the core population dwindled from about 1000 to around 400. The ebb and flow of transients was steady; they came from nowhere, sometimes created a bit of stir, and then, like the red dust willy-willies which blew up out of nowhere and stung your legs if you got caught in them, they disappeared without trace.

For anyone wanting to vanish, Gwalia was the last stop – a refuge for married men dodging alimony payments and wanting to keep one step ahead of their wives. The town was also a safe haven for a few nonconformists and recluses; they kept to themselves and were accepted as part of the community.

There was an unwritten law: If they didn't tell, you didn't ask. Single men arrived, and always with the same grand scheme – to save money and move on. During his three years as Gwalia policeman, Bob Primrose made a habit of meeting the train and casting a casual eye over the new arrivals, who sometimes numbered as many as twenty men, all looking for work on the mine. If someone aroused his suspicions, he made a point of striking up a conversation, even driving them to one of the boarding houses, all the while asking questions. Mr Primrose was strict but fair. A bit on the shortish side, he always wore the police uniform of khaki shirt and shorts, long socks and a white pith helmet, which caused some hilarity the first time he appeared in the public bar of the State Hotel. 'Oh gawd. Get a look at this, would ya.'

The bar went silent and Constable Primrose eyeballed a smirking customer. He asked his name and said, without a smile and holding the handshake: 'What's the joke, Andy?'

There was a moment of embarrassment: 'Nothing, really.'

Mr Primrose moved to establish his authority: 'You're not laughing at me, are you?'

Perish the thought. 'No … no.'

Mr Primrose had made his point: 'Well, I'm glad about that. I'm sure we both wouldn't want any misunderstanding to get us off on the wrong foot.'

Mr Primrose was known by the locals as 'Mister Bob', which came out of deference to his role in the town. He and his wife June had three children, one of whom was intellectually disabled. Their fourth child, a daughter, was born at the Leonora hospital. The infant suffered breathing problems and, despite the best efforts of Dr Morrison, she died within an hour of being born.

Dick Leaney, a bit of a card, nicknamed Bob Primrose 'the flower of the force'.

―――

The towns of Leonora and Gwalia were different in both style and spirit. Gwalia's population was 60 per cent Italian, 20 per cent Eastern European – with the larger percentage of the latter being Yugoslavs – and the rest 'Britishers'. It was a European community and the first stop for some of the new arrivals. At one time there were twenty-eight different nationalities working on the mine. After overcoming their culture shock they found friendship and security. For many it became their new home, while others stayed only a few months. The first group of displaced persons who arrived in the town were astonished when Vic and Melda Mazza allowed them instant credit in their shop; to book up and pay once a fortnight when they collected their wages from the mine. These poor souls, who'd lost everything in a devastated and war-torn Europe, were grateful for the trust and became loyal customers. The percentage of bad debts was minuscule compared to the amount of money they spent in the shop.

The Italians in Gwalia brought many of their traditions from the old country, and since they made up such a large percentage of the population the town was, in many ways, akin to an Italian village. They celebrated saints' and name days. Christenings, engagements, weddings and Christmas were all excuses for a party. The women cooked a feast of food and sweets from their own regions of Italy, which Australians soon came to appreciate and never knocked back an invitation.

The Italians painstakingly decorated the hessian and tin interiors of their houses with simple patterns from home. With no available stencils they improvised, carving a pattern into the face of half a potato which they dipped into a mixture of kalsomine and daubed the entire area. An intersecting diagonal theme appeared in a number of houses and soon became known as the potato pattern.

The Italian women put their energies into their houses and the preparation of food. Interiors, however basic, were immaculate. They brought from Italy a range of coloured glass and decanters, ornately embroidered tablecloths and lace-trimmed bed linen. Traditional 24-carat gold-trimmed coffee and liqueur sets were displayed on elaborate trays and used for special occasions. Collectables were housed on shelves. Framed hand-tinted and sepia photographs of parents, some of whom they never saw again, hung on the walls. They pointed proudly to scenes from the Italian villages and the countryside where they were born.

Leonora was the business centre and superficially more polished. It had a National Bank of Australasia, the Registry Office and Courthouse, a pharmacy, the telephone exchange, several halls, including the Freemasons and the Country Women's Association, St Catherine's Dominican Convent, the undertaker and fire brigade, and the municipal offices. Leonora tended to be more British. The White House Hotel was not for hoi polloi, and was where bridal parties went to have a celebratory drink after the wedding ceremony.

I couldn't walk past the two front windows of the chemist shop in Leonora without stopping to gaze at the range of upmarket jewellery and the selection of presents. It was where I saw the sugar Father Christmas which Beria bought for me, and which every year sat on top of her Christmas cake. The pharmacist, Mr Porteous, was an alcoholic – a problem attributed to his period of active service in the Second World War. Everyone felt sorry when Mr Porteous, dressed in full army uniform with a baton tucked under his arm, marched back and forth outside his shop, shouting commands at the top of his voice. Mr Porteous had been a major during the war, and under the influence he argued he outranked Dr Moore, who had only been a captain, and was therefore better placed to know which drugs patients should be taking. On occasion he refused to fill scripts as they were written. It was good fortune which saved Bernice Quarti. Puzzled by the medication, she telephoned Mr Porteous, who, in a sober state, advised her to tip the potentially fatal medicine down the drain.

Gwalia sprawled over approximately three square miles of cleared bush and the remaining scrub grew to the back fence of houses perched on the edge of the township; some were completely surrounded. Narrow corrugated dirt roads and long winding tracks picked their way through the low-lying brown and dark green vegetation. Paths crisscrossed through and around the shallow gullies and creeks, which ran fierce during the spectacular electrical thunderstorms that struck without warning. Spindly, stunted brown brush trees provided shelter for feral goats and kangaroos. Wild hops, native tomato bushes and saltbush shrub flourished. The quartz and rocky slopes surrounding the town sheltered brown centipedes, scorpions, red-back and trapdoor spiders, lizards, racehorse goannas and small insects. Fine red-gravel mounds surrounded the entrance to the dozens of red and black bull ants' nests. We knew from the local Aborigines – the Wongi people – that frenzied ant activity was an unmistakable indication of approaching rain. Crows, magpies, butcher birds, bronze-wing and top-notch pigeons, galahs, 28 parrots – more correctly the Port Lincoln parrot – and wedge-tail eagles flew about the town.

During the week it was an early start but no one needed an alarm clock. As the dawn broke the roosters in chookhouses across the town performed a contrapuntal fugue of crowing, signalling everyone to be up and about. The procession of men walking up the hill started from seven o'clock. Before he got the job on the wood line, my father left home at precisely ten past seven every morning. In high summer, the sun rose over Mount Leonora a little after 5 am. In the middle of winter it was as late as a quarter to seven, and disappeared at about a quarter past five. By nine at night, and certainly ten o'clock at the latest, most houses were in darkness. A quiet descended on the town. The streets were deserted except for those men making their way home around midnight after working on the afternoon shift, or a few stragglers returning from the pub.

The picture theatre operated on Wednesday and Saturday nights, and during the summer evenings the pool brought a little more activity onto the streets. On Tuesday and Thursday evenings many people went to the station to watch the train come in and have a chat with friends. It was also a chance to see who was arriving in town and what parcels people were collecting from the guard's van. Those people with post office boxes sometimes came out in the early evening to collect their mail.

∞

We lived in the house down near Halfway Creek for a few months and Steve came to stay every weekend. He nagged Beria about the long walk to and from the hotel and the betting shop. She agreed to move when he found a house just around the corner from the Co-Op, the butcher's shops, the picture theatre and the Catholic church, and only two minutes from the State Hotel and the betting shop where he spent all his spare time. A week or so after we settled in, Steve arrived carrying a small cardboard suitcase of clothes. He stayed, permanently.

The house, officially camp number 94 and with a rateable value of £12, was owned by Joe Radalj, a Slav friend of Steve's. Joe was an ungainly giant with an enormous frame, olive skin, large forearms covered in tight curly black hair, a shining bald head and an oversized, sweating moon face. He never stopped grinning, revealing a number of gold teeth. Beria took one look at him. 'God, it's Grinning Joe,' she said, and the name stuck. I thought it was his name and called him Mr Grinning Joe. Unlike his mate Little Charlie, who lived 100 yards away from us in the next camp, Grinning Joe was clean. He wore navy blue or bottle green workman's cotton trousers held up by a thick leather belt, a matching shirt and black working boots with reinforced toes and long leather laces.

Beria paid fifteen shillings a fortnight in rent for the four-roomed house and we lived there for five years. Grinning Joe lived in the next street and looked after any repairs. He came to collect the rent and if there was something wrong with the house Beria wouldn't pay him until it was fixed. She always inspected his handiwork to make sure it was done to her satisfaction. 'I'm not accepting that. Do it again, and I'll pay you when it's done properly.' The house was built on a slope and my bedroom was a step lower. Constructed from galvanised iron, it was lined with plasterboard and pressed tin ceilings featuring kookaburras on one, and an effigy of Queen Victoria on the other. I asked Beria about her. 'How the bloody hell would I know?' she said. I lay in bed staring and wondering: Who is she, and why is she on the ceiling?

The two larger rooms measured ten by twelve feet, and the smaller bedrooms eight by ten. The floors were laid with jarrah and it was Nita's job to hand-polish them – on her knees using Fisher's polish wax which was applied with a cloth, allowed to dry, and then buffed to a sheen. When she neglected to polish under the bed, ten-year-old Nita was made to do it again before she was allowed to go to the pool. Her tears bounced off the floor as she polished in the sweltering heat. Beria applied the same exacting standards to Nita as those the officers had applied to her in the Salvation Army home:

'If it's worth doing, it's worth doing properly.' Desperate to go to the pool, Nita pleaded: 'No one looks under the bed.' That wasn't how Beria saw it: 'I do, and that's all that matters.' Nita had an old pair of yellow woollen bathers which not only looked awful but they also itched, and were so heavy when wet they almost pulled her to the bottom of the pool. She grumbled and asked for a new pair, but Beria was indifferent. 'If you don't like them, don't go swimming.' Beria made her wait for a new pair.

Beria and Lewie shared the cost of furnishing the house. Between them they bought a kitchen table and four chairs, and a cream and green kitchenette with leadlight doors patterned from clear and emerald green dimple glass. Down one side of the kitchenette was a cupboard pantry. In the centre, next to the set of double drawers, was a tin-lined breadbox which caused the bread to sweat and created a pungent odour that tainted the bread with a slight metallic taste. When I complained Beria said I was talking bunkum.

She bought the four-piece bedroom suite – a double bed, a triple-mirrored dressing table and two double wardrobes – from an advertisement in the *West Australian*. It cost £30. The mesh wire base of Lewie's second-hand single bed had the spring of a trampoline but I only ever dared stand and bounce up and down a couple of times. Beria would have hit the roof, and me, had she known. The kapok mattress was studded with soft brown leather discs.

Lewie bought the Kelvinator refrigerator on time payment; it cost 102 guineas (a guinea being one pound one shilling). Beria was forty and this was her first fridge. I was not allowed to open the door without asking, or to take any food or fruit without checking. There had to be an apple and an orange every day for Steve's crib. If I asked for either, Beria always checked the number before answering.

When Beria heard someone was selling up, she bought an oak china cabinet for £8. It sat in the corner of my bedroom displaying her fine bone English china cups and saucers, none of which she used, and her collection of china ornaments, which I spent hours rearranging. Some were Christmas presents, others were won at the funfair which came to town every year. The full blown metallic magenta rose sat in a silver snowstorm dome the size of a large orange. The Dolly Varden figurine was six inches high. Her three-tiered skirt, the cover of her opened parasol, and the trim on the brim of her picture hat were made from layers of glued and lacquered pastel lace.

My favourite was a water set – a jug and six glasses, all rimmed with a 24-carat gold band and made from lightly smoked brown fine crystal. Each glass and two sides of the jug were decorated in rough relief, with the thick outline of a pink rose head. 'I bought it at the Co-Op,' Beria recalled. 'Six pound I paid for it. I don't think I ever used it. For years it sat in the china cabinet. I bought it when Joan was born in 1955. I knew Steve wouldn't give me anything, so I bought myself a present. Ronnie loved it. He used to get it out and stare at it.'

Nita and I shared a bedroom until Beria decided Nita was too old. She moved into Lewie's bedroom and he slept on one end of the enclosed front verandah. He made a window over his bed by cutting a three-sided opening into the unlined galvanised iron wall. It was rolled up in the summer, and weighted down from the outside with a couple of heavy posts during the winter.

The front verandah had a green wooden stable door, the bottom half of which was always closed to help shut out the fine gravel and twigs of tumbleweed which blew in the wind. The yard was a mixture of gravel and small rocks, and apart from the vegetable garden there was no other greenery. The chicken-wire fence was slung between roughly dressed mulga trunks and secured with roofing nails.

The inside of the flimsy tin bath was painted with a pale green enamel, which peeled off and floated on the water; consequently, the bottom of the bath was rough and chaffed your bum. Beria bought a chip-burning bath heater. She conserved water and insisted we all use the same bath water, adding more hot as it was needed. Nita, who liked a really hot bath and came out looking like a lobster, always went first. Sometimes Beria sprinkled Rinso washing powder into the water, which I swirled around for a bubble bath. I didn't have a bath every night but before Beria threw out the washing-up water she added a bit more hot, placed the tin dish on the floor in front of the fire, and I stood in it, rubbing one foot on top of the other. She ignored any mention of the grease and bits of food floating on the surface. 'Stop your grizzling. It won't kill you.'

The lavatory, chookhouse and woodheap were at one end of the yard and the washhouse, rainwater tank and vegetable garden were on the sheltered side of the house. The washhouse was a wooden frame with a tin roof and torn double hessian walls. It had no door or window frames. The copper was free-standing and the floor crudely slung planks with gaps between. Two brass cold-water taps over the tin washing tubs were the only luxury. Beria physically hauled the tubs to empty the used rinsing water onto the garden. The rainwater tank was coated with a lime wash, which hissed when you wet it. Steve watered the vegetable garden every afternoon, but it was Beria who did the weeding and sprinkled it with chicken manure. The rich soil was filled with giant earthworms and produced huge watermelons that cracked like a stockwhip when you cut them, rockmelons that perfumed the hot air, fennel, peas, beans, red and white radishes, carrots, lettuce, Slav cabbage four feet tall, huge capsicums that we ate like apples, bushes of hot chillies, and tomatoes the size of saucers.

Beria was not allowed to have a flower garden. 'Waste of time,' Steve sneered. 'You can't eat them.'

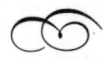

Running along the outside wall of the butcher's shop was an open cement drain about six inches deep which was used to dispose of animal waste products. The drain fed into a twelve-inch cement pipe which ran under the road in front of the shop. It was the job of the teenage butcher boys to keep the drain and the pipe clean using a large rubber water-hose and a length of freewheeling heavy-gauge chain, which ran the inside length of the pipe. With a butcher boy positioned at either end of the pipe and physically heaving the chain back and forth between them, their repetitive action and the flow of water kept the waste moving and the pipe clear of blockages.

The bloodied water, waste meat, offal and lumps of animal fat emptied out onto the vacant flat directly in front of the shop, where it was eaten by the birds or decayed in the sun. Some days were worse than others, and the stench as we came around the corner of the shop turned my stomach. Even Beria commented: 'Hold your nose, Ronnie. It's putrid today, isn't it?'

There were approximately a hundred houses in Gwalia, most of which were in one of the four machine-graded streets. The others were built at random around town, giving it a higgledy-piggledy aspect. The houses were much of a muchness, four rooms built from corrugated iron with a central passageway and a front and back verandah. The outside was rarely painted. Lucy Tognali's father, Lorenzo, was a carpenter so their house was a cut above.

Some of the single men's camps were one or two rooms and so small they were like a house in miniature. My father lived in the two-room pink camp with only inches between the top of his head and the ceiling, and he was not a tall man. The six management houses on Staff Hill were finished to a higher standard but only the mine manager, Vic and Melda Mazza, the State Hotel, the police station, the state school and the headmaster's house had a pull-the-chain lavatory and septic tanks installed.

The house that Beria moved to in Tower Street belonged to Mrs Stewart and was built to an exceptional standard with materials pilfered from the mine. Later, her house down by the railway line was put together almost entirely from recycled materials. The floors of the back and front verandahs and two additional bedrooms were cement. The others were a combination of timber and discarded gelignite pine boxes collected from the mine. The bottom half of the walls were lined with mismatching pressed and ripple-corrugated tin, the top with plasterboard. The white enamel built-in kitchen sink was connected with cold running water and considered a luxury. In summer Beria rolled down the heavy canvas blinds on the front verandah, hosed down the cement floor, and closed the doors and windows to keep the house cool.

Gwalia was not an impoverished town but still, nothing was wasted and building maintenance was minimal. In some houses the laundry doubled as a summer shower. The end of the garden hose was fitted with a rose nozzle and attached to the wall with a makeshift connection. The Paravicinis' bathroom in the backyard was freestanding, a couple of feet away from the door. In the winter the wind whistled through the gaps in the walls and around the doorjamb. Some of the gaps were wide enough to see through, which sometimes disconcerted the women.

Tower Street ran through the centre of both towns and was a crudely constructed strip of blue-metal gravel coated with tar, which melted in the summer and stuck to the soles of your sandals and burnt your bare feet. The road was hardly wide enough for two cars to pass. On one side was a footpath supported by a retaining wall. On the other side the distance from the edge of the road to house fences was almost the equivalent of two lanes of traffic. This was where we played.

Sometimes I rode my bike but mostly I walked everywhere. Quite a few of the men working on the mine rode to and from Leonora every day. There weren't as many sedan cars as there were utilities, and some, like Ike Nye's, had a tin cabin with no doors and a timber tray. Ike always parked his truck on the mound outside the State Hotel, and when it came time to leave he released the handbrake and rolled away to a self-start. At various times, my brother Lewie drove a jalopy with wooden running boards and no canopy, a small Bedford truck, a left-hand-drive army jeep, a motorbike fitted with a sidecar, and a new black Holden utility.

Everyone, except those men living in one- and two-room humpies, was connected to the electricity supply and mains water. Some meters erratically ran backwards, and when Alf Peterson came to take a reading you had to run around and make sure everything was turned off, including the fridge. Sinks and hand basins were unusual and few houses had a tap in the kitchen or power points. Beria said it constantly: 'Ronnie, go and fill the kettle with rainwater.'

Ironing was a laborious ritual requiring damping-down and wrapping the clothes in towels to keep them moist and easier to iron. The connection on the iron had been altered, and Beria stood on a chair to plug it into a double-adapter attached to the light fitting hanging in the middle of the room. The heavy metal iron had no temperature gauge and was prone to overheating and burning out if Beria forgot to switch it off at regular intervals. Eventually, Lewie fitted a four-point power board in Beria's kitchen but if she plugged in more than one appliance it blew a fuse. There were no hot-water systems and Mrs Quarti had a commercial-sized electric immerser, akin to those used in an electric kettle, which hung over the edge of the bath.

Front verandas were closed in with flywire and green lattice and hidden behind scarlet bougainvillea, climbing fern, oleanders or jade. Space was at a premium and families converted either end of the verandah into a sleep-out – a permanent bedroom for the girls and boys, divided by curtains, and strictly off-limits to each other. Until her brothers left home, Clara Paravicini slept in the lounge room. When she moved into the second bedroom she shared it with her youngest brother up until the day she got married. Those boys who didn't leave town and went to work on the mine lived at home until they got married. Some of them continued to sleep in the same backyard sheds put up for them years earlier when the house became too small to accommodate all the children. The girls stayed inside and as soon as the boys were old enough they were moved out. It allowed the boys an independence and a certain freedom denied the girls.

Every three months the slime-coated heavy-duty cotton duck from the sluice vats was replaced. After being squirted with a pressure hose, the cleaned filter cloth was much sought after; it made the perfect house lining and lasted for years. The interior walls were painted with pink or white kalsomine, a powder containing zinc oxide and glue and mixed with water. Cement floors were painted or polished, and the doorjambs were goldfields green. Beria had four thick-pile bedroom mats which featured large sprays of European flowers, a bucolic English landscape, and Australian flora and fauna. From the Co-Op she bought me a glazed two-foot china kookaburra sitting on a tree stump with a snake in his mouth, and a pair of plaster of Paris black and white Springer spaniels, which she used as doorstops.

Tin chimneys, of all shapes and sizes and in varying states of disrepair, were attached to the sides of the houses. The return sides of the chimney had a small window, allowing light onto the top of the lead-blackened wood stove, which was the focal point of the house and more often than not the only source of heat in the winter. As soon as boys were big enough to swing an axe they were expected to chop the wood. Barefoot, and swinging the axe high into the air, I missed the log and almost severed my little toe. Beria washed and wrapped the wound in some strips of sheeting and left it to heal for a week.

Most families had a vegetable garden, but Bernice Quarti maintained the earth was so hard the carrots grew in the shape of a corkscrew. In summer the ground was so hot we ran barefoot from the shade of one lamppost to the next. The earth was so compacted the water pipes were laid on the surface and by mid-morning in the summer the tap water was almost boiling. Anyone planning to take a bath during the day ran it first thing in the morning. There was no shortage of water, and the levels at Station Creek water supply never dropped. It was estimated the natural underground storage contained billions of gallons.

I was expected to do little around the house, but it was my job to carry and stack small loads of wood in the kitchen wood-box and to bring in the morning's wood every night. With the stove the only means of boiling water to make Steve's tea, my rare lapses were guaranteed to incur Beria's wrath, especially if there was a heavy frost.

Mrs Patroni's boarding house was in the centre of Tower Street and was home for about twenty single European men working on the mine. The standard of Mrs Patroni's food made up for the lack of facilities. The dining room served three meals a day and some of the surface workers came back for a hot midday meal. Full board included a crib of sandwiches, cake and fruit for the underground workers.

I often saw Mrs Patroni standing in the doorway on the front verandah watching the passing parade. With one hand on her hip and the other resting high on the door frame, it was an alluring sight.

Whenever she saw me she waved, and invited me in to eat: '*Ciao bello, vene qua. Vene qua per mangare.*' She took a shine to me and I was one of the few kids allowed inside her boarding house. Mrs Patroni was an outstanding cook – her cotoletta and rissoles were irresistible. For a while Mrs Robinson, our next-door neighbour and Ollie Garbellini's mother, was the cook at Mrs Patroni's. Mrs Robinson was formidable, standing six foot two and weighing about eighteen stone. She was married to Pop Robinson, her second husband, who was more than a foot shorter and about half her weight. Mrs Scolari was the housemaid at Mrs Patroni's. When we lived opposite I would see her every afternoon setting off on her bike to the boarding house. There was something alluring – almost scandalous – about Mrs Scolari. She was a slim, attractive woman with dark hair. 'What are you talking about? Of course she dyes it.' Beria scoffed.

Together with her husband, Bonaventura, and their one-year-old son Macca, Dina Patroni landed in Fremantle in 1910. Her other two children, Italo and Ida, were born in Australia. The family came from Sernio, Lombardy, a small village nestling into the side of the Italian Alps. Bonaventura died in 1948 and from that time Mrs Patroni ran the boarding house alone. She had a boyfriend, Emilio Quislini, a miner who eventually went home to his village in Italy.

Mrs Patroni lived in the two suitably decorated front rooms of the boarding house. Her parlour had beautiful curtains, framed pictures and comfortable chairs. Her double bed was made up with fine lace-trimmed and embroidered Italian linen. One end of the front verandah was converted to a sleep-out, the other end was her kitchen pantry, which Mrs Scolari's son Peter raided – helping himself to the dried apricots. The boarders lived in two rows of single and shared unlined tin huts, measuring about eight feet square, made from corrugated sheeting and lined with hessian and ripple tin – a smaller gauge version of the corrugated form. They were furnished with a single bed, a kapok mattress and pillow, bed linen and blankets, a small wardrobe, a bedside locker, an overhead light bulb and a small window in the back wall. They were freezing in the winter and hot in the summer.

It was difficult to guess Mrs Patroni's age. She was a shapely woman with jet black hair pulled back off her face and fixed in a tight chignon on the nape of her neck. Always fully made-up, impeccably dressed in crepe with Italian leather high heels and a double strand of red crystals around her neck, she was an intriguing character. I never once saw her walking in the street but she did own a Vauxhall car which she sometimes drove to Leonora. Beria worked for a while doing the house washing – bed linen and the white linen tablecloths Mrs Patroni insisted should be starched. Beria couldn't work out when Mrs Patroni had a bath. The only bathroom was next to the row of six pan lavatories in the backyard, 'and I'm damn sure she didn't use that'.

The policeman Tom Clews correctly suspected Mrs Patroni of running a sly grog shop, and a couple of times the boys from the Kalgoorlie liquor branch came to town to investigate, but she was too cunning for them and was never charged. She sold the grog at an inflated price to the men living in the boarding house, and anyone else in the town who came asking. Every week she took delivery of four crates of beer from Kalgoorlie, which were stored along with other contraband in a square hole in the ground under her bedroom floor. The trapdoor entrance, which the police never discovered, was concealed under a rug.

Dina Patroni and Melda Mazza were the town's shrewdest businesswomen. Mrs Patroni ran a lucrative cash trade, employing a waitress, a yardman, laundry staff, and, at one time, a half-caste Aboriginal housemaid, Bessie, who was always arguing with her husband and seemed to have a permanent black eye. Both were drinkers. One night he began accusing her of being unfaithful and before long the argument turned violent and he started hitting her. He was naked, and when he wouldn't stop Bessie grabbed a knife and almost completely severed his penis. Screaming and bleeding like a stuck pig, he was rushed to the Leonora hospital where it was sewn back by Dr Kristian Wilson.

Someone once tried to poison Mrs Patroni by lacing a couple of bottles of red wine with cyanide stolen from the mine. The culprit put so much cyanide in the wine it made the drinkers vomit and brought on convulsions. They were taken to the hospital and they all survived. The poisoner was caught and sentenced to five years' gaol.

Before we arrived in Leonora, Father Brennan was the Catholic priest, and he was something of character. People still talked about him long after he was gone. He was replaced by Father Keith Spain.

Every second day Beria raked and swept out the chookhouse, and scrubbed and filled the water bowls with a solution of Condy's crystals. It was my job to turn the tap on and off at her command. Once, she didn't hear Father Spain calling, but with the front door open and the wireless blaring he knew she was home. He wandered through to the back of the house and was standing in the doorway just as Beria stood up and hit her head on a piece of protruding water pipe. 'Oh shit!' she yelled. 'You rotten mongrel bastard of a thing.'

Rubbing her head, and checking her fingers for blood to see if she had broken the skin, she saw Father Spain, who said before she could apologise: 'It's alright, Rocky. I've heard all those words before.'

Father Spain always wore a black Roman cassock with thirty-three buttons down the front – one for each year of Christ's life. He was a popular figure in the town and spent his days visiting in the parishes. Even Steve liked him and always bought him a beer when he joined the men for a drink at the State Hotel. He was the first priest we knew in Gwalia and he often came to the house to see Beria. It was Father Spain, on the advice of the sisters, who arranged for Nita to go as a boarder to Dominican Ladies' College. It mattered little that Beria was not a Catholic, he was suspicious of Steve's behaviour in the house. She always made Father Spain a cup of tea. 'Have you got any of your boiled fruitcake, Rocky?' he asked in reply. The mutual respect turned to friendship and he insisted she call him Keith. According to the church Beria was living in sin but Father Spain never allowed it to taint their association. When they started talking I was sent to my room. 'Off you go, Ronnie. Little pigs have got big ears.' Complaining of being thirsty cut no ice with Beria. She could read me like a book. 'Are you? Well, don't worry, you won't die. You can have a drink of water when Father Spain goes. You stay in your bedroom and read your book, and stop interrupting us while we're talking.'

Things changed after Father Spain went, and we weren't included in the Catholic community. The next two priests, Fathers Moffatt and Tobin, never once came to our house, and I was ignored. Beria had no time or regard for either priest, and barely exchanged a word with them.

In his youth, my father went to Mass in Italy, but he was not interested in attending church with me or Nita. Roman Catholicism in the goldfields was the prerogative of women and children who believed implicitly in sin and heaven and hell.

Father Moffatt's hands trembled. He was a complex personality whose rapport with his parishioners was strained. When the mine manager, Reg Barden, made his annual appearance at Christmas Mass, Father Moffatt used his sermon to condemn part-time Catholics who appeared only rarely in the congregation. The jibe was pointed and

Mr Barden was incensed. His sister was a fully professed Dominican nun and he helped financially support the sisters in Leonora.

Father Tobin used his sermons to rail at the young women in the congregation, accusing them of treating the Mass as a competitive fashion parade.

One priest's reputation as a casanova was common currency in the goldfields. Beria's friend insisted the neighbours' children were locked out as soon as he arrived at a particular house, while the rest of the town tried to work out why his car was parked there at all hours of the day and night. Another priest enjoyed a drink and spent a great deal of time in the hotel. He was known by the men – some of whom were hardened drinkers – as someone who could 'hold his liquor' and who didn't live his life by the standards he imposed on his parishioners. The policeman said: 'He was a bit of a scallywag, and something of a hypocrite. When I asked him if he was going to join in at the dance he said, "I can't be seen dancing with a woman!" I had to stop myself from saying, "I don't know why. You're bedding half of them!"'

One priest was a snob with only a perfunctory interest in ordinary parishioners, spending his time instead with those involved in the town management, or the owners of the surrounding sheep stations. The priest didn't have a permanent housekeeper and was looked after by the women of the parish and the sisters, who provided the majority of his meals. As a matter of course he was also invited to eat with the parishioners and had regular nights with a couple of them. The majority of the Italian women in Gwalia came from the north of Italy and, as their mothers did in their villages, provided the priest with traditional spaghetti, gnocchi and risotto made from recipes they brought from the old country. It was considered, even by the other Italian women, that Alma Mazza made the best spaghetti bolognese in Gwalia.

One priest began making unwelcome daytime visits to the home of Bernice Quarti, an attractive blonde. They weren't Catholic and his unambiguous attention made Mrs Quarti uncomfortable. When she mentioned it to her husband, Doug, he wasted no time in contacting the priest and telling him in straightforward, salty language to stay away.

When I lived in one of the back streets with my father, Nita and her boyfriend Italo Cher, it was a short distance from Mrs Tognali, and Father Tobin visited regularly. What he lacked in height he made up for in talent as a pianist. He spent hours playing the piano on the front verandah and providing us a free concert while Mrs Tognali kept up a supply of her famous tomato sandwiches.

Beria was not of the faith, but having married Catholics and promised, she was as good as her word, and all four children were raised in the faith. During her time in the Salvation Army home Beria went to the Citadel every Sunday and had community hymn singing on Sunday night. She said she believed in God but she was not what she called 'churchy'. However, it didn't stop her from helping us observe the simple rules of the church. We didn't have to eat meat on Friday and I wore the brown scapular of Our Lady of Mount Carmel and a small crucifix around my neck.

When it became clear Beria was not sending me back to the convent, Father Tobin made no attempt to include me. I enjoyed the mystery of the church and was envious and unhappy at being excluded from the organised activities. Father Tobin never called at the house to discuss it when other Catholic boys of my age were being prepared for their first Holy Communion. Nita gave me her old missal from boarding school and I spent hours moving the coloured ribbons from one page to the next, learning the prayers and the names of the vestments and the liturgical vessels. I didn't need to be reminded about Mass on Sunday, benediction on Tuesday night, and the rosary on

Friday night. I was disappointed when Father Tobin cancelled benediction and the rosary, complaining that not enough people were attending. Father Tobin said Mass so quickly Lena Beccaria and her friends decided to time him. 'It was all over in twenty minutes.'

I was excited when Father Tobin announced at Mass he was recruiting new altar boys. I checked with Beria before I volunteered. There were four of us, including Nat Garbellini, and once a week after school we gathered in the sacristy at the St Francis of Assisi Church. Latin instruction lifted a veil on a world which I loved, and with my knowledge of Italian I found it easy to learn and read. My Dutch friend, Albert Van Der Haydn, lived on the block and after school we sat in the backyard of his house testing each other with the prayers. I was first to learn the Latin form of the Confiteor, the Lord's Prayer and the Nicene Creed.

Of the group, I was the only one not attending the convent. Ollie had taken Nat and the other Garbellini children out of the state school after Maurice Reilly, the headmaster, lost his temper and thrashed Billy around the legs when he caught him walking on the school verandah wearing his football boots. As weeks went by and the classes continued, Father Tobin pressured me about attending the convent. I knew what Beria's reaction would be and I didn't know what to say. After a month of instruction we began serving the Mass and benediction as a regular group. When the new school year started and we met for our first Latin class of the year, Father Tobin turned on me. 'I made the situation quite clear,' he said. 'You are obviously not coming to the convent so you can't go on being an altar boy. You'll have to go.'

I ran home. With tears streaming down my face, I explained and pleaded with Beria to be allowed to attend the convent. She listened in stony silence and then let fly. 'Is that what he said? Well, you can go back and tell that mongrel bastard of a priest I said he can go to buggery, because I am not sending you back to the bloody convent; and as far as I'm concerned he can shove his church right up his arse. And anyway, who the bloody hell does he think he is? He's not a patch on Father Spain. And another thing, I'd like to know what's he doing spending all that time with married women when their husbands aren't there? Tell him to answer me that one, why don't you?'

That was the end of the discussion. The next Sunday, Beria asked if I was going to Mass. 'No,' I told her. 'If I can't be an altar boy I don't want to go anymore.'

I never did, and from that day on I more or less ignored Father Tobin, and he certainly never went out of his way to speak to me.

As a result of growing up in the Salvation Army children's home, Beria was a perfectionist, doing everything at double speed, even walking. Whenever we went out I held her hand, but keeping up took an effort.

'Ronnie, will you hurry up? And how many times do I have to tell you, don't drag your feet when you walk.'

I cried easily.

'Stop that,' Beria growled, 'or I'll give you something to cry for.'

Beria was never familiar, addressing those ladies she considered to be only casual acquaintances in the most formal manner. While she was known to many by her nickname of Rocky, neighbours she had known for years were always addressed as 'Mrs'. I never dared to call an adult by their Christian name: 'Did I hear you correctly? I'll tell you what, if I hear any more of that I'll box your bloody ears. Now get outside and play, and don't come in until I call you.'

Beria didn't have to say a word; she controlled me with a look, a glance, an almost imperceptible movement of her head. If someone offered me a second piece of cake, I looked to Beria, and from merely the flicker of an eye I knew the answer. The slightest backward tilt of her head meant: Outside and play – now! If I dallied, or pretended not to notice, it only needed for her to raise her voice a little – 'Ronnie' – and give me a dirty look and I was gone without a word.

Beria made a point of ignoring Steve when he told her to stay home all day while he was at work. Sometimes she'd spend time with Wint, leaving to be home in time to light the fire before he knocked off, and providing him with no clue as to what she had done for the day. One time she was surprised but not worried to discover he was already home and pacing like a caged lion. He had been home for two hours and was furious, abusing her and making all sorts of accusations: 'You think you're more clever than me. You pretend you stay here all day on your own and then come back in time to light the fire.'

Beria was not prepared to give in to his ranting. 'For God's sake, Steve, I went to see Wint, and if you don't believe me, go and ask her, why don't you?'

He became abusive: 'What you want to go and see those bitches for?'

She wouldn't let him have the last word: 'Because I want to. I don't have to stay here all day on my own just because you say so.' Steve continued to bully her, but whatever the consequences, Beria was not going to be bossed around: 'You don't stay home, so why should I? And nothing you say is going to make me change my mind. I don't know how many times you want me to tell you – you are not my boss!'

When Steve realised he was fighting a losing battle he retreated to the pub.

∞

Most kids in Gwalia learned to swim in the cement swimming pool on the top of Staff Hill, which was also a holding tank for the boilers on the Sons of Gwalia. The daily water level varied, depending on the needs of the mine. The pool was open for three two-hour sessions from 1 December through to the last weekend in March. I rarely went at night. I was scared of the dark, and I hated the hundreds of iridescent green stink beetles which came out at night. Attracted by the fluorescent light suspended across the middle of the pool, they flew through the air and landed on you. If you tried to handle them or accidentally sat on one, they squirted a foul-smelling secretion from their tail, and no matter how many times you washed your hands with soap and water the smell wouldn't disappear. One year the beetles came in such plague proportions the men killed and shovelled them into 44-gallon drums.

Our next-door neighbour, Vido Ivankovich, or Little Charlie as he was known, was the pool attendant for five years. Like so many of the foreigners in the town he was a mystery. We knew nothing about his life in Yugoslavia. Unsmiling and socially inept, he kept to himself. His only friend was Grinning Joe, who lived about 100 yards from Little Charlie's camp. Most nights the two of them sat on the verandah drinking muscat and talking. Neither of them went to the pub and Charlie was in bed by nine o'clock.

His was a three-room camp – a kitchen and two bedrooms. There was no bathroom and it seemed that he wore the same clothes every day. The rank smell which hung around him and all these camps was a combination of ingrained grease and dirt, body odour, smoke, candle wax and lumpy kapok. Little Charlie lived for most of the year on his open verandah, but in the winter he moved into the bedroom. His bed was a pile of thinning fusty army blankets and a stained mattress-ticking pillow.

Steve and Little Charlie were on genial terms and I often played around in his front vegetable garden, which was dominated by Slav cabbage. There was no electricity and Charlie relied on candlelight, although he preferred to sit in the dark. Scattered throughout the camp were a number of barely recognisable white enamel candleholders hidden beneath mounds of melted wax which he let me break away to amuse myself. After years of working at the pool, Little Charlie was sick to death of the sight and sound of children. The older kids and the young men who worked on the mine recognised his antipathy and went out of their way to torment him. Nita was a ringleader. They knew exactly what it took to test his patience, and once provoked he was irascible to the point of being dangerous.

Little Charlie sat at a combined wooden table and bench just inside the gate, sheltering under an awning. He hated water and, unfortunately for him, the table which was at the shallow end of the pool was perfectly positioned for anyone wanting to splash him. A strong swimmer, Nita was one of the worst offenders. He blustered and cursed in his Slavic tongue, rushing to a handy pile of ready stones, then charging up and down the side of the pool waiting for an opportunity to stone the culprit. The battles sometimes raged for as long as half an hour, with everyone clearing the pool. The more exasperated Little Charlie became, the more the cheering crowd egged him on. Little Charlie never conceded defeat, waiting until closing time if necessary to have his revenge.

Little Charlie was responsible for the cleaning of the changing rooms and the daily chlorinating of the water, which was so haphazard the walls and floor of the pool were coated with two inches of green slime which we peeled away in chunks and threw at each other during water fights. The powdered lime came in 44-gallon drums and every morning Little Charlie mixed a solution in a metal bucket and walked the length of the pool, tipping as he went. From time to time one of the older kids would run by, yank the bucket from Charlie's grip and throw it into the pool. Since he couldn't swim, he had to convince one of the kids to retrieve it. I felt sorry for Little Charlie, and if he asked me I always obliged.

Some kids were never allowed to visit the pool, their mothers branding it a public health hazard and calling for it to be closed. Thankfully, their harping fell on deaf ears; however, during the first poliomyelitis epidemic of 1948, when Johnny Sheridan contracted infantile paralysis, the pool was closed for a time.

Although he was only five foot three, Little Charlie was agile and strong, and not beyond scratching at your face with his longish fingernails. Nor was he timid about engaging in fisticuffs, and there was no discriminating between boys and girls. Woe betide you if he got close enough to grab hold during an argument. Using a closed fist he bashed many a kid around the head, including Nita, and bodily threw them out of the pool, or banned them for weeks. He knew to the day if you had served your time, and to be allowed back required some slick talking and a litany of false promises. Nita was a tomboy, and taunted him mercilessly. Their feud went beyond the pool, and his loathing of her, which was etched into his face, only made Nita more determined.

Little Charlie was a mostly disagreeable neighbour and was responsible for the death of my dog. Beria took me with her to Kalgoorlie in 1953 when she went to finalise her divorce arrangements. We stayed in Boulder with Joan Coe, a cousin, who gave me a white puppy as a present. He had a black patch over one eye and I called him Patchy. He was my first dog and I loved him. We brought him home on the steam train. Beria hid him in a bag and he travelled in our compartment with us, which was against the law.

For a time Little Charlie had two boarders, a couple of young men who worked on the mine. Every time they walked past they teased Patchy, kicking the gate, poking at him and pelting him with stones. 'Hey, cut that out!' Beria yelled at them. 'What the hell do you two think you're up to? If I catch you throwing stones at the dog again I'll come out and throw stones at you. Now get on your way before I let him out, and then we'll see how brave you are.' Little Charlie was also the cleaner at the state school and if he thought no one was watching when he passed the front gate, he poked at Patchy with the handle of a broom.

Not surprisingly, Patchy hated the three of them, barking and snarling whenever they passed in front of the house. By mistake, somebody left the front gate open and when Patchy saw the two boarders walking past he went for them. They turned to run back to the camp but they were too slow. One managed to make it inside the gate, but Patchy gave him a decent bite on the backside. They complained to the policeman, Jim Lemon, who came to the house. Beria abused the three neighbours for their persistent teasing but it was too late, Patchy had to be taken away and shot. Beria wrapped him in a sugarbag and Lewie threw him into one of the mine furnaces. I was heartbroken.

Little Charlie retired at the end of 1958 and once he went into hospital it was obvious he was never coming home. Aged sixty-six, he died the following August. His death went more or less unnoticed in the town. Steve, Grinning Joe and a couple of fellow Slavs were the only ones at his funeral. In the week before he died Steve helped clean out his camp. He didn't have much – a bed and a couple of pieces of dilapidated furniture. They doused his clothes with kerosene and made a bonfire of them. Grinning Joe took all his personal papers. When I went to visit Beria after school, she told me Little Charlie was dead. 'Poor old bugger. It won't be the same without him around. And you kids won't have anyone to torment at the pool now.'

In the early 1950s, Gwalia had two general stores – V.B. and M.M. Mazza and the Co-Op, which was owned by the locals and managed by Jimmy Caruthers. The shops traded all day Saturday and a half-day on Wednesday. They closed every day for an hour from 12.30 while the staff went home for lunch. For a time, the Co-Op, which was Beria's preferred store, traded on Sunday. Sadly, through lack of patronage, it closed its doors at the end of 1956. While the rest of the town was enjoying Christmas Eve around the tree in the park, a neighbour broke into the Co-Op and helped himself to the remaining stock of Onkaparinga blankets, Actil sheets, pillowcases, towels, kitchen utensils and, according to Beria, 'anything else he could get his hands on. She won't have to buy anything for years.' Beria laughed the next day when the thief's wife told her what happened. Just as he was loading the stock into boxes an old Aboriginal man appeared out of the darkness. 'He got such a fright, he nearly shit himself. He gave the old boy some tobacco from the shelf and told him to piss off!'

Harry Gray was the Gwalia butcher. There were two churches – Anglican and Catholic. Maurice Reilly was headmaster at the state school and Mother Xavier Superior at the Dominican convent. There were four boarding houses – including the purpose-built mine mess run by Mrs Saunders – a pokey two-roomed doctor's surgery, the Australian Workers' Union Hall, which doubled as the picture theatre, and the swimming pool and football oval. For a time Ernie Sheer had a pie shop opposite the State Hotel. Mr Sheer was missing part of one arm from halfway between the elbow and wrist. I believed it when I was told he lost his hand in the mincing machine.

With no competition, Vic and Melda Mazza put their shop on a jinker and moved it to the centre of the town. The Mazzas were an astute, hard-working business couple and the shop made them arguably the richest family in the town. Vic believed in a day's work for a day's pay. 'Don't stand around idle,' he used to say. 'Even if there is no one in the shop there's always something to do.' When he thought I was spending too much time talking to Peggy Garbellini while she was meant to be working he told me to buy what I wanted and leave.

Two of Vic Mazza's brothers worked at the shop. Dino served behind the counter and Bob did most of the deliveries. For twenty years Bob was in and out of every house on a weekly basis. He, more than anyone else in the town, knew what was happening.

Christmas in Gwalia was a community celebration – you could smell the excitement and the town was abuzz. It was the busiest time of the year at Mazza's shop. The beer came in sixty-bottle boxes by train from Kalgoorlie and you had to have your order in two weeks in advance. In the days leading up to Christmas Bob Mazza was run off his feet delivering dozens of boxes around the town. Just as he was about to make his delivery to a house in Tower Street, the wife appeared on the raised front verandah, screaming for help, saying her husband was going to shoot her. Knowing them both, Bob raced around to the back door and got a hell of a fright when he met the husband, clutching a rifle. The two men chatted for a moment, and when the husband calmed down he assured Bob everything was fine and he'd put away the gun.

When Melda and Vic were away in Perth on one of their rare holidays they left Dino in charge of the shop. A man came in wanting one size 9, right-foot tan riding boot. Dino made the sale, and charged for only one boot. When Vic was stocktaking some months later he questioned Dino about the missing boot. Only then did the penny drop and Dino realise the improbability of finding another one-legged man with the same shoe size wanting only the left boot. Melda and Vic kept the boot as a souvenir.

Both the inside and outside of the store were impeccably maintained and commercial travellers said it was the cleanest shop in country Western Australia. The raised gravel verandah at the front was swept and watered each morning. There was no air-conditioning and canvas blinds were lowered when the afternoon sun hit the front of the shop. The staff cleaned the windows of their department every day using Bon Ami, a compressed white powder which was applied with a wet cloth. The residue of dry white film was removed by rubbing with newspaper or a clean cloth. Bob Mazza polished a thick plate-glass front door so expertly it became invisible in the sunlight. A traveller, thinking it was open, tried to walk through and hit his head.

Mazza's was a three-in-one walk-through mini-emporium for groceries, fruit and vegetables, men's, women's and children's clothing, haberdashery, mercery, confectionery and newsagency. The household furnishings were stored out the back and for a premium price you could order anything you wanted. My father bought a Silent Knight kerosene refrigerator, the tank of which had to be filled once a week. Mazza's delivered the kerosene in a returnable four-gallon drum.

The haberdashery and mercery section was in the centre of the shop and the dark brown linoleum was polished to a sheen. The bulk of the stock on sale was English. The range of J.P. Coates' plain and variegated blue, mauve, lemon, pink, green, red and brown fancywork threads hung in twists from a small spiked revolving stand on the end of the counter. I turned it slowly, marvelling at the kaleidoscopic colours. Rolls of paper-backed pure satin ribbon in every width and hue of the rainbow, cards of Beautron pearl buttons, imported cotton lace and fine silver-threaded organdie scarves were carefully displayed. Meticulously stacked bolts of dressmaking fabric were on shelves behind the counter. A yard-long brass dressmaking ruler, polished to a glint, was screwed into the edge of the counter.

Twice a year Vic and Melda went to Perth on a buying spree. They stocked leading brands: Leroy dresses, Sportscraft skirts and Merle slippers – 'the best in Australia!' Beria wore Maxwell brassieres, which came in white and tea rose. The concentric machine stitching stiffened and pointed the conical-shaped cup. Pelaco and Whitmont shirts, Marshall shoes, Casben sportswear and Jantzen bathers, with its red diving-girl logo. John Brown and Crestknit fine wool jumpers and cardigans started at £5. Before I left for boarding school my father bought me a pale aqua Crestknit jumper with a black fleck and silver thread, and finished with a shawl collar. Made from the finest merino wool, I wore it for best. The two glass showcases displayed watches, crockery, English china dinner sets packed in pine boxes filled with straw, jewellery and a comprehensive range of men's felt and straw hats. Mazza's carried two perfumes: the German cologne 4711, and Mitcham Lavender which came from one of the great lavender-growing areas of southern England. Beria used Gemey – 'the perfume that captured five continents' – Goya carnation talcum powder and Angel Face powder. For men they stocked 1808 Brilliantine, Potter and Moore lavender hair oil and Crystalline rapid hair restorer.

Mazza's sold the best and charged accordingly. The fruit and vegetables arrived twice weekly by train from one of the leading Chinese market gardeners, Ah Sam, in Wellington Street, Perth. The peaches, plums and apricots were hand-packed in slat jarrah boxes lined with white butcher's paper; pears and apples were hand-wrapped in a square of pale green tissue paper. The one-pound bags of Watery Hall grapes from the Sandalford vineyard in the Swan Valley were packed in airflow plastic bags. The single Italian men bought and ate them sitting on the benches outside the shop. We only had cherries on Christmas Day; big, dark and juicy, they were a taste explosion in your mouth.

The refrigerated smallgoods section catered for a migrant population. Watsonia legs of cured ham, Hutton's pineapple ham packed in oats or wheat husks and wrapped in a muslin cloth. The Tibaldi and D'Orsogna air-dried, gnarled, fat-oozing Italian sausages and salami were looped in overhead swags. The pork and beef mortadella di Bologna sausage was the genuine article; the Roman and pecorino provolone cheese came in small wheels. The gorgonzola was imported, and Bel Paese was the most expensive. Mazza's stocked Soprano pasta and Ciro's tomato paste. The giant dried apricots, peaches, pears and the Five Crown juicy Australian prunes – packed in seven-pound tins – were sold loose, wrapped in greaseproof paper. We had fresh fish once a year – Good Friday. Roll mops and pickled herrings were for the Dutch.

The staff needed a ladder to reach the top of the ceiling-high wooden shelves stocked with tins of camp pie, Swift's sardines – which sold by the gross – Imperial and Globe brand corned beef in a pyramid-shaped tin with an attached key, braised steak and onions, and sausages and vegetables. Tinned spiced ham was the bestseller, especially with those living out on the wood line.

The family-owned cake company, Mills and Ware's, made madeira, sultana and thickly iced rainbow cake. The Swiss roll, coated in fine castor sugar, made a perfect base for wine trifle. The moist one-pound Ritz fruitcake was cellophane wrapped and weighty with fruit. My father ate it spread with butter or slices of Roman or goat's milk cheese. The centres of the coconut macaroons were wet to perfection. Mazza sold the full Rosella range of products, including the lumpy solus apricot jam, which I ate straight from the tin. Beria loved Mira dark plum and my father ate only Rayner's chunky fig jam. Rosella's award-winning green tomato pickles were always amongst Mazza's top-selling items, especially with the Europeans, who spread it on their cribs of well-buttered cold lamb or pork sandwiches.

Peak, Velvet and Signal soap were sold in twelve-inch bars and easily cut to a manageable size with a breadknife. Solyptol and Liptol disinfectant soaps prevented minor cuts and scratches from turning septic. The most popular hair oils for men were Brylcreem, Californian Poppy, Vaseline, and Potter and Moore. Faulding's setting lotion held the most unruly hair in place. Beria used green Herco hand lotion which came in a circular glass container with a flat base and the screw cap on the side.

Mazza's had a 'gallon licence' for the sale of beer, wine and spirits. The licence allowed them to sell any combination of alcohol providing it totalled a measure of one gallon.

Valencia No. 1 claret was their bestseller with the Slavs and Italians. Matured in ten-gallon oak barrels, it came from two Slav brothers in the Middle Swan. Mazza sold it in crudely corked recycled beer bottles and it was the job of the after-school spud boy to fill the bottles, first rinsing them in a galvanised tub of cold water at the back of the shop. The claret dregs in the bottom of the beer bottles attracted cockroaches which climbed in and had to be carefully flushed out and scooped off the top of the water with a cupped hand. Mazza also used recycled beer bottles to store kerosene and the pungent thick black disinfectant phenyl, used in lavatory pans. The spud boy was under strict instructions to smell each bottle to make sure the two lots remained separate. In the summer the syphoning was sometimes risky work. The combination of his tippling, the claret fumes and the build-up of heat under the tin roof was so overwhelming, the spud boy needed regular breaks in the fresh air to stop from passing out.

Peter's ice-cream carried the slogan, 'the health food of a nation', and came in five-gallon tin churns transported in purpose-built containers made from dark green, thickly quilted tarpaulin. You had a choice: vanilla, chocolate, strawberry or rainbow – a combination of the three. The Co-Op made its own ice-cream. My favourite was vanilla with diced glacé maraschino cherries. The five-gallon light aluminium milk containers were stored at freezing temperature and Mazza's milkshakes were filled with the finest particles of ice. The revolutionary quarter-pint pyramid-shaped tetra pack for storing and transporting milk was made from plastic and aluminium-coated paperboard. Frozen solid, it was a delicious milk iceblock.

Sullivan's garage was in Leonora, so Mazza's put in a seven-foot petrol bowser at the front of the shop. With each heavy back and forth pump of the handle a measured spew of pinkish brown petroleum inched into the glass top section of the bowser. The escaping fumes shimmered as they rode the hot air and evaporated. The underground source remained a puzzlement and I daydreamed of being big enough to pump the three-foot-long handle on the side of the bowser.

∞

After Mazza's went, the block closed down. Consequently, Steve Nemes moved his barber shop into his house, next door to Mrs Patroni's. Steve came to Gwalia as a penniless, displaced person, and was now a man of many parts. He was not only the barber, but he also worked full-time on the mine, and was the town's tailor. He made all Steve Salinovich's suits and trousers. He never seemed to sleep. Not to inconvenience his customers, he did fittings in the evening, cutting and sewing into the night. Bob Mazza had a haircut at half past four in the morning – on his way to work.

Steve kept our hair very short, using electric shears, a pair of thinning scissors – which reminded me of Beria's pinking shears – and a pair of long-bladed scissors. He had two brown leather barber's chairs, and as he didn't open the shop until he had finished his day shift on the mine, they were both constantly occupied. There were no appointments; you joined the queue and waited. For a couple of hours from half past three, and for the best part of Saturday, Steve snipped without a break. He worked alone between the two chairs and as soon as one became vacant the next person in line jumped in and sat waiting, staring at himself in the mirror. Steve had two large bottles of European cologne, and an especially fine talcum powder, which he sprinkled liberally onto a soft, white-haired oblong brush that he used to clear away the freshly cut hairs on your neck and prevent any itching.

To help pass the time while you waited, there was a large pile of dog-eared reading matter, mostly *Man* magazine, a risqué glossy publication of girlie photographs, together with *Pix* and *Australasian Post*. From time to time my father would visit Steve the barber to be professionally shaved with a cut-throat razor. My father always shaved with a cut-throat, and although he owned a strop he always called on Steve when his razor needed to be sharpened.

∽

The brown bakelite HMV wireless sat on the top of our kitchenette, connected to a length of quarter-inch copper cable which ran to the home-made aerial – a 25-foot metal pole attached to the front corner of the house. The daytime signal was strong but night reception depended on weather conditions and cloud cover. We sat straining, hearing one word in three as the wireless crackled and hissed, and the reception came and went. Beria's patience was tried when the programme disappeared just as the murder was about to be solved. Steve insisted the new wireless was faulty, demanding it be replaced. It turned out the wireless was in perfect working condition and Steve had wired the aerial incorrectly; however, he refused to believe he was at fault and continued complaining.

The wireless was turned on first thing in the morning and it played until bedtime, except when Beria went to the shop. Sometimes I asked one too many questions. 'For God's sake, Ronnie, you're driving me mad; go and listen to the wireless, why don't you.'

The two networks provided a balance of news, music and entertainment: 6KG broadcast from its studios in Kalgoorlie, and 6WN, the classical network, and 6WF, the light entertainment and education network of the Australian Broadcasting Commission, broadcast from the studios in Perth, on relay through 6GF Kalgoorlie. The ABC was directly opposite the Berkeley Flats where my Aunt Silvia lived with her second husband, Les Watkins, a cobbler.

Beria listened almost exclusively to the ABC. Our day started with the breakfast programme, compered by John Juan, who was blessed with a mellifluous voice and some trite jokes. He had been half of a successful Adagio dance act, Juan and Zelda, working at the Moulin Rouge in Paris. Beria had a love–hate relationship with him, and from the way she shouted at the radio I thought they were friends.

There were as many as 200 daily radio serials running across Australia. The morning programming on 6KG brought 'Portia Faces Life', 'When a Girl Marries' – 'dedicated to all those who are in love, and all those who can remember' – and 'Doctor Paul'. On the ABC, 'The Hospital Half Hour' with the theme music 'Look for the Silver Lining' was a cheerio programme dedicated to a different hospital and its patients, in particular the Home of Peace in Subiaco and the Wooroloo sanatorium for tuberculosis and leprosy. When I asked Beria about leprosy, she said: 'I'm not really sure. It's some sort of disease you can catch and your arms and legs fall off.'

That pricked my imagination. 'Really? How do you catch it?'

Beria saw the look on my face and stopped me. 'That's all I know, Ronnie. If you want to know any more, go and ask your teacher.'

From the time I was four, and the moment I heard the first notes of the haunting theme for the ABC's daily serial, 'Blue Hills', written by Gwen Meredith, I ran looking for Beria: 'Quick, Mum. Gwen Meredith's on!' 'Blue Hills' was the spin-off from 'The Lawsons', a wartime serial set in rural Australia. The final episode of 'The Lawsons' went to air on a Friday in February 1949, and the following Monday 'Blue Hills' commenced. At its zenith, thousands of Australian women tuned in daily at ten minutes to one. A couple of years later, as I walked past the houses on the way back to school at lunchtime, the wafting sound of the recognisable theme was a sign to hurry up.

Outside the kitchen door on the front verandah was a shabby velveteen lounge chair where I sat to read, play games, and listen to the wireless as Beria went about her chores. 'Yours for the Asking' and 'For You at Home' were request programmes; listeners wrote requesting a song for a nominated loved-one. The ABC sent a card to the nominee advising the date and time, and on the day a personal greeting was read on air. While Nita was at boarding school she wrote several times with a request for Beria; always the same song: 'A Mother as Lovely as You'.

I loved being alone with Beria in the kitchen, especially in the winter. She worked at her sewing machine or we sat together in front of the fire, listening to the wireless. Jack Davey, Bob Dyer and Mo (Roy Rene) were stars. Keith Smith's 'Pied Piper' was Beria's favourite – sometimes embarrassing but always funny as children candidly answered a range of questions, often concerning their parents. Howling with laughter, she said, often: 'What they say! Those kids are as bad as you.' The musical variety programme, 'The Village Glee Club', was broadcast once a week. Beria knew: 'Ronnie, come on – your favourite programme's on.' I sang along: 'To hear again when lights are low, the voice in the old village choir.'

The pool closed at the end of March, marking the end of summer but not the heat, and we turned to the wireless for our amusement, tuning in from four o'clock until half past six listening to a succession of fifteen-minute serials: 'The Sea Hound', 'Dick Tracy', 'The Air Adventures of Hop Harrigan', 'Superman', 'Tarzan', and 'Biggles', based on the books by Captain W.E. Johns about the fictitious Squadron Leader James Bigglesworth.

The ABC's Argonauts' Club was part of Children's Corner, and boasted 50,000 members aged from seven to seventeen. The members were assigned to a ship named after a mythological Greek character and allocated a crew number. I listened, longing to join. They took a pledge: 'Before the sun and the night, and the blue sea, I vow to stand faithfully by all that is brave and beautiful; to seek adventure, and having discovered aught of wonder, or delight; of merriment or loveliness, to share it freely with my comrades, the Band of Happy Rowers.' The brainchild of writer Nina Murdoch, it was innovative children's programming presenting cultural content in an area which, until that time, was dominated by bunnies, kookaburras and birthday calls. The programme encouraged writing, music, drawing and painting, and its presenters at various times included the poet A.D. Hope (Anthony Inkwell) and painter Jeffrey Smart. There were book readings, and serials, including 'The Muddle-Headed Wombat'. Fifteen thousand children were sending contributions to the programme.

With the sawdust-filled windjammer pressed against the bottom of the closed kitchen door to stop the draught, and a roaring fire in the stove – 'Ronnie, don't put so much wood on the fire' – Steve and Beria sat at the kitchen table playing cards and listening to their favourite serials, a combination of American and English productions, and Australian programmes from the studios of Hector Crawford in Melbourne and Grace Gibson in Sydney. They listened each night to a police serial – 'Inspector West', 'Police File' and 'Night Beat'. Even the theme music gave me goosebumps. The authentic sound effects and the curdling screams of the murder victims left me too frightened to move.

The wireless was also a major part in our school lessons. The ABC, in conjunction with the Education Department, produced and broadcast weekly singing, health and hygiene, folk dancing and literature and history lessons. When the Olympic Games in Melbourne commenced on 23 November 1956, it was almost the end of the school year. Written lessons were set aside and for two weeks we gathered around the classroom wireless, listening, as we marbled paper using paint floating on water and made Christmas cards, leather purses and cane baskets.

On 4 October 1957 came the incredible news that the USSR had launched Sputnik into outer space. It was the first man-made satellite to circle the earth and we talked of nothing else at school. Overnight the words 'satellite' and 'Sputnik' slipped into our vocabulary.

Announcers broadcast the times Sputnik could be seen with the naked eye. Night after night I stood on the woodheap, watching and wondering what it all meant. It was exciting stuff. One night Beria and I were walking home after a meal at Wint's house and we stood in the Tower Street, watching, hand in hand, as Sputnik moved across the sky like a bright shining star. Neither of us spoke.

A month later, Russia launched a second Sputnik with a dog, Laika, on board. There was a technical problem and Laika died the following day when her cabin overheated. At school Mr Reilly told us: 'This is very exciting, and the scientists say that one day they might even be able to put a man on the moon.' I was speechless.

The Christmas school holidays didn't start until late December, by which time it was too hot for lessons. With our exams out of the way the last two weeks were spent at the pool completing bronze swimming medals, tidying up the school for the following year, and preparing for Christmas. There was a piano in the spare school room and in 1954 Ian Watson, a boy in the last year of his education, played to entertain us. It was the first time I had seen a young man play the piano. Petula Clark had recorded 'The Little Shoemaker', which became a hit. When I asked Ian, he sat down at the piano, tinkled for a second, then played it for me. His ability reinforced my determination to play the piano.

Patti Page, Jo Stafford, Rosemary Clooney and Teresa Brewer were the singing stars, along with the singing cowboys, Gene Autry and Roy Rogers, and the yodeller Slim Whitman. I knew the words to all the songs on the wireless – 'Mocking Bird Hill' and 'On Top of Old Smokey'. Lewie's wife Jean had a true clear voice and sang 'I Went to Your Wedding' and 'The Tennessee Waltz'; I sang 'Dear John' and 'Lay Down your Arms'. Beria's favourites were 'Beautiful, Beautiful, Brown Eyes', 'Forever and Ever' and the yodelling ranger Hank Snow's 'Blue Velvet Band'.

When Mrs Chamberlain was playing the piano at a wedding reception I was standing close by, singing along quietly to the hit song, 'Oh My Papa'. She heard and called me closer. She played it again, told me to sing louder. She listened for a bit then turned and said to the rest of the band: 'This little boy can sing.'

Nobody took any notice.

F or Beria and me, they were 'Wint' and 'Pop'. Their real names were Emily Victoria and Joseph Edward Winter. He was as thin as she was solid. Wint had curly grey hair and wore glasses. If she wasn't cooking, she was always busy doing something around the house. In the hot weather her cheeks were red and her face dripped perspiration.

I went to stay with Wint many times, sometimes for a couple of days and sometimes for months, depending on how things were at home between Beria and Steve. She was a second mother, always there, and took me at a moment's notice. She hugged and kissed me for no reason. I knew that Wint loved me, and I loved her. I could hear the beat of her heart as my tiny frame disappeared into her ample bosom and she squeezed the breath out of me. Wherever Wint went, I followed, chatting and asking questions which she was never too busy to answer. Sometimes she would laugh and ask: 'Ronnie, do you ever stop talking?'

As much as I loved Beria, I was never homesick when I was with Wint, even when I didn't see Beria for weeks on end. Somehow, Wint made the separation tolerable.

I was staying with Wint at the same time her eldest daughter Jess and grand-daughter Lorraine were visiting from Perth. Lorraine and I were the same age and, apart from jealousy over Wint, played together for the most part without fighting. Across the town, everyone was cleaning up after a week of uncharacteristic winter winds and rain storms had wreaked havoc. Fences and chookhouses were blown over, sheeting was ripped from rooves, branches snapped from trees, and as we made our way to the butcher's shop I spotted the wooden cross from atop the Catholic church. I pointed to where it lay broken on the ground.

'Look,' I said to Wint, 'de cross is broken. De rain did it.'

'Didn't!' Lorraine snapped back.

'Did,' I said adamantly. 'De rain broke de cross.'

'Didn't.' At which point Lorraine burst into tears.

I had a supply of clothes at Wint's, including hand-me-downs from her children. She gave me an English herringbone double-breasted overcoat with two deep pockets. It was a favourite; thick and heavy, it made me feel safe when I wore it. Beria had a clean-out and it disappeared from my bedroom. 'I gave it away,' she told me when I asked where it was. 'Anyway, it looked silly on you. It was too big.'

Wint's house was in Manning Street, just down from the post office. It had two main rooms – a lounge, and Wint and Pop's bedroom, the door of which she always kept shut. A closed-in verandah ran on three sides of the house and was partitioned off to form other bedrooms, a dining room and a bathroom. The large kitchen was tacked onto the back verandah. The lounge room, where Pop sat each night to listen to the wireless, starting with the ABC news at seven o'clock, was furnished with a three-piece cut-velvet suite. In winter Pop lit the open fire, above which the mantelpiece was covered in framed photographs. I slept on the louvred front verandah.

The bathroom was at one end of the verandah and Pop and Wint's daughter, June, had a bedroom at the other end. Wint was a fine seamstress, and June's single timber wardrobe was bursting with a collection of pastel nylon and tulle ball gowns. I was allowed to look and, occasionally, to touch these glorious creations. It was my favourite place in the house. Sometimes, while Wint worked in the kitchen or hung out the washing in the backyard, I would sneak into June's bedroom, quietly turn the key in the mirrored single wardrobe door and stare in wonderment, touching and rolling the fabric between my fingers. Leonora and Gwalia were social towns and during the winter ball season the young men and women thought nothing of travelling to the nearby towns of Menzies and Laverton, or almost 150 miles to Kalgoorlie, leaving on Friday night and returning late Sunday afternoon. I would stand silently, watching Wint pack June's suitcase with one or two of her creations.

Everything was always in the same place in Wint's kitchen. In winter, when it was too cold to eat on the verandah, we had the evening meal at the kitchen table, which was usually covered by a floral-patterned cream plastic cloth with a scalloped edge. On the verandah, the burgundy crushed-velvet tablecloth reached almost to the floor, its edge trimmed with gold cotton pom-poms about the size of a sixpence, a few of which had broken away and hung by a thread. On the coldest days, Wint stood in front of her green enamelled kitchen fire, lifted up the back of her skirt, and sighed and wiggled with pleasure as she warmed her bum.

Every morning was spent cooking for Pop, who came home at midday. First we went to the butcher and then Mazza's shop. I trotted along beside Wint, holding her hand and chatting. The combined food smells in the kitchen hung in the air like a swirling fog. I sat at the far end of the table, out of harm's way, watching as Wint made curried sausages, stews or sweet curry and rice.

Sometimes for lunch we had left-over Sunday roast leg of lamb with hot mashed potato, and lettuce and tomato covered with an English salad dressing made from Nestlé's sweetened condensed milk, vinegar and Keen's dry mustard powder. For pudding Wint made lemon sago and creamed rice with tinned fruit. She filled the light-as-a-feather double sponge cakes with Nestlé's tinned cream and apricot jam.

Pop sat at the head of the table in a Victorian carver with a brown leather sprung seat. The table was permanently set with a traditional EPNS and cut-glass triple cruet set, a dome-shaped butter dish and a milk jug, all protected from the flies with a fine throw-over net edged with evenly spaced, coloured glass beads. The table had heavy turned legs with metal and enamel casters which sat in round, thick glass holders to stop it from sliding on the cement floor partly covered in linoleum.

Pop was a fitter and turner and was appointed a foreman on the mine when Mr Lethlean resigned. He wore long-sleeved navy blue overalls and had his own particular reassuring smell – a mixture of grime, sump oil and kerosene. A couple of minutes after they blew the noon whistle on the mine, Pop appeared from behind the corner of the St James' Church of England. He came into the yard through the back gate. The rainwater tank was at the side of the house next to Pop's timber carpenter's workbench, at one end of which was a vise made from wood and steel and a steel blacksmith's anvil. Next to the anvil was Pop's Sunshine milk tin filled with kerosene-soaked cotton waste from the mine which he used to wipe the grease from his hands. Leaning over the bath, Pop scrubbed his hands with Trusol, a grey abrasive cleaning paste which came in a round airtight yellow tin. It was also used to clean enamel baths and saucepans. If you left the Trusol exposed to the air for a few days, the paste dehydrated and was unusable.

Wint lit the bath heater every night. I was a ticklish child, and from the squeals of laughter you would have thought she was trying to drown me. It was pandemonium and Wint always ended with a wet pinafore.

Beria was a pernickety seamstress who learned from a professional in the Salvation Army home. The officer in charge of the sewing room was a society dressmaker before she joined the Army, and she taught all the girls to sew. 'Matron Pratt used to get me to darn her black silk stockings. She said none of the other girls could do it as finely as I did.'

When a commercial traveller came calling, he soon convinced Beria it was time for a new sewing machine. For £127 cash, they could purchase the newest top-of-the-range Singer sewing machine. The salesman suggested they trade in the treadle Singer machine my father bought for Beria in 1939. A superb piece of mechanical design, it had cost £27. It had three carved drawers and the black metal head of the machine was ornately decorated with the company logo and swirling hand-painted gold filigree. After fourteen years of constant use it needed only a new wheel belt, and was in such excellent condition they offered a £25 trade-in.

Singer's latest piece of engineering wizardry was Beria's pride and joy, and when they heard about it the other ladies came to have a look at it. It did zigzag stitching, ran back and forward with the flick of a lever, and even made buttonholes. Double needles meant Beria could sew in two colours at the same time, and by changing a series of black plastic discs and metal feet it embroidered and did a variety of stitches. The sewing machine folded from sight into a solid wooden cabinet with double doors. The top of the leather-padded stool was removable, and housed dozens of wooden cotton reels and various sewing accoutrements. 'These are not toys for you to play with,' Beria said when she noticed my interest.' And if I catch you cutting paper with my dressmaking scissors, I'll skin you alive.' Eventually, she taught me how to sew and I was allowed to make handkerchiefs with squares of old sheeting edged with lace.

Beria thought nothing of spending the whole day sewing, and was not frightened to work with delicate fabrics. She drew her own patterns, and made Nita several voile dresses with full-flared skirts. The standard 36-inch width of fabric was not wide enough to cut a full skirt, and 'a piece' needed to be added to the hemline to complete the circle. In the summer I wore red and blue gingham, and green sailcloth bib-and-brace combinations. Beria decorated around the edge of the bib with white rickrack – a zigzag trimming. The straps buttoned at the front and were crossed at the back to stop them slipping off my shoulders.

When someone gave Beria a bag of wool scraps, she turned them into a technicoloured striped jumper for me. It buttoned across the shoulder and was my favourite. When it came to dressmaking, crocheting or knitting, she had unlimited patience, and would do something time and again until she considered it to be perfect. She unravelled a hand-knitted jumper, wound the wool into balls, and re-knitted the yarn. Sometimes a knot would take twenty minutes to untie. For the best part of one winter, Beria spent the evenings sitting in front of the wood stove, listening to the wireless and knitting for Steve two two-ply sleeveless cabled pullovers: cream with navy blue trim, and the other a bottle green.

Beria was pedantic about perfect hemlines and used an upright wooden measuring stick fitted with a sliding red plastic arrow. She had an unerring eye and commented in the street: 'Look at the hem on her dress, it's a disgrace. It's up at the front and dipping at the back. Somebody should tell her.'

When Wint's daughter June married Mick Pavlovich, Wint made the wedding dress. She brought a length of fabric around to embroider it on Beria's machine. I couldn't understand why Beria wasn't invited to the wedding. 'It doesn't worry me,' was Beria's reaction. 'If she doesn't want me there, I'm not going to lose any sleep over it. I won't have to buy her a present now, will I?' The wedding was never discussed, and Beria and Wint remained close friends.

***

The mine manager's house was at the top of Staff Hill and formed the apex of our small community. The house was built by Herbert Hoover, who passed through Gwalia on his way to becoming the thirty-first president of the United States. Mr Hoover was an engineer based in Kalgoorlie and travelled to the many mines under his control, including the Sons of Gwalia. To cut mining costs he hired mostly Italian labourers, as a result of which the town's population was made up mostly of immigrants. On their first day of work many of them arrived wearing the only clothing they possessed, a tailored suit.

Mr Hoover chose the site and supervised the building of the Oregon-lined manager's residence. It was a grand design which looked out over the town. The house, which was completed in 1899 at a cost of £750, was surrounded on three sides by a wide wooden verandah. A small back room accommodated a full-time cook. Each room was fitted with a servant bell pull and during winter a yardman was needed to supply the wood for the kitchen and the four fireplaces. A tank behind the house was used as a pool.

Reg Barden was the manager of the mine, and he lived in the house with his wife, Eileen, and their four children. On the occasions I dared venture close to the house I was intimidated by its high wrought-iron fence, the imposing gates and concrete steps, the manicured lawns and gardens, and a magnificent display of roses planted by Mrs Barden. The vegetable garden and grapevines were located in the yard behind the house and the chicken and turkey pen a short distance down the back of the hill. One night four drunken teenage lads, led by Vergie Cugini, stole a turkey, which they killed, plucked, cleaned and attempted to cook on an open fire behind the South Gwalia hill. Having done with the turkey, they decided to borrow the mine's green utility to take a joy ride around the town. One of the lads became nervous and headed home, later confessing to his father. Their high-spirited prank turned sour when the Gwalia policeman wanted to press charges, but Reg Barden was opposed to the idea. 'No. I was young once,' he said and let the matter drop.

Most houses in Gwalia had water and electricity but there was no sewerage system in the town. The bathroom water ran into the garden, or out onto the flat through crudely laid drainpipes where it stagnated into a thick black smelly slime, ensnaring passers-by who ventured unaware into the night without a torch. Often we played near these polluted areas, and sometimes inadvertently strayed too near. The sensation of the hot, stinking sludge oozing through the toes of my bare feet sent a shudder through my body.

The lavatory was hot in the summer, cold in winter, dark in the dead of night, and foul all year. Underneath the wooden seat was a favourite nesting place for red-back spiders. The thought of them made me cautious and, like my father, I squatted European style with one foot firmly on either side of the hole. Some people installed a candle in their outhouse. My friend Jan Quarti lived in one of the staff houses on the hill, and her mother had an electric light installed in theirs. We had neither, and I never went after dark. I used the woodheap, or the ground.

Mazza's store sold boxes of toilet paper but we used squares of newspaper stuffed into a rotting canvas waterbag, which hung from a rusting nail hammered into a dried post. Attached to the back of door, a fading deaf-and-dumb sign-language chart was disintegrating in the dry heat. My father placed a bundle of English *Daily Sketch* newspapers in a wooden box in the lavatory. Brittle and yellowed with age, they attracted clucky chooks who sought them out as a nesting place. There was an established protocol to reading in the lavatory; always tear the sheet of paper from the top of the magazine or the newspaper. There was nothing more irritating than getting halfway through a story only to discover the next page was missing. The squares of soft green tissue paper used to pack fruit in timber crates were saved and put to good use.

The brimming tar-lined pan was replaced twice a week through the ground-level door at the back. The decomposing raw waste, used Kotex sanitary pads and Durex condoms attracted swarms of blowflies, turning the pan into a rich feeding ground for thousands of heaving maggots. The use of ashes or phenyl in the pan made it almost bearable. Beria didn't bother with such details and left the contents of our pan just as nature delivered.

It puzzled me why they called it the night cart. In Gwalia the open utility truck went down the main street in the middle of the day. In the summer, and about 150 degrees in the sun, it was putrid, and even though the pans were covered with a lid, it turned your stomach; the smell lodged in the back of your nose and throat. I hated it and tried to hold my breath until the smell disappeared. Beria was mystified and wanted to know why I threw a half-eaten ice-cream into the bin after the cart went past.

'Because it will be covered in germs from the night cart,' I told her.

Beria shook her head as she so often did with me. 'I'm buggered if I know where you get some of these ideas. Sometimes I think you're not all there. Next time if you don't want your ice-cream, give it to me. I'm not worried about the germs!'

When we had nothing to do, my friend Nat Garbellini and I would sometimes lurk in the lane behind his place, waiting for someone to go into the lavatory. After allowing them time to get comfortable we would sneak behind, quietly open the flap, and jab their bum with a long pointed stick; or we'd bash as hard as we could with both hands on the tin wall. In no position to venture out, the startled occupant swore and cursed. Thank God we were never caught. Nat's mother, Ollie, didn't put up with any nonsense, and neither did Beria. She had a fifteen-inch strip of leather suitcase strapping which hung from a nail next to the fireplace. It was soft enough to wrap round your legs and the tails Lewie cut into it tripled the sting and the number of welts it left behind.

When Lewie's son Trevor threw a lighted twopenny bunger into the lavatory pan, showering his maternal grandmother Mary from head to toe with the contents, Beria couldn't contain her delight. The bunger went off with a hell of a bang, almost wrecking the lavatory. Mary flew out, with her skirt around her shoulders and her knickers down around her ankles, calling out to her husband: 'George, George, come and help me.'

Steve never went out to the lavatory at night. A couple of times I saw him peeing into the tin bath on the back verandah. He kept a large Sunshine milk tin under the bed, into which he relieved himself and spat lumps of phlegm. Beria was not too particular, and the tin sometimes remained unemptied for several days. If I happened to be around, the job of disposing of this foul-smelling liquid fell to me. It turned my stomach.

With my hands wrapped around the brimming tin, I tentatively carried it outside. My awkwardness set up a rocking motion, pushing the urine over the edge and trickling down the side of the tin, wetting my hands. I was not allowed to tip it into the pan. Insisting the contents would raise the level, Beria told me to throw it out onto the flat. The milk tin was originally airtight with an aluminium seal, the removal of which left a razor-sharp edge, and several times I cut my finger, badly. I had not mastered the art of throwing the slopping contents in one clean action and every time, without fail, some of the putrid liquid slopped back onto my legs, running down to my feet and soaking my sandals. The phlegm stuck to my legs. I dry retched, but my protests to Beria were dismissed. 'Oh give over, and stop your complaining. Just wash it off under the hose; it won't kill you.'

***

A few months after we moved to Grinning Joe's house in 1950, Beria got a full-time job as laundress at the Leonora District Hospital. She worked a five-day week and was paid £7, out of which she paid Wint £1 a week to look after me during the day. A little before seven o'clock Beria dropped me off before meeting up with three or four girls who worked as wards maids and together they rode in a group to the hospital.

On those rare days Wint couldn't look after me I went to work with Beria, riding on the passenger seat of her bicycle. The hospital was at the top of a steepish rise, and with me on the back of the bike it took some pedalling power for Beria to keep up with the other girls.

For several weeks Beria complained to Lewie and Steve about a slow leak puncture. She had to pump up the tyre before she left for work, and then again before she set out for home. After an especially hard day she arrived home in a temper and, throwing the bike on the ground, vented her spleen. 'I am sick of asking, and I am not going back to work until one of you fixes that bloody puncture.' It was done in half an hour but Beria was still fuming. 'I hope you're not expecting me to say thank you, because I'm not. You should have bloody well fixed it for me when I first told you about it two weeks ago.'

Occasionally, Beria took me with her to the hospital and I couldn't have been happier. I spent the day helping and wandering around, and in the afternoon I slept in one of the nurses' rooms. In the extreme far corner of the hospital grounds was a small brick building with a tin roof. It was the morgue. Beria knew I was itching to look inside: 'If I catch you going near the morgue, you'll get a belting.'

As the girls rode around the side of the hospital to park their bikes, they could smell the ether heavy in the air. That was enough to make Beria feel green around the gills. It was midday before she stopped feeling squeamish. One of the side effects of ether is post-anaesthetic nausea and vomiting. The couple of times Beria went into hospital for an operation, she heaved her heart out for days. The operating theatre was a brick room on the side of the building. It was not air-conditioned and in the summer Dr Moore operated at five in the morning. There was no anaesthetist so he started the anaesthetic, and it was maintained by the theatre sister and regulated by checking the patient's eyes.

Beria washed and ironed from 8 am until 4 pm. She never once arrived late, left early, or took a sick day. The washing was done by hand, copper boiling and individually rinsing each item. She did all the linen, including the bloodstained. Depending on the number of patients, and the weekend activity, the Monday wash was sometimes a heavy load. Beria started her working life in service, and she wouldn't leave until every last item had been washed. It was a matter of pride. 'Matron Stokes said she never once had to check on me, because she knew I wouldn't leave anything for the next day.'

Sometimes it was five o'clock before she finished. Matron and the six or so nursing staff wore two pure cotton uniforms a week, which Beria starched and ironed, using Reckitt's raw starch mixed with hot water. On the back of the starch packet was a scene from a Victorian laundry, with the lady of the house checking as the laundry maid dashed away with a smoothing iron. Matron Stokes was so impressed with Beria's efforts she carried a uniform through the wards showing patients how expertly it had been ironed. Only Matron wore white; the nurses wore blue because of the red dust.

The free-standing laundry was crudely constructed from sheets of galvanised iron and a couple of empty window frames. It was away from the hospital block, behind the kitchen, and just along from the natives' wards. The laundry backed onto the rocky scrub and was unprotected from the sun. It had a wooden floor, running cold water, a large ironing table and two concrete rinsing troughs with a hand-turned wringer in between. The troughs were so rough they took the skin off your knuckles if your scrubbing hand slipped. The second cold water rinsing trough was dipped with Reckitt's blue, a laundry whitener to stop old linen turning yellow. The huge boiling copper was set in bricks. Jack Cudini was the yardman, and every morning it was his job to light the fire in the copper and to stoke it throughout the day. In summer the temperature in the laundry reached as high as 125 degrees.

It was also Jack Cudini's job to wheel the occasional body to the morgue on a six-wheel trolley. The yard was stony, which made for a bumpy final ride. Jack was somewhat taken aback one day when the supposed corpse of Mr Adamini sat bolt upright. 'Jack, where are you taking me?' he asked. Only later did they tell Jack it was a joke.

Jack had a pronounced stutter which Beria couldn't resist mimicking. With her back to the door in the staff dining room she was in full flight on one occasion, and the more the girls laughed the more Beria continued. She didn't realise Jack was standing behind her, watching. 'You bloody bitches. Why didn't you tell me he was standing behind me?'

Beria argued with Steve and handed in her notice after thirteen months. 'No, bugger you,' she yelled at him. 'Why should I work and pay for everything in the house with my money, and you keep all yours so you can drink and gamble?' On Beria's last day Matron Stokes made her a personal gift of ten shillings.

༺ ༻

The Half-caste Act of 1886 defined as 'Aboriginal', every Aboriginal native of Australia, every Aboriginal half-caste, or child of a half-caste – whom we called quarter-castes. The half-castes – those of mixed blood with citizenship papers – were allowed to live in the town and were employed as domestics in the hotels and boarding houses, and at the hospital.

The 'full bloods' – those not of mixed blood – worked on the sheep stations as stockmen and domestics. The Half-caste Act introduced employment contracts between employers and Aboriginal workers over the age of fourteen but there was no provision in the act for contracts to include wages. Employers were expected to provide 'substantial, good and sufficient rations' – usually flour, tea, sugar and meat, clothing and blankets. If they were paid it was at a lower rate than their white co-workers. The act also gave them the right to keep their families together.

Gwalia was a designated mining precinct which, by law, banned Aborigines. That changed in 1944 when the government decided to give citizenship rights to some Aboriginal people if they promised to give up their traditional ways, prove they had severed all ties with family – except parents, siblings and their own children – and friends, were free from disease, could speak English, had been 'civilised' in behaviour for two years, could manage their personal affairs, and were industrious in their habits.

Any white person could make a complaint to a magistrate, and their citizenship could be revoked if they were found guilty of rejecting 'civilised' life, were convicted twice of any felony, found drunk, or had contracted leprosy, syphilis, granuloma (small nodules that are seen in a variety of diseases) or yaws (a tropical infection of the skin, bones and joints).

British law didn't recognise Aboriginal laws and practices, or their right to own property. Legally, these citizenship certificates meant they were no longer Aboriginal, and while the blackfellas referred to them pejoratively as 'dog tags' or 'dog licences', the certificates granted them voting rights, allowed them to go into hotels and shops, provided for their children to go to state schools, and removed them from the restrictions of the stringent state protection laws. In Gwalia, those with citizenship papers lived in the town in rented properties, but they weren't allowed to swim in the pool, and weren't encouraged to be part of the community. It was illegal to sell blackfellas alcohol, and even those few in possession of citizenship papers were discouraged from joining the white men in the public bars.

Aborigines without papers were controlled by the Commissioner of Native Affairs. Summarily, they could be tried for a range of criminal offences, could not press charges at law, were not permitted to give evidence in court, and could not vote. If they tried to enter a banned area everyone chased them, shouting, 'Get out of here!' calling them 'boongs' and 'black bastards'. They could be forced to live on reserves, and had no access to social welfare.

The nomadic Aborigines lived in bark, tin and scrap-metal shelters in the bush, or under the trees on the fringe of the town. They wandered around by day but had to be gone by four o'clock, and could not return until nine the following morning. Those caught after hours were locked up for the night, regardless of the explanation.

The district hospital was segregated. Even those natives with citizenship certificates were not hospitalised in the whites-only wards, and expectant Aboriginal women were denied access to the labour or maternity wards, except in a medical emergency. A full-time Aboriginal wards maid was not allowed to sleep in the white staff quarters. My sister Joan was born at the Leonora hospital. When they brought her to Beria for the first time her face was hidden from view. Beria lifted back the bunny rug and discovered an Aboriginal baby. The nursing staff and the other women in the ward laughed.

In 1954, for the first time, the children of the few full-blooded Aboriginal families who lived in Gwalia, and a number of half-caste kids, were accepted into the state schools. While they weren't actively denied a place, there were no Aboriginal children at the local convent. I couldn't work out what it meant when I was told the Aborigines were pagans and could corrupt our Christian souls.

The Commissioner's power to remove children was abolished by the Native Welfare Act, 1954; however, he remained the legal guardian of all indigenous children. Even those children being cared for by a relative or friend could be removed if maintenance was not being paid, regardless of the circumstances under which the child was living. Full-blooded children considered in any medical danger, or living in a health-threatening environment, were separated from their parents and placed permanently into the care of the United Aborigines Mission at Mount Margaret, a Christian establishment founded in 1921 by the Rev. Rodolphe Schenk and his wife Isobel, a typist who taught crafts to the women on the mission.

Schenk was notorious for the many savings he implemented in the mission's operating budget. Beria didn't mince her words. 'Everyone knows he's a crook. He's making a fortune out of the blackfellas.' The Rev. Schenk's unsympathetic and fundamentalist interference with traditional practices attracted strong criticism from visiting anthropologists, and resistance from Aboriginal elders. Aboriginal mothers were denied access to their children, the majority of whom were converted to Christianity and taught to speak only English. Their ancient heritage was ignored.

We came face to face with Aboriginal mission children once a year when they arrived on the back of a truck to compete in the inter-school sports. Several were exceptionally fine athletes, who easily beat their competition. However, from time to time there seemed to be confusion about their age. Some of the ten- and eleven-year-old boys against whom we raced seemed to be showing signs of growing a beard.

∞

Relationships between Aboriginal women and white men were frowned upon in most quarters. Alberto Bernardi lived with an Aboriginal woman in Leonora in a run-down camp near the convent, at the back of Lewie and Jean's house. He was referred to as a no-hoper, and no one in the town had much to do with him. Aboriginal women were called 'gins', and white men who had a sexual relationship with them were 'gin jockeys'. Their children were 'half-castes' and, if the relationship ended, the kids were forcibly and permanently removed from the mother's custody, and placed in a state or religious institution.

The mine didn't operate on Sundays, and it was a day of quiet in Gwalia. Even the steam whistle was silent. Bob Mazza was having a nap before midday dinner and was startled by the sound of two gunshots and a woman screaming. He went to investigate and discovered it was coming from the house opposite the mine mess, where Davies, a white man, and Jedda, an Aboriginal woman, lived in a permanent and often volatile de facto relationship. A friend, McConaughey, was also living with them. As they did every weekend, the three were drinking and arguing when Davies learned of Jedda's infidelity with McConaughey. Davies tried to shoot Jedda, who managed to escape with a grazed arm. Before turning the gun on himself, Davies shot McConaughey, fatally.

∞

The blackfellas in Gwalia were Wongi people, whose original country is around Maralinga, the remote spot in South Australia where the federal government granted the British permission to conduct a series of nuclear tests throughout 1956 and 1957. For a couple of years there was an old Wongi whom Beria used to feed. Three or four times a week he would come and stand at the back gate. He never called out; he just waited patiently till she spotted him. Steve would say to her: 'Eh, your boyfriend's down the back.'

He was tall and skinny, and always looked so sick. He never had shoes, not even in the winter. Beria always gave him hot soup, meat and bread, and some tea and sugar in a brown paper bag. All he ever said was: 'Thank you, Missus.' I used to watch him as he wandered off down the back lane. One day he stopped coming. When I asked Beria why, she said, 'I don't know, Ronnie. He probably died, poor old bugger.'

There were two full-bloods in the town, Billy and Nina. They lived in a makeshift tin and chaff-bag shelter under the old pepper tree down behind the railway line, not far from the football oval. Their skin was black as pitch and Billy's hair was matted and tied back with a red scarf. Nina always wore three or four dresses and walked a few paces behind, followed by a couple of kangaroo dogs with clearly visible ribs. They wandered around the town collecting food and clothing. They never caused trouble, nor did they speak to anyone.

My sister Joan was about four, and scared stiff of them. From the back door Beria would call out, 'Billy, Nina, you can come and get her now'.

It was enough to send Joan rushing to her room, crying hysterically. It was a torment which amused Beria, Lewie and Jean, and they laughed at her terror. I watched without saying a word when Joan ran and hid under her bed. She had to be physically dragged out, rigid with fear and fighting and screaming at the top of her voice: 'No, no!' Beria had to calm her with promises it was only a joke.

Lewie found a wallet in the street which contained a large sum of money. He contacted the police. About an hour later they called to say a husband and wife, with a couple of kids, were on their way. They were most grateful, explaining it was their pension money for the next fortnight. They left, and after closing the door Lewie turned and said: 'I'd have kept it if I'd known it belonged to a bloody Abo.'

In 1952, after thirteen years of marriage, including the legally required three years of separation, my father filed for divorce on the grounds of Beria's adultery with Steve Salinovich, who was named as co-respondent. According to the divorce papers, my father 'remonstrated with Beria about her behaviour towards, and her association with, the Co-Defendant Steve Salinovich. When she refused to end this association, he ordered her to leave the matrimonial home, and thereupon cohabitation ceased.'

Divorce was messy, expensive, and carried with it a social stigma. It was not recognised by the Roman Catholic Church and was deemed a mortal sin, which the parish priests brazenly visited on the children. Children born of second marriages which were not approved by the church were deemed illegitimate.

Beria and my father were on civil terms and when she asked him for a divorce he agreed without argument. He was the innocent party but never once made a disparaging comment about Beria, nor were we involved in any tension which had been between them. When the papers were served on Beria, Lewie and Steve drove to Kalgoorlie to make arrangements with Beria's solicitor, Mr Hartrey. The two men, both of whom were six foot and a bit, completed the seven-hour, 294-mile round trip over one weekend. Steve rode pillion on the strut-metal seat of Lewie's Bantam motorbike, the smallest in the range, which resembled a bicycle fitted with a lawnmower engine. Perched on the metal seat with his knees up under his chin, Steve needed a pillow for seating protection as they bounced over the corrugated dirt road.

On Monday, 31 August 1953, the divorce case was heard in the Eastern Goldfields Circuit Court, Kalgoorlie, before Commissioner T.A. Draper, Esq. Both my parents were in court but neither was required to take the stand. It was an uncomplicated, uncontested session with no disputes from either party. By law, Beria's adultery made her the guilty party and liable for my father's costs; however, he chose to pay his own legal fees. They had to wait another year before the marriage was finally dissolved, freeing both parties to marry again.

As Beria was leaving the Hannan Street courthouse she stumbled on the steps and snapped the high heel from her shoe. She turned to my father who was walking close behind, removed the damaged shoe and, to my father's consternation, threw it at him.

'Now look what you have done. It's your bloody fault!'

Beria was having none of it when Mr Hartrey later explained it would cost a further £25 for the court to make a custody decision.

'You can bloody well go to hell. I'm telling you straight, I am not paying you another penny!'

With that she slammed down the receiver of the public telephone and the living and financial arrangements remained as they were before the divorce.

I could read by the time I turned four and was obsessed with the idea of attending school. I played schools on my own at home and I pestered Beria, pleading to be allowed to go to the convent with Nita. In 1951, Nita's final year in primary school, Beria finally relented. 'For God's sake, Nita, will you ask Sister Mary Bertrand if she'll take him? And you can tell Sister from me, I said he's driving me mad about it. Every bloody day it's the same thing, wanting to go to school. He won't stop harping on it.'

Unofficially, I started school in the third term after the August holidays. I couldn't have been happier, trotting alongside Nita every morning for the remainder of the year. In 1952, a couple of weeks short of my fifth birthday, I was officially enrolled at the St Catherine's Dominican Convent.

When asked if we knew any poetry I leapt to my feet, keen to share my repertoire taught by Beria. They were poems she had learned during her years in the Salvation Army children's home. I recited my favourite:

Dan, Dan the dirty man,
Washed his face in the frying pan.
Combed his hair with the leg of the chair,
And told his mother he didn't care.

I was pleased when everyone laughed, enthusiastically. However, several days later, my next poem was not received with the same degree of enthusiasm:

Kikey Moses, King of the Jews,
Sold his wife for a pair of shoes.
When the shoes began to wear
Kikey Moses began to swear.
When the swearing began to stop,
Kikey Moses bought a shop.
When the shop began to sell
Kikey Moses went to hell!

The next time my teacher met Beria, she suggested perhaps I should be taught more suitable poems in the future. Beria was puzzled. 'I'm buggered if I know what she's talking about.'

I was at the convent two years before Beria sent me to the state school. 'They're not teaching him fast enough.'

When a school report said, 'He has a keen interest and a wide general knowledge, but needs to learn to control his tongue, and moderate his language,' I was baffled. Beria made no comment, and it was never investigated. I wondered if I had been confused with some other kid as I never swore. Beria did, often. When her small Hoover washing machine, overloaded with heavy working clothes, struggled to turn the tangled weight, she whacked it impatiently with her dowelling pot-stick, cursing at the top of her voice: 'You rotten mongrel bastard of a thing.' Like me, the washing machine was obedient. 'If ever I hear you swearing,' Beria warned, 'I'll bloody well wash your mouth out with soap and water, and then I'll give you a belting. And don't think I won't.'

A couple of years before I was born, Beria's friend Ollie Garbellini left Curly and nicked off with another bloke. She went to Kalgoorlie for a couple of months. She took her oldest boy, Ken, and left Peggy, Billy and Ann with Curly, who brought them around for Beria to look after. Billy was a handful: 'God, he was a bugger of a kid.' She warned him about his swearing. When he ignored her, she grabbed him by the scruff of his neck, marched him into the bathroom and forcibly shoved the cake of Lifebuoy Red soap into his mouth. When Ollie returned, Billy told his mother. Ollie laughed: 'The way she swears, someone should wash out *her* mouth with Lifebuoy.'

Beria never made an idle threat. Ann was about twelve months at the time. 'She was a dirty little bitch,' Beria said later. 'She'd take the mess out of her nappy and smear it all over the cot and the walls. I told her: "If you do that again I'll bloody well rub your nose in it." She did, and I rubbed her nose in it. She never did it again.'

Beria was feisty, and after a fight with the local baker she started ordering her bread from Kalgoorlie, 147 miles away. It arrived twice a week by train. She sent me to the station to collect it from the guard's van. One night, unbeknownst to me, Beria arrived just as I was struggling with the sugarbag and its contents. She overheard something I said, which she considered out of line. Throwing the sugarbag to one side, she grabbed me by the arm, and on the crowded railway station, belted me: 'Now bloody well get home, and don't stop running till you get there.' Blinded by tears, I took off with Beria following behind. I was strongly attached to my mother, and happy to be around her, watching whatever she was doing. No matter how upset I was after a belting, Beria never hugged me to 'make it better': 'Don't come to me looking for sympathy. You've got no one to blame but yourself. Learn to behave, and I won't have to hit you.'

∞

From age five I suffered from migraine, a debilitating condition which in the 1950s was a medical mystery. After several years I was diagnosed as being nervous and highly strung and was prescribed daily doses of Phenobarbital. I took the tiny tablets twice daily for two or three years. No one mentioned to me or my father that it was a habit-forming barbiturate.

My migraines were called bilious attacks. I would wake in the morning unable to lift my head off the pillow, and wracked with temple-thumping pain. Sometimes I thought my skull would crack open and my brains spill out. In my disturbed sleep the blankets became thick and heavy and my fingers and hands seemed bloated and difficult to move. With the imaginary weight resting on me I couldn't move. I sweated, profusely. The migraines started about the time the postmaster's daughter and I went wandering around the vacant flat on the boundary of the mine and overdosed on wild hops, which grew in abundance. We ate so much of the edible dark green spade-shaped leaves we vomited, violently.

The attacks became so regular Beria took to keeping a small tin bucket on hand and I would spend the morning vomiting bright green bile. An attack usually lasted for about three hours. When the vomiting ceased, the headache was gone. I would pass out for a couple of hours and then be up and around, if somewhat exhausted and incapable of any activity which required energy. It took two days to fully recover. Beria described me as 'green around the gills' but the doctor was never called.

The worst attack occurred in January 1958 when I was living with my father and Nita. It was an abnormally scorching day and I wandered for some hours in the sun without a hat. Quite suddenly, and late in the afternoon, I recognised the symptoms and went to rest on my bed. Within minutes I was moaning in agony. It was my father's first encounter with my migraines and there was nothing he could do but stand by helplessly, staring. Eventually I vomited, then fell asleep for several hours. The next day he took me to Mazza's and bought for me a large straw hat, which he insisted I wear whenever I left the house. 'Where's your hat?'

became his catch-cry. He was convinced the attacks were the result of intense heat.

※

Like every other kid in the town, I looked forward to the arrival of the twice-weekly steam train. The sound of the whistle heralding its imminent arrival as it came round the sweep of track and crossed over the wood-line bridge brought us running from all directions.

The back gate at Grinning Joe's house was made from sheets of galvanised iron nailed to a Z-shaped frame. It was too big for me to open and Beria warned me on numerous occasions not to climb on it. In my haste to see the train I ignored the warning, lost my footing, slipped and caught myself on a piece of jagged tin which tore a half-moon gaping gash into my inside upper right arm. With a flap of hanging flesh and pouring blood, I ran screaming into the house. Beria wrapped my arm in a towel and Harry Gray drove us to the Leonora hospital in his delivery truck.

I was five years old at the time and devoted to Beria. The pain was made even worse when, in the midst of the mayhem, concerned and distressed, Beria said: 'It is your own bloody fault. How many times have I told you not to climb on the gate?' I didn't answer. 'Well?' And as she so often did, she shook her head and tutted in disbelief.

The gash required two stitches. I began to cry again at the sight of the suture. 'Shut up,' Dr Moore said. 'I haven't even touched you yet.'

※

There was only one footpath in Gwalia. The winding dirt tracks elsewhere were minefields of double-G prickles and seed pods from the hundreds of tumbleweeds which blew in the hot wind. Following behind Nita, I stepped onto a piece of tumbleweed, which disappeared into the ball of my right foot. For several days Beria was unsympathetic when I complained about the pain. 'It's your own fault. How many times have I told you not to take your shoes off?'

Finally, she took me to the doctor, who insisted it was nothing more than a scratch. The pain persisted and I continued to complain. I was unable to wear shoes or place my foot squarely on the floor. In the bath one night I yelped in agony as Beria attempted to wash my foot. In irritation, she grabbed a hold, and using her thumbs either side of the wound she sharply squeezed the affected area. I screamed in agony as the wound exploded. There was a sharp spurt of pus and blood, and out popped the offending tumbleweed spike, which Beria fished out of the bathwater. After a bit more squeezing, the pain disappeared. The next morning she marched me to confront the doctor. Showing him the piece of weed, she snapped: 'You said there was nothing in his foot. So what the bloody hell is this then?'

Sunday lunch was either roast pork or chicken, although Beria preferred rooster: 'It's more tasty.' First thing after breakfast she chose and caught the bird and handed it over to Steve to chop off its head. The plucking and cleaning was Beria's job, and the ritual never altered. She blanched the bird in hot water before plucking and singeing the remaining down with a rolled-up piece of burning newspaper, creating a lingering acrid smell, like burning hair. When it came to cleaning the chook Beria was not at all squeamish. She cut a hole in the underbelly, put in her hand and pulled out the gizzards, separating the giblets, the feet, neck and unlaid egg yolks. Beria cooked the chook and potatoes in a camp oven, a cast-iron pot with a handle and lid designed to sit in the ashes of a stockman's camp fire. To make it fit into the oven of the stove Beria had Steve saw off the three small legs. She used a knife to string the beans, and the peas were out of a can.

When Beria and Steve went to have a sleep after lunch I was told to keep quiet. My curiosity got the better of me and I went to investigate. Beria and Steve had the back bedroom with two windows, one of which opened onto the enclosed verandah. I was about three at the time and, with the window sill too high for me, I moved a nearby oil tin into place and climbed up. I could see everything. Beria and Steve were naked. He was on top with his bum bouncing up and down. After a few moments Beria caught sight of my face pressed up against the window pane, watching. Without arousing Steve's suspicion she waved viciously, once. I knew from the gravity of her action exactly what was meant and I moved outside to play, at double speed. 'Thank God Steve didn't know he was watching,' Beria said to Joan Gray later. 'I'm not joking when I say he would have killed him!'

Since Beria never had a headache or caught cold, she was not a sympathetic nurse, although she did take notice when I complained about a pain in the lower right-hand side of my stomach. I was in the bath and I squealed when she touched me. The next morning she took me to Dr Moore, who diagnosed appendicitis. It was the winter of 1951, and within a few days I was a patient in the Leonora District Hospital.

There was a bright light, a mask on my face, and then the smell of ether. I struggled momentarily, trying to pull off the mask. When I came to, my appendix had been removed. In a few days I was sitting in the sun in a cane chair on the verandah facing the lawn, wearing a check dressing gown and drinking a cup of soup. Beria visited and I was happy, but from the moment she left I cried and, no matter how much they tried, the nurses couldn't settle me. After two or three visits Matron Stokes took action: 'Rocky, he frets when you leave, and I think it'd be best if you stayed away until he's ready to go home.'

Matron was right. I was so involved in what was happening I failed to notice Beria was not visiting. My father visited several times, and although I loved him, I was not upset when he left. At the end of two weeks Dr Moore removed the two stitches and I went home with a neat scar.

∞

The Leonora District Hospital was funded jointly by the state and federal governments and provided free medical service for families living and working in the goldfields. The doctor and matron, helped by a small nursing and domestic staff, ran efficient men's, women's, children's, native and maternity wards. There were live-in quarters for the staff and the matron, and the doctor's residence was attached to the hospital. Dr Harry Moore was so poorly paid, £25 a week less rent, he threatened the board with resignation unless he was given a raise.

The grounds of the hospital had several grass areas and a lot of trees for shade. The maternity ward had its own lawn with benches and was out of sight from the more public areas. The domestic and medical section of the hospital was housed under one huge galvanised-iron roof and surrounded by silent bush. The wards had polished wooden floors, wooden bedside lockers, green privacy curtains on wires, sturdy hospital-issue iron bed frames with wire bases, firm mattresses and pillows, and government-issue bedding. The bars of the metal bedhead were hinged at the top, allowing the bottom to pull forward and form a back support for patients sitting up in bed. The wireless was piped to each bed and connected to an aluminium tear-shaped earpiece which rested on your pillow. The doctor held morning surgery six days of the week, assisted by the matron, who changed dressings and gave injections. She also did her daily rounds visiting every patient, at the same time checking the condition of the wards.

The Leonora hospital was supported by the Royal Flying Doctor Service based in Kalgoorlie, an hour away by air. There were no X-ray facilities but the doctor reset broken bones, sutured cuts and wounds, patched-up injured miners, delivered babies and performed general surgery. There was no dentist or veterinarian in the town, so in an emergency he performed their duties as well. The burden of responsibility was enormous and varied, particularly for a 28-year-old doctor. After her regular check-up one day, Mrs Steel left the surgery only to return three minutes later, saying, 'Doctor, I have a pain.' Then the baby arrived, a fourteen-pound child, which Dr Moore delivered. His first caesarean was performed at midnight, on an Italian woman. He did it by the textbook, but was so nervous he had a diarrhoea attack and had to scrub up three times before he could start.

The hospital had a succession of excellent matrons and they were always addressed by their title, even in the street.

Mining was a dangerous business and accidents were commonplace. Steve was hurt several times. A falling rock took a large piece out of the tip of his nose, leaving him with a permanent scar. On another occasion his lower leg was badly gouged by a sharp rock. There were many anxious days and nights as Matron Corner battled to stave off gangrene. Her dedication was extraordinary and she won. As a thankyou, Steve bought her a large double-layer box of MacRobertson's chocolates, which cost £5. Steve was off work and on compo for three months. Having him around the house for that time drove Beria mad. For the sake of peace, and to keep me out of harm's way, I was packed off to stay with Wint until he went back to work.

Matron lived in the hospital quarters, and it was not unusual for a seriously ill patient to wake in the middle of the night and find her standing next to the bed, checking, wearing her dressing gown. Matron Corner trained in Victoria because the Western Australian training hospitals refused to offer a place to an Aboriginal student nurse. One of the stolen generation, she grew up on the Mount Margaret Mission, and after finishing her training came back to Leonora and the hospital as a nursing sister. An Aboriginal rights campaigner, she fought for her people, implementing a programme fully integrating Aboriginal in-patients with general wards, and finally was able to do away with the primitive native wards which caused her distress and embarrassment.

Nurses were recruited Australia-wide and word of a new arrival at the hospital spread fast, the young men using any excuse to meet them. Some married local boys and settled into the community; others did their stint and moved on.

Agnew, where I was born, didn't have a hospital. When my parents arrived in 1943 Matron Pridiss was in charge of the nursing station. She worked from a room in a small purpose-built house equipped with basic instruments, and a supply of mixtures and tablets which she administered at will.

When Nita was four years old, complaining of a sore stomach and screaming in pain at Beria's touch, Matron Pridiss diagnosed constipation and recommended a large dose of castor oil. The pain intensified and my parents drove her the eighty miles to Dr Wilson at the Leonora hospital. Nita had acute appendicitis, exacerbated by the massive dose of castor oil, and was prepared for immediate surgery. She was lucky. Her appendix burst during the operation and if she hadn't been in hospital she could have been dead in a couple of hours.

Within weeks of the outbreak of the Second World War, the baker in Agnew was called up and Beria, who was short of money, decided to take on the job, even though she had never before baked bread. 'I found a bread recipe in the Country Women's Cookbook. I brewed my own yeast from potatoes and yeast powder, a starter which I ordered by post from Perth.' During the war, potatoes were rationed to half a pound per person, per week. Beria sold her bread on a permanent order and insisted everyone provide a potato for the yeast. Six days a week, for twelve months, she made ten loaves of bread, selling them for a shilling each. Every night before going to bed she made the dough, then got out of bed and punched it back at three o'clock and started baking at five. Her oven was so small she could bake only four loaves in a batch. When she burnt her finger attempting to turn a hot bread tin without a potholder, Matron Pridiss insisted she had a whitlow and lanced her finger to remove it. When the finger became infected Beria went to see Dr Wilson, who was livid that Matron Pridiss attempted an invasive surgical procedure. The bone was decaying and he had to operate. For three months Beria was in and out of hospital while he battled to save her right-hand middle finger. Soon after this Matron Pridiss resigned.

The five or six standard cure-all remedies were purchased from the store. Some of them lasted for years and were used by successive children. Beria kept her meagre supply in the kitchenette. When I scratched myself: 'Just put a bit of goanna salve on it.' Dr Morse's Indian Root Pills 'cleansed the blood'. 'Too fat to fit the Ford Pill figure? Be slim and be smart, follow the Ford diet chart.' They kept you regular. The Italians drank Fernet Branca. Cod liver oil extract was a child's cure-all. The smell was enough to put me off. Both Nita and Lewie's son Trevor loved it, swallowing two or three spoonfuls at a time. Chlorodine cured 'the runs' – instantly. You added two or three drops to water. It had a similar flavour to the big brown cough lollies which tasted like chloroform. Beria preferred cornflour and water: 'That'll bind you up.' Boils were drawn with a hot poultice of antiphlogistine – a thick grey mixture containing kaolin, a fine white absorbent Chinese clay, which acted on the pus-infected areas. The antiphlogistine was spread onto a piece of clean cloth and heated in the oven. Beria tested it with the back of her fingers and no matter how much I screamed she never believed it was too hot. 'What are you talking about? Just stop your whining, will you?'

Heenzo, Australia's largest selling patent medicine, was an addictive, aniseed oil–based family cough syrup which was mixed with water; Saunders' Malt Extract was a sweet, molasses-like concoction which was doled out by the tablespoon. Beria kept a bottle and a tin of each in the kitchenette for herself and took them regularly.

In January 1952, my sister Nita, accompanied by my father, left Gwalia to begin school at the Dominican Ladies' College in Dongara. Beria and I walked to the railway station to see them off on their journey, which would take two days and one night. My sister was wearing her tan summer tunic and as she and my father settled into the dogbox carriage, with its canvas waterbag hanging off the side, I watched in silence, stricken with sadness.

Nita and I spent more time together than you would normally expect of a brother and sister with an eight-year age difference. To Nita's annoyance, Beria argued: 'If you don't want to take Ronnie with you, then you really don't want to go, do you?' I became an ever-present thorn in Nita's side, and she sought to get her own back. If she had to comb my hair, she pulled it. When Beria told her to put my shoes on me she tied the laces so tightly it hurt. When Beria quizzed me, I innocently told tales which got Nita into trouble. More than once it was my fault she was not allowed to go to the pool for a week.

When it came time to say goodbye at the railway station that hot January morning, I put my arms around Nita's neck and held on so tightly I had to be prised away. I watched the train vanish down the long sweep of track, trying to hide my sobs, trying to catch my breath. As Beria and I walked home, she held my hand more firmly than usual. I was still sobbing.

Nita was away at boarding school for almost three years. As the holidays approached, Beria marked, and I counted, the days to her return. The calendar, which invariably featured a picture of the Queen, hung from a nail in the kitchen wall and was the only decoration. I was surprised when in late 1954 Nita returned unexpectedly, announcing that she had left school for good. Nita had written Beria, claiming the other girls were making her life a misery because they had somehow found out that Beria was divorced and an adulteress, living in sin with another man. According to Nita, the revelation raced through the college and she was immediately ostracised.

The sisters at Dongara routinely read the incoming and outgoing student mail, but Nita secretly posted her letter to Beria seeking permission to return home. Beria was riled by what she read and wrote back, agreeing – a decision she took without consulting my father. The prioress, Reverend Mother Emmanuel, who knew nothing of the gossip before reading Beria's letter, set about trying to fix things. She wanted Nita to stay; academically she was in the top group of her year and was only months away from completing her Junior Certificate; she played A-grade tennis with the strength of a man, and would flatten any girl who got in her way on the basketball court. Reverend Mother flushed out and admonished those girls involved but it changed nothing. Once Nita made up her mind she could not be cajoled.

My father was furious when he learned of Nita's return and the surrounding circumstances. A day or so following, he came after work to see my mother and Nita. The three of them sat together outside in the shade, talking. Knowing I was trying to listen in, they sent me inside to read a book, well out of earshot. Mother Emmanuelle wrote to my father, telling him she was confident Nita had a bright future if she stayed at school. Like many young women of her generation, Nita was fifteen when she left school and without any qualification. My father cried at the waste of her ability.

Valma Giovanazzi was also at Dominican Ladies' College. She was only a year younger than Nita and the two girls were friends, but Nita told my parents she thought Valma was responsible for the gossip. Some days later I was with my father when he called to see Valma's parents. They were friends and talked at length, sitting at the kitchen table.

Valma returned home for the Christmas holidays and started working at Mazza's store. She loved it and never went back to Dongara, despite letters from Reverend Mother to her parents, pleading for Valma to complete her Junior Certificate. She even offered a cut in fees, but like Nita, Valma had decided her school days were over. 'I loved working in the shop, and once you start earning money you don't want to go back to school.' Valma was fourteen years and four months old, legally old enough to join the workforce.

At night, both sides of Tower Street were lit from regularly spaced wooden lampposts, each fitted with a single bulb which generated a soft yellow light, bringing to the darkness a romantic eeriness which belied the tough nature of the town. The streets were safe, and incidents of rape and sexual assault weren't common. The majority of people left their doors unlocked, day and night, and apart from the occasional prowler or peeping Tom everyone felt safe, except for the chooks. In the dead of night they were stalked by the foxes, or pinched by neighbours in search of a free meal.

It puzzled Beria that I was scared of the dark. 'You and your fertile imagination. I'm buggered if I know why you're so frightened.' Day or night, I didn't like being alone in the house. If Beria was out when I came home at lunchtime, I went hungry rather than stay and eat on my own. The silence and the stillness of the air set my imagination racing and my nerves jangling. At night I jumped and screamed when I imagined shadows at the window. I heard strange noises and checked behind doors and under beds. I wouldn't venture out after dark without Beria, or someone, being with me. I lay in bed, paralysed, too frightened to move, convinced there was someone in the room. I slept with my head under the blankets.

For a month or so a prowler terrorised the town, shining a torch into the faces of women who happened to be out after dark. He stopped several on their way home from benediction. Beria insisted a well-known station owner was a habitual peeping Tom. 'He's a bloody nuisance,' she told anyone who mentioned his name, 'always peeping through bathroom windows. I just wish to Christ his missus would keep him at home.' Beria also accused Harold Morgan, Wint's son from her first marriage. 'Wint would be horrified if she knew that Harold was peeping in other people's windows.'

Nita told Beria how she and her girlfriend were riding their bikes between Leonora and Gwalia when they were terrorised by one of the single guys, riding a motorbike. He followed, playing a game of cat and mouse, cutting across in front of them until they had to stop and wheel their bikes back into the town. Beria sent Steve to confront him. 'You go and have a word with him, because if you don't, I bloody well will, and I can tell you right now, I won't be held responsible for my actions.'

While Nita was away at boarding school I slept alone in a bedroom. My bed ran against the wall, under the window which had the best summer breeze in the house. When I woke in the middle of the night, convinced there was a face at the open window watching me, I jumped out of bed and raced to Steve and Beria's bedroom. It was a bright moonlit night. Standing at their bedroom door, frightened, I caught sight of my own reflection in the window opposite. 'Look, there's someone at the window.' Beria was irritated by my imaginings: 'Stop being so bloody stupid, there's no one there. Now get yourself back into bed, and don't get out again.'

One night just before the Christmas of 1953, Beria explained, while tucking me in, that she would wait until I was asleep, and then she and Steve were going to visit their friends, Joan and Bob Tagliaferri, who lived at the other end of the town. 'Joan and Bob are having a get-together, and children are not invited.' A couple of hours later something disturbed me. The house seemed strangely silent so I went looking for Beria. Finding she was not there, I panicked. I went back to my room, changed into my clothes and ran to the Tagliaferris'. I knew from the glare on Steve's face that he was livid. So too was Beria. 'Why can't you do as you're told? I said to stay in bed. You're a bloody little stickybeak, always scared you might miss out on something. Now go and sit over there and wait until we're ready.' Within minutes they finished their drinks and we set off for home. Beria held my hand and she and Steve walked at a pace which had me running the entire distance. Not a word was spoken. She changed me into my pyjamas and bundled me back into bed. 'Now this time, bloody well stay there. I don't want to see you, or hear a peep out of you, until the morning.'

At one time the Bennetts were our next-door neighbours. One of their sons came into our house in the middle of the night wearing only his underpants and got into bed with Nita, who was twelve. He told her not to be frightened. 'It's alright,' he said to her repeatedly, 'you know me.' He was in there for some time and then went wandering into Beria's room, unaware Steve was also there. Beria shouted: 'Steve, there's someone in the room!' Steve jumped out of bed and the intruder ran, but not before they recognised him. Nita, who was wearing a nightdress, was discovered curled up on the end of the bed. The next morning Beria confronted the parents: 'You bloody well keep your son home at night, or I'll report him to the police.' She was ropeable that the young Aboriginal boy had the gumption to come into her house.

A few days after my father returned from settling Nita in Dongara, he called around after work to give Beria news of the school and to discuss the fortnightly maintenance payment. I was sitting nearby, eavesdropping. When he suggested halving the amount since Nita was away at school, Beria bridled. My father explained he only earned £22 a fortnight and couldn't afford £4 a fortnight. She was most indignant when he mentioned the quarterly Government Child Endowment payment, which she collected for both of us. In a fit of pique she said: 'Right! I've had enough. You bloody well take him and look after him. I'd like to see you keep him for a pound a week. And you can take him now if you want.' My father left without any further discussion.

'Contrary' was one of Beria's favourite words. She often accused me, and Steve, of being 'so bloody contrary'. Once Beria made a decision she never went back on her word, no matter how much it hurt her. A few days after the row with my father, and still fuming, she dumped me at the Garbellinis' for the second time in my life. The first time was with Nita when I was coming up for four and Beria, Steve and Lewie went to Perth for a two-week holiday. Every morning as our father rode past on his way to work at the mine he left a shilling hidden under the cake of soap on the trough in the outside washhouse.

This time I was on my own. Having settled me in, Ollie made it clear I was not to leave the yard, nor was I allowed to visit my mother, under any circumstances. Lewie, who lived with Beria and Steve, visited regularly. One day after he'd left, Ollie said: 'Lewie's only your half-brother, you know.' I had just turned five, and I didn't understand what she meant. 'He's not Ginger's. Sergio Gherardi is his father.' It meant nothing to me. I loved my big brother.

Most days my father stopped by on his way home from work, but it was for Beria that I watched and ached. I'd been at the Garbellinis' for a couple of weeks when, one Saturday afternoon while no one was around, I took off out of the side gate and headed for home. When I arrived, Beria was sitting on the bed in the shade at the front of the house. She hugged and kissed me. She cried when I pleaded to be allowed to come back. In the end, she had to tell me to go. Crying, I trudged the beaten track across the open stretch of flat between the house and the road proper. Before I passed between the huts and Beria disappeared from sight, I looked back. She was still sitting outside the house. Further up the hill, the mine's chimneystack trailed black smoke into the sky.

One day, without warning, there was a flurry of activity after one of Ollie's kids came running into the house to tell her they'd seen Beria and she was on her way to get me. Ollie grabbed my arm and, half dragging and half carrying me, raced me to the back gate, down the lane and into the backyard of her neighbour, Lill Johns. Before they could get me into the house and out of sight Beria was in the yard. She grabbed a hold of me and shouted at Ollie: 'Get your hands off him. He's my bloody kid and I want him. Now hand him over!'

When Beria moved to open the back gate she was blocked by the two women. Fortuitously, at that moment I spotted Lewie and a friend, Andy Fassanini, walking by: 'Mum, there's Lewie. Call him.' She shouted and he came to her assistance. While Ollie and Lill continued to block the gate, Beria took a hold and swung me bodily into the air and over the five-foot wire and tin fence. Lewie caught me on the other side. She turned and faced the two women: 'Now if the pair of you don't get out of my bloody way I'll give both of you a backhander.' With that she shoved Lill and Ollie aside, let herself out of the yard, grabbed my hand, and together we marched off down the lane. For a couple of weeks there was a bit of bad blood between them but they soon forgot about it. Ollie and Beria could have been sisters; both were uncompromising and fearless.

In the early years I spent so much time with the Garbellinis I felt part of the family. Their youngest son, Nat – short for Natale which means Christmas – was two months older than me and we grew up as virtual brothers. We shared a single bed sleeping head to toe. At the state school we sat next to each other in class, and we always played together.

Ollie and Curly Garbellini were friends with both Beria and my father. They met in Laverton in 1938 and the two men were interned together on Rottnest Island during the war, while their wives shared the wartime discrimination experience. Curly always said their internment was a disgrace and Australia should be ashamed of what they did to the Italians in the goldfields.

Living with the Garbellinis was the antithesis of being with Beria. Ollie and Curly had five children, closely spaced. The oldest, Ken, was in the army and occasionally returned home. The others were Margaret Irene, whom we called Peggy, Billie, who was known as Bunter, Ann and Nat.

Ollie Garbellini was a tall, thin woman, cursed with advanced varicose veins. Her voice was loud and strident; a sharp tongued virago whose manner and language were plain and straightforward.

She was not easily won over and not afraid to disagree. 'That's bullshit!' she said sharply, and often. Most kids in Gwalia were terrified of her, but I wasn't. I had no reason. The other kids knew they weren't allowed in the house. If they came to visit they could play in the yard, or sit on the steps at the front door. Ollie always looked after me and I was treated no differently from her own, included in any punishments she handed out. The kids – especially the two girls – had chores, and the evening meal was served on time and eaten at the kitchen table, even on the hottest of days. Never once did I see Ollie hug or kiss any one of her children.

Curly, whose name was Enrico, was fifteen years older than Ollie. Unlike my father, I never heard Curly swear or even raise his voice. He tried to settle disputes with talking and reasoning, but when he 'did his block' he was not beyond using his shaving strop as punishment. When he arrived home from work he always made a point of greeting his children, and me. Ollie was a talented cook, and if I happened to be there at mealtime, even when I was not living with them, Curly made sure I was fed. One time, when she dished up the spaghetti and there was no plate for me, Curly asked, 'What about Ronnie?'

'We've got enough kids of our own to feed,' she said without looking at me. Curly stopped her with a curt 'Eh!' and the sharp point of a finger. It was the only time Ollie ever made me feel I was not welcome in the house. Curly saw the tears welling in my eyes. 'Come on, Ronnie, that's enough of that,' he said. 'Just sit down and eat.'

The Garbellinis' house was a converted state school in Tower Street in the middle of the town, two doors away from Mazza's store. Old Louie Columbo lived on the other side of the fence in a derelict two-room camp. For no reason, he hated Nero, the Garbellinis' dog. He threw rocks and poked at him through the fence with a stick, and was always threatening to poison him. One day someone threw a piece of baited meat into the yard, which Nero ate and then died. When the policeman investigated, he couldn't establish who was the culprit.

Ollie and Curly were quite social. They drank together only on the weekend, and on Saturday night while the kids were at the pictures, they went dancing at the State Hotel, cutting quite a figure on the dance floor. Ollie also drank during the week, usually with her neighbour, Lill. She would send Billy scuttling down the back lane to buy two bottles of beer from Mrs Patroni. To disguise her breath, Ollie ate packets of Minties.

Curly was nearly killed when he was blown down the stope after another miner set off a charge outside of blasting time. He had a broken arm, leg and ribs and wasn't expected to live. He was in hospital and off work for six months. After that he worked on the surface at the mine. When Ollie heard the emergency twelve whistle blasts, she said she had a funny feeling it might be Curly. The miner who set off the explosion was fined £20.

When we were living in Grinning Joe's house, Ollie came around to see Beria one day – something she never did; we always went to her place. Ollie already had five children and she was pregnant again. The doctor wouldn't do anything for her so she asked Beria to help her get rid of it. The woman who ran the boarding house in Wiluna, where Beria had worked twenty years earlier, had told her what to do. Beria did it for herself four times. 'I didn't have any choice. Otherwise I would have ended up with a tribe.'

The next morning she went around to Ollie's place and did it for her. She used an old-fashioned wooden pen with a steel nib, coated in soap. Beria kept the pen in one of the drawers of her sewing machine. Once when I decided to play with it, Beria was quick to chip me: 'Just put that back where you found it, and don't let me catch you touching it again.'

My father had no relatives in Australia, and he was not much interested in talking about his family in Italy. Whenever I broached the subject he answered perfunctorily and never provided an opportunity to continue the conversation. On the other hand, Curly told us all about his own childhood and the family he left behind. Aunts and cousins came to Gwalia to visit, and I knew more about Nat's relatives than I did about my own.

Curly's sister, Anna-Maria, was missing the thumb on her right hand. We were told it was a result of being captured by the Germans during the Second World War and strung up by her thumbs using piano wire. The truth was, Curly cut it off on the chopping block when they were children in Italy. However, Anna-Maria *was* a partisan heroine who worked with the resistance against the Germans. She owned a black mule which she used to transport hand grenades to the Allied soldiers in the Italian Alps. Several times she was arrested and gaoled by the Gestapo. She and a group of fellow partisans escaped from gaol the night before they were due to be shipped to a concentration camp. Her brother, Benito, who was also a partisan, was captured and shot by a German firing squad.

Cousin Bruno, Anna-Maria's son, came to Gwalia as relieving station master. He was our hero – tall and handsome. When Bruno and the older boys returned from a daytime shooting trip, he unloaded the .22 rifle at the kitchen table and dropped a handful of unspent bullets into an ashtray, which was soon filled with cigarette butts. Everyone was sitting around the kitchen table, waiting, while Ollie was at the stove stirring the polenta for dinner. When Ann picked up the ashtray and emptied it into the roaring kitchen fire the bullets started exploding. Ollie took off down the back lane, screaming at the top of her voice. When everyone stopped laughing and persuaded Ollie to return, she didn't find it the slightest bit funny. She was convinced Ann, 'the bloody little bitch', had done it intentionally.

My father was a talented amateur boxer and Curly asked him to teach the kids, including the girls, how to protect themselves. Bobby Beccaria, a friend who lived nearby, joined in. Peggy was about twelve and quickly mastered the basics. Following a couple of weeks of instruction Bobby challenged her to a fight. They pulled on the gloves, and with my father refereeing, began throwing wild punches. In a matter of seconds Bobby was lying on his back seeing stars. He shook his head, jumped up and took off for home, crying. Peggy was looking around for her next bout.

∞

When Beria suffered a miscarriage in 1952 she was hospitalised for three weeks. As far as Beria could tell the pregnancy was quite normal. She had spent the best part of the day washing, and the evening sewing on the treadle Singer machine. I heard her talking to Joan Gray about it and the pair of them wondered if the combined vibrations from the washing and sewing machines had caused the miscarriage. The haemorrhaging started in the early hours of the morning and Beria was already in hospital by the time I got out of bed.

Dr Moore had trouble stopping the bleeding. Beria overheard him and the matron talking about her. He said she needed a transfusion and he wondered if maybe they should bring in the Flying Doctor and transfer her to Kalgoorlie. For two weeks Beria slept in a bed the foot of which was raised at a steep angle. Nurse 'Squeaker' Moore was efficient and popular with patients, but following a couple of days off duty she was unaware of the seriousness of the situation and asked Beria to take a shower. Beria put her feet on the floor, stood up and fainted. The fall started more serious bleeding. When the doctor came to see her, Beria told him it wasn't Squeaker's fault. 'She wasn't to know, and anyway, I should have said no when she told me to get out of bed.'

Lewie took me and I stayed with Wint for more than a month. Both my father and Lewie, who was not yet married, came to see me every couple of days. When Beria came home she struggled to regain her strength. It was the only time I ever knew her to be ill. Wint took me to see her a couple of times. When it came time to say goodbye, Wint had a way of distracting me. Filled with all sorts of promises, and clinging firmly to Wint's hand, I trotted across the flat, happily waving goodbye to Beria.

I grew up with the sounds of the Italian, Slav, Polish, German, Hungarian and even Russian languages ringing in my ears. Some kids spoke only their native tongue until they went to school. In the early 1950s 'displaced persons' from Europe were still arriving by train in Gwalia. For a time I thought being a displaced person meant a life-threatening disease. It remained a puzzlement and Beria laughed when finally I asked. 'You silly bugger,' she said. 'It means they don't have anywhere to live back in their own country.' She saw that look on my face and stopped me before I could say anything: 'Ronnie, I've told you all I know about them!'

The boarding houses in Gwalia catered specifically for the European men and served food to their taste, but it was not unusual for three or four men to share a house together – 'batching' as it was known. Sometimes they even shared a housekeeper and the sleeping arrangements amongst them were fairly loose.

Three German merchant seamen, August, Gerhard and Karl, jumped ship in Fremantle and ended up in Gwalia. The policeman arrested them on a warrant, which was withdrawn when the shipping company learned it was responsible for their transportation costs from Gwalia to Fremantle. Everyone laughed when Karl took to wearing his lederhosen around the town.

Bob Mazza's curiosity was aroused when the Germans started ordering excessive quantities of expensive Bols cherry and apricot brandy, blue curacao, crème de menthe and Gold Wasser, a citrus-flavoured liqueur with flakes of 22-carat gold-leaf floating in it. To Mazza's delight and bewilderment, the ordering went on every second weekend for several months. Word of their extravagance soon spread through the town and, given their reluctance to answer questions, it took a bit of detective work on Mazza's part to unravel the story.

It emerged that two German girls, Christina and Marianne, officially displaced persons, had arrived in town a few months earlier, and through Christina's job as a waitress at Mrs Patroni's the pair had met up with the seamen and become friends. The five Germans spent every weekend together and the supply of liqueurs soon rid them of their inhibitions and brought the weekend partying to a satisfactory conclusion.

In fact, the behaviour of the three Germans was not so unusual. Steve and his mates had a regular Saturday afternoon interlude with a former Gwalia girl who had gone away, married, and returned to live in the town. Her husband worked on the mine. Beria knew but never mentioned it to Steve. 'I couldn't be bothered, but I knew that Steve and three or four of his mates used to go and visit some tart who lived over in the street behind the state school. They used to take it in turns with her. One day Steve was taking so long the other blokes were getting sick of waiting. She had a pile of clean washing on the kitchen table, and to help pass the time they folded it for her.' When the same woman seduced the sixteen-year-old butcher boy, he took to throwing the meat from her front gate. He couldn't keep up with her demands.

Gwalia was also a snobbish little town. At the top end of the scale was an eclectic group who, having sought out their social equals to play bridge and tennis, held supper parties.

The Leonora and Gwalia society was lorded over by a self-aggrandising matron who lived in Leonora and whose husband occupied a minor government position. Her guests were those she considered her social equal – government and bank employees, and the occupants of the houses on the Staff Hill. She also included owners of the outlying sheep stations. I was captivated by the wives and daughters of the station owners as they proceeded along the main street, sheltering from the heat under the continuous bullnose verandah, which ran the length of one side of the shopping strip. The shopkeepers' esteem was apparent from the unctuous bowing and scraping. Even strident and independent characters seemed to buckle in awe. They stayed overnight at the White House Hotel, considered by the town's upper echelon to be superior to the Central and Commercial hotels, where the working men drank in the public bars and spilled out into the street in the summer, jabbering in their own lingo. Although drinking in the street was technically illegal, that law was never enforced. My father lived immediately behind the White House Hotel. I passed by often, and regardless of my apprehension, I yearned to see inside. From the street, with the front door opened, it appeared dark and mysteriously cavernous.

I recognised the social queen and sometimes passed her by in the street. She never acknowledged me and I doubt was even aware of my existence. As far as Beria was concerned, this commonplace middle-aged woman with mousy hair was a figure of fun. Invitations to her exclusive supper parties were deemed a tangible indication of entry into goldfields society. I tried to envisage her soirees and asked Bernice Quarti who, together with her husband Doug, was sometimes invited. I was agog when she explained how the men drank beer while the ladies were served sweet sherry and dry ginger ale, or advocaat and cherry brandy with a lemonade dash. The gatherings, Mrs Quarti assured me, followed a familiar pattern. The guests arrived soon after the evening meal and at around ten-thirty the hostess served her guests offerings of mostly sweet and sometimes savoury dishes. Home-made sausage rolls were a favourite. Everyone went home at around midnight.

'I don't know why she's got tickets on herself,' Beria said when I mentioned the social queen. 'Before she married him, she was a barmaid.'

At the other end of the social scale was the indomitable spirit of Beria, who had no time for hoity-toity ways. Her life was filled with more pressing issues. 'I'm not interested in gossip,' she used to say, 'and as long as they mind their own business and leave me alone, they can do what they bloody well like.'

∞

I was days away from my sixth birthday when my friend, Jan Quarti, asked if I was having a party. 'Of course I am,' I said without hesitation. 'Would you like to come?' She went home and asked permission, and the next day at school, accepted. Beria paid no attention when I mentioned it. 'What are you talking about? You're not having a birthday party.'

When Jan arrived at the front door, wearing a party frock and clutching a present, Beria and my sister-in-law Jean, who happened to be visiting, realised I *was* having a birthday party. Beria immediately gave us two shillings each and sent us to the Co-Op to buy lollies while she and Jean set about preparing a party for two.

Neither of them could stop laughing. When we returned, each clutching a giant bag, they had created an instant birthday cake and some other party bits and pieces.

***

Gwalia didn't have a ladies' hairdresser, so four times a year Phyllis Sparling came from her salon in Kalgoorlie, and for a week the ladies waited in a queue at the State Hotel to have their hair cut and permed. Steve always made a point of reminding Beria. 'She's here. Go and get your hair done!'

Like many of the other women, Beria had a tight perm, which made her look like a fuzzy-wuzzy – not that I ever said it. Beria's friend, Joy Miller, sometimes did her hair using a home-perm kit bought at the chemist. There were two brands – Richard Hudnut and Toni – and each smelt as bad as the other. Beria insisted on Richard Hudnut, which, according to her, 'held longer'. When you walked past the houses on the way home from school you could smell the overpowering combination of peroxide and setting lotion, which seemed to take forever to dissipate. I was wide-eyed at stories of women who failed to follow the instructions, and applied setting solution of such strength it burnt their hair off at the root. Some over-cooked their hair in the tiny burgundy plastic rollers, turning it green and gelatinous.

***

Beria was a good cook who lacked imagination. Her speciality was a hearty plate of ham and eggs, which Steve's cronies loved. With the skill of a butcher, she cut thick slices off the leg of ham which hung from a hook on the front verandah, rubbed down the cast-iron top plate of the wood stove with screwed-up newspaper, smeared it with a spoonful of dripping, and threw on the slices of ham to sizzle and brown. She cooked the bright yellow eggs, often double-yolkers, in a heavy iron frying pan using the dripping collected from the Sunday roast and stored in the fridge. She toasted thick slices of pipe loaf bread over the coals using a long toasting fork made from heavy, twisted, galvanised coated wire. The aroma wafted through the house.

After the hotel closed at eleven o'clock on Saturday night, Steve sometimes invited three or four of his gambling mates back to the house for a feed before setting off for an all-night euchre session. On one such night they were tucking in to Beria's ham and eggs when Lewie and his fiancée Jean arrived back from the pictures. As Lewie drove his motorbike and sidecar into the gravel road in front of the house his headlight picked up the partially concealed body of a man lying in the dirt up against a neighbour's side fence. It was uncharacteristic; there were no vagrants in the town. When Lewie mentioned it, Steve was suspicious and went to investigate. In the torchlight he could see it was the same man he'd argued with in the hotel earlier in the day. He became even more suspicious when he couldn't wake him. Back inside he asked Lewie to call into the police station on his way back to Leonora and speak to Roy Patterson. Woken by the activity, I wandered out to the kitchen and overheard enough of the conversation for the blood to drain out of my face. Beria caught sight of me standing in the passageway beside the Kelvinator fridge: 'Have a look at Ronnie, will you. It's always the same when he gets a fright; he turns as white as a sheet!'

When Roy Patterson arrived, the man continued to feign sleep until Roy asked for a bucket of cold water. With that he sat up and Roy took him away for an interview and put him in the lock-up overnight. It turned out, after drinking all day and mulling over the argument with Steve, the man wanted revenge. He planned to wait until everyone in the house was asleep, then creep in and smash open Steve's skull with a rock. Roy Patterson gave Steve the confiscated rock as a memento and it sat on the top of the kitchenette. I talked about it for days and asked questions. To set my mind at rest Beria said eventually: 'Ronnie, will you stop worrying. He's gone. Roy Patterson ran him out of town.'

I stared at her.

'Don't look at me like that. I'm telling you the truth. I saw Roy Patterson put him on the train.'

Beria and my father talked it over and they agreed Nita and I should visit every Saturday and even stay with him some weekends. Beria encouraged us and it was a Saturday treat to which I looked forward. Not even the possibility of catching sight of Mrs Ansley in the street could spoil my stay in Leonora.

My father lived in the same rented house he shared with my mother. His weekend routine and menu never altered. For lunch we ate rump steak and eggs, pan-fried in butter. He poured the cooking juices over the medium-rare meat and the plate was wiped clean with fresh white bread and butter. Like my mother, he was not much of a vegetable eater. Every week we had SPC tinned Bartlett pears, and Nestlé's tinned cream. At night he cooked his famous rigatoni.

For breakfast on Sunday morning he gave me Weetbix, which was the one meal I didn't enjoy. Using boiling water, he mixed the Sunshine powdered milk in a large, elegantly shaped white English china jug with a large handle, which was part of a set of three and remained from when he was married to my mother. The milk was too hot and he used too little. The stodgy pile of dry brown cereal sat in the bottom of the bowl and was hard to swallow. My father tried hard to please me and, for fear of hurting his feelings, I didn't complain.

For Sunday lunch we had leg of lamb, which he sprinkled with rosemary, or a roast chicken, with baked potatoes, baked onion, beans and tinned peas, smothered in a thick, dark brown gravy.

Beria was protective of me. I was not part of the rough and tumble and didn't always fit in with the other kids. I was never invited to birthday parties, not even by Beria's closest friend. I was a naturally tidy child; my clothes were always clean and I can't remember ever having dirty hands. I was an easy target when older kids were looking for someone to torment.

Peter Passeri was the bane of my life, tormenting me for two or three years. He was a nuggetty kid, about four or five years my senior, short for his age and a bit of a ringleader with a particular group of kids. He was 'too big for his boots and needed his ears boxed', Beria said. His brother, Gino, was the opposite and worked in the office on the mine. Beria rather hoped Gino would one day marry Nita. Peter went to the convent school so I didn't know him that well, but for some reason he had a set against me. He lived on the edge of the town at the bottom of Staff Hill in a cluster of higgledy-piggledy camps and houses. I avoided him as much as possible but he never missed an opportunity. If I saw him at the pool, I turned and went home. If I was in the water he deliberately bombed me time and again. If I sat on the bench he sat next to me and pushed me, always wanting the exact spot where I was. He hid my towel or threw it over the fence. Beria came to the pool and told him off a couple of times but it made no difference. It was a relief when he started work on the mine, but if he called in for a swim after work or on the weekend, I went home.

At three o'clock one morning in the middle of winter, Beria thought she heard someone tapping on the front door. Steve was asleep beside her and she got up to investigate. Wearing only her nightie, she wandered around outside the house and, discovering no one, she went back to bed. At five o'clock she and Steve were woken by the sound of moaning coming from the front verandah. They went to investigate and found a man huddled under Beria's white ironing sheet. Shivering and wearing only his underpants, his feet were filled with prickles. The noise of them talking woke me and I wandered out. I saw the man and the blood drained out of my face. 'Ronnie's gone as white as a sheet again!'

Steve knew him, but only from seeing him in the pub. He explained he lived in the boarding house near the railway station, where he and his roommate had been drinking. It didn't take long for the discussion to turn nasty and when a butcher's knife was produced to settle a disagreement, the man, fearing for his life, jumped out of the window, ran through a bed of double-G prickles and came to Steve for protection.

Beria sent me back to bed and, after they had warmed him up and removed the prickles from his feet, left him to sleep in the spare bed on the front verandah. The next morning Steve took him to see Roy Patterson, who went to the boarding house, issued the assailant with a warning and confiscated the knife, which he gave to his wife to use in the kitchen.

Roy Patterson and his wife, Christine, sometimes came for tea and we were invited to the police station. Mr Patterson used to put us in the lock-up if we misbehaved. One day as Beria and I were taking the shortcut around the back of the police station, their oldest girl, Erica, popped her head up over the top of the fence. Spotting Beria she called out: 'Mrs Rocky, Mrs Rocky, my mum and dad had a fight, and my dad tipped his dinner over my mum's head.'

A panorama of Gwalia from the top of Mount Leonora, where I sat with my dogs, Tippy and Puppy, and stared at the distant horizon.

RIGHT: My father, Nello, aged seventeen. This was taken for his passport before he came to Australia in 1926, and is the only picture of him.

BELOW LEFT: The Certificate of Registration of Alien recorded all his details, including the scar on his arm.

BELOW RIGHT: Beria in the yard of Grinning Joe's house. The dress was made from nylon – the new wonder fabric – in a bright floral pattern of reds, blues, yellows and greens. It was one of her favourites.

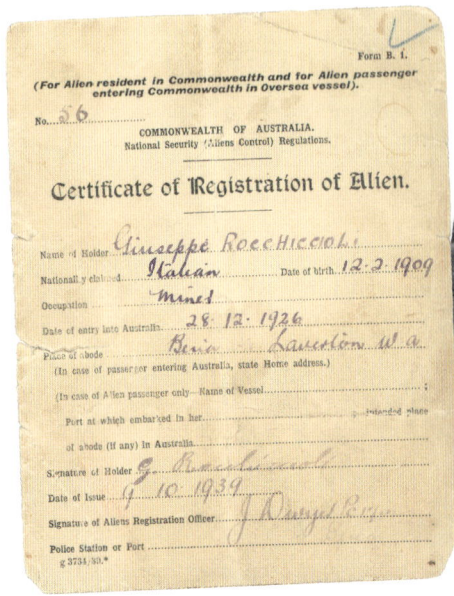

The Salvation Army Children's Home, 'Kia Ora', Broome Street, Cottesloe. The building on the right is the school room. Beria was there for thirteen years.

This photo was taken around 1920, when Beria was nine. She is in the front row, sixth from the left.

TOP: Leonora, 1949. Billy and me, between the back of the house and the chookhouse.

BOTTOM LEFT: Gwalia, 1951. Dressed in Nita's calico petticoat, with Beria's bike and the tattered washhouse in the background.

BOTTOM RIGHT: Me, wearing Nita's confirmation cloak and veil. Mrs Turich's house is behind me.

Gwalia, 1951. Lewie and me in the lane outside the Parkinsons' house. The mine is in the background.

RIGHT: Nita and me, outside the house in Leonora, 1948.

BELOW: Gwalia, 1953. Beria and me in the yard of Grinning Joe's house. Beria's dress was white linen, with rows of red stitching. On the left, a kangaroo skin is nailed to the ground to dry.

I have only the slightest recollection of this studio portrait taken in York, where my father took Nita and me for a holiday.

The debutante ball in 1958: (L to R) Peggy Garbellini, Nita, Thelma 'Tuppy' Hay, Kay Quarti, Norma Steel (Miss Eastern Goldfields), Pat Pennefather, Helen Williams and Pearl Hay. Flower-girl Carol Chomley is in the front.

Peggy and Quirino Ferrari's wedding in 1961. St Francis of Assisi Church, Gwalia. (L to R) Ollie Garbellini, Robyn Matthews, Rino and Peggy, Ann and Curly Garbellini.

ABOVE: Lewie and Jean's wedding at the Sacred Heart Church, Leonora. Nita, Beria, Steve and I are standing on the side. Beria said it was the unhappiest day of her life.

LEFT: 17 December 1953 – on the way to Lewie's wedding. (L to R) Lewie, Beria, me, Nita, Jimmy Millar and Steve, who was best man.

BELOW: Gwalia, March 1959. Nita and Frank Mafrici's wedding.

TOP: 'Going shooting': Lewie, Ian Jones, me, Stefano Fanetti and Beria, outside Grinning Joe's house.

LEFT: Val Parkinson and me. Beria thought Val was the right girl for Lewie.

BOTTOM LEFT: Gwalia, 1954. Nita, in her Dominican Ladies' College winter uniform, and me.

BOTTOM RIGHT: Steve and Joan, at her christening, 1954. (Photograph by Ben Poole)

TOP LEFT: School Sport's Day 1954, Gwalia oval. Peter Passeri, Don Conlon and me.

TOP RIGHT: Joan and me. The shed in the background was my favourite reading spot.

LEFT: Beria and Joan in the backyard of Mrs Stewart's house, 1957.

TOP TO BOTTOM: The open cut, a view of the town from Staff Hill, and the workshops on the Sons of Gwalia mine. (Pictures courtesy Mrs Eileen Barden)

The pool, with the electric wire strung across the water! (Courtesy the Gwalia Historical Museum)

The Sons of Gwalia mine on the slope of Staff Hill was the centre of town. Its smoking chimneystack, which dominated the skyline, could be seen from everywhere.

Tower Street, the main street of Gwalia, from Biggs's corner. Steve the barber, Patroni's boarding house and Mazza's shop are on the right.

ABOVE: Nita and Italo Cher. The picture, taken by a travelling photographer, was for Nita's eighteenth birthday.

RIGHT: Emily Winter and Beria. She was 'Wint', and was always there when we needed her – no matter what.

(L to R) My aunt Silvia, my great aunt Gladys, my aunt Edith and Beria.

(L to R) Cousin Don McGregor, my aunt Silvia, and Father and Nana McGregor in the front parlour of 23 Knebworth Ave, Perth.

Beria and me, with Oscar and Luci in South Yarra, Melbourne. It was Beria's ninetieth birthday.

Beria ignored her and told me to do the same. 'Just keep walking and don't look at her.' The further away we got the louder Erica shouted, and the more Beria laughed.

Mrs White was different from the other ladies in the town. She was an ebbing silhouette from another generation and I thought she was very old. Her name was Catherine but they called her Cate. She was born in Clunes, Victoria's first goldmining town. She lived with her daughter Eileen Barden, who was married to Reg, the general manager of the mine. Once a week Mrs White walked down from the top of the hill to check on her house, which was behind our place. It stood alone in the middle of the flat a short walk from the butcher's shop.

As Mrs White walked past at a measured pace I stood with my fingers hooked in the wire of the fence, staring. I willed her to speak, but she never did. Her face was framed by snow-white hair and in the summer she wore a large white straw hat. She looked straight ahead in the direction of the little rusting tin house which, unoccupied for some years, was a cheerless sight of creeping decay. It had developed a noticeable lean and appeared in danger of blowing away in a strong willy-willy. The wind rattled the loose sheets of the corrugated-iron roof, which was entirely coated in rust. The front flywire door was permanently ajar, hanging by one hinge, and the canvas blinds behind the disintegrating green latticework were rotting and coated in fine red dust. The house had no fence and the front door, which opened onto the gravel beaten path, looked across to the back of our lavatory and chookhouse and to the alleyway which ran beside Little Charlie's camp.

Mrs White was unaware that Beria and I watched her from the corner of our chookhouse. Through the open front door we could see into the living room, crammed with furniture and bric-a-brac from her married life. Her weekly routine never altered. She sat for an hour or more rummaging through a tin trunk filled with what appeared to be baby and children's clothes. At the end of her stay Mrs White would close the trunk, turn out the light, lock the front door and, with her sights set straight ahead, begin her long walk home to the top of the hill.

In summer the days started early. It was light at half past four and the mercury was often hovering around the century by ten o'clock. It was too hot for sport or physical games. During the holidays, groups of kids gathered at one or other of their mates' houses and sat around talking, reading comics or playing board and card games.

I was visiting a friend. Six or seven fourteen- and fifteen-year-old lads were sitting around, bored and wondering how they might amuse themselves for an hour or so until the pool opened at three. Their collective imaginations turned to one thing when a well-developed, flirtatious thirteen-year-old girl arrived to visit my friend's sister. She had a reputation for being 'friendly' and pretty soon things started to happen. One of them asked: 'Wot would you do if we all knocked ya off?'

She giggled. It was hot and the boys were bursting out of their shorts. The tomfoolery gave way to fondling her breasts and putting their hands between her legs. It went on until, in one quick action, they removed her shorts. In a couple of minutes it passed the point of no return. They picked her up and carried her bodily, laughing and squealing, into the bedroom. In seconds she was stripped naked and pushed onto the bed. From where my friend and I were sitting it seemed everyone was enjoying the fun. The oldest and biggest of the boys went first.

He ripped off his shorts and, completely naked, jumped onto the bed, and bounced away to happiness while the other lads stood around, watching and giving encouragement. Each of the boys followed in turn. A couple of them went back for a repeat. The sister, whom the young lady had come to visit, didn't approve and kept threatening, 'If you don't stop, I am going to tell Mum what you're doing!'

Normally the wrath of this particular mother would have stopped them dead in their tracks, but not today. When it was all over, the girl jumped off the bed, put her clothes on, and they all sat around talking until it was time for the pool to open.

∽

The moisture content and malleability of the mine slimes sparked the imagination of two of the older boys. With sex constantly on their minds, and possibilities restricted, they gouged circular cavities into the sloping wall of the embankment. Three or four inches in diameter and about six inches deep, the holes, located at crotch level, were well used by the boys in their continuing self-education. The same two lads climbed into one of the empty railway trucks and manually helped each other to relieve their itch. When they spotted the stationmaster's son peeping at them through a hole in the truck, they jumped up and ejaculated over his head.

∽

Two brothers who lived in Gwalia went to the convent in Leonora, and although the convent operated a bus service they rode their bikes instead. When a girl asked the older of the brothers for a ride home he agreed, providing he and his brother could stop at Halfway Creek for payment in kind.

It all happened and a few days later the older brother said to me, as he compared two experiences: 'She was a dry root, not like the other one, she was wet.'

I had no idea what they were talking about but was keen to find out and I knew that Barry Loftus was sexually experienced. It took a few days, but having mustered the courage, I attempted to engage him in a question-and-answer sex lesson.

It was summer and the sun was setting. I was standing on one side of the cyclone wire front gate, and Barry Loftus was on the other, seated on his bicycle and supporting himself against the post. He seemed quite amenable to answering my questions until I asked: 'What happens when you put it in? Do you wee inside them?'

An obvious look of disbelief crossed his face. 'No,' he said, pausing for a moment. 'I'll see you later.'

He was gone, and I was none the wiser.

∞

Billy Garbellini and Alan Pennefather were walking down the back lane, not far from the Pennefathers' house down near the railway line, when they heard part of a conversation coming from behind the high tin fence. There was a lot of huffing and puffing, and frantic whispered dialogue: 'Hurry up! It's my turn', and 'Hold her still!' When Billy and Alan climbed up onto the fence to look they were horrified at what they saw. Two brothers, whom they knew, had hold of a goat, one at either end. With that, Billy and Alan jumped down and started throwing rocks at them over the fence. When they told a mate what they'd seen, he went round to the brothers' house and thumped both of them.

Going to the Gwalia pictures on Saturday night with Beria and Nita was a regular event, except when Steve lost his money on the horses and there was trouble in the camp.

The hall was just around the corner from Grinning Joe's house. The films were screened inside in winter, and outside in summer. Beria had a permanent reservation – aisle seats in E row – and woe betide the box-office girl if she sold them. The whites sat down the front in the blocks of slung canvas deckchairs, and the blackfellas, who paid the same price, sat on a couple of rows of wooden-slat benches at the back. Everyone stood to attention for the national anthem. Shot in glorious technicolour, it was the 1952 vision of Queen Elizabeth riding side-saddle to the Trooping of the Colour.

Alf Dorph-Peterson, a former RAAF leading aircraftman, ran the pictures; he also worked for the municipal offices reading the water and light meters, and owned and operated one of the Leonora cafes which boasted 'grills at all hours'. The two projectors involved a series of reel changes and the audience cheered and hooted when a projector broke down, regularly. Alf showed lots of cowboys and Indians, and Beria's favourite – Ma and Pa Kettle. I had nightmares after *The Creature from the Black Lagoon* and *Jedda,* an Australian-made film in which the leading man, Marbuck, forced Jedda to eat cooked snake.

When I was younger, I fell asleep as soon as the lights went out. Beria took me home at half-time – it was only 300 yards away – put me to bed and went back for the second film. One Saturday night, something frightened me and I woke up. I went to her bedroom, searching. Discovering I was alone in the house, I panicked and raced back to the theatre. Beria was sitting with Nita and my unexpected appearance sent them into paroxysms of laughter. Incapable of speech, and with tears streaming down their faces, they could only point. I had my clothes on inside out and my shoes on the wrong feet. Beria took me home and put me back into bed.

It was not easy keeping me awake on the way home. Beria reckoned it was as good as a comedy show. When she stopped for a moment to talk with friends I disappeared. A quick search found me curled up and sound asleep on the nearby church steps. It was only a few paces more before I sat down on the Co-Op store steps, leaned against the wall, and again fell asleep.

Beria always bought a glass bottle of soft drink at interval with a returnable refund of threepence on the empty. Every kid in the town collected and cashed in bottles for pocket money. Most houses had a bottle heap, and the bottle-o called regularly for the empty beer bottles, paying a halfpenny each. At the end of the night I was always too tired to be bothered carrying the empty bottle, dropping and picking it up all the way home. Early Sunday mornings I climbed through a hole in the back fence of the picture theatre and searched under the seats for money. I always found a handful of coins, sometimes a ten-shilling note, and occasionally a pound.

Katie Adamini was considered to be a bit of a handful. She was a free spirit who didn't care what other people thought. Rope and stiffened petticoats were the latest fashion craze, and Katie's were stiffer and bigger than everyone's. She showed me once; she was wearing four.

Katie had been educated at the local convent and regularly attended Mass. For a time she lived with the Weston family, helping with the children. When she was seventeen she had a relationship with Tino Delpup. Every night they would sit together on the large water pipe outside Tony Demeis's house on the way up the hill. When Katie got pregnant, she refused to hide away and went to Kalgoorlie for the birth of her son, Peter. When she returned to Gwalia the new mother proudly wheeled him around, ignoring the town gossips. She had the courage to keep her child, in the same way Beria had in 1933, and my aunt Annie before her. Three of the girls with whom Katie played basketball were pregnant when they got married in Gwalia. Eventually, Katie and her son moved to Kalgoorlie. She raised him on her own, at a time when being an unmarried mother carried a social stigma.

Nita was friends with Katie's older sister Lucy. They met up often and, much to their chagrin but at Beria's insistence, I tagged along. Nita was home from school for the May holidays of 1954. Petula Clarke's 'The Little Shoemaker' was top of the hit parade. The two girls were almost fifteen and discovering the opposite sex. The pair of them were keen on a good-looking young man who lived diagonally opposite the Adaminis. He was probably eighteen or nineteen, and shared with a fellow worker from the mine.

One Sunday afternoon when Nita was visiting Lucy, the boys were home and the pair of them went visiting. Naturally, I followed. It was a small two-roomed shanty and I was uncertain about the rough and tumble and the loud laughter. I was seven and

I knew Beria was not happy about Nita talking to boys and once went to check on her at the pictures. When she discovered Nita and several other girls innocently standing at the back under the projection box, talking to a couple of lads and waiting for the film to start, she assumed the worst. She charged in and gave Nita a telling-off loud enough for the whole theatre to hear. 'Now get home,' she shouted.

I sat watching Nita, Lucy and the two boys and then, without a word, ran home to tell Beria, who moved with the speed of light from one end of the town to the other. Despite Nita's pleading, she had to stay home for a week. It was a little while before she spoke to me.

Somehow in the turmoil of Beria's home affairs, the 'special days' between me and my father were lost. I didn't know my father's birthday until I was eleven, and I was never encouraged to buy him a Christmas or Father's Day present, although, for the sake of peace, Beria always made sure I had something for Steve. Beria never talked to me about my father, and I never wondered where he was, or what he might be doing, on the special days. I went to live with my father when I was ten – and that was the first year we saw each other on Christmas Day. For the two years I lived with Beria and Steve in Tower Street, my father rode past the front door on his bicycle at the same time every morning and afternoon, but I didn't think, and no one mentioned, to look out for him. Sometimes we met by chance. He was delighted to see me and stopped to talk. When I told Beria, she always asked the same question: 'Did you ask him for some money?'

Following my parents' divorce, I never saw my father with another woman, apart from a brief dalliance with a half-caste Aboriginal waitress he met while we were staying at the Hostel

Manly, on a holiday at Cottesloe Beach. He had not been lucky in love. He said: 'Women! They're all bitches; there's not a good one amongst them.' However, he always considered Jean a worthwhile woman. 'She's one out of the box,' he used to say.

A few years later, my father's anger boiled over when Ollie Garbellini left Curly and moved in with one of the Guild brothers. He called her a slut, which I repeated to Ollie. He was embarrassed when she confronted him and later at home he abused me in the most humiliating manner, refusing to speak to me for several weeks. When I tried to start a conversation he spat at the floor and turned his head away. He cooked only for himself, leaving me to my own devices.

Talking about her marriage to my father, Beria said, 'I suppose I really should have stayed with Ginger, but he was such a miserable old bastard. Not once in ten years did I ever hear him laugh.' He was a curmudgeon and given to outbursts of uncontrollable rage. He pulled off his shoe and threw it at people, and sometimes let fly with whatever he happened to have in his hand, even the teapot. He had a habit of dismissing people with a contemptuous scoff: 'Phew! Bloody rubbish.'

It was rare that anyone came to visit my father, although he had a couple of Italian friends, Bob de Maria and Sebastiano lo Presti. Sometimes in the summer he would visit for an hour or so. Mostly he sat alone, smoking. The kettle was always boiling and he brewed Amgoorie tea in a one-cup aluminium teapot elaborately etched with a lotus flower motif. In the summer he perched on the front or back doorstep. In the winter he pulled a chair close to the kitchen fire and sat hunched over, legs apart, elbows on his knees and his chin resting on his hands, staring vacantly into his thoughts, which he never shared, and slurping his tea which he drank from the saucer. He went to bed at nine o'clock and was up at ten past five every day, even on the weekends. When both silicosis and tuberculosis ravaged his body and the recovery from major lung surgery was excruciating, he cried and talked to the nurses of committing suicide. He yearned to contact his brother Flavio in Italy.

After Beria and my father separated, their acrimony and pig-headedness quickly gave way to civility, even concern. When my father was in hospital with a crushed toe, Beria went several times during the day to see him. My father's concern for me and Nita never wavered, and Beria did nothing to spoil our relationship with him. If there was a doubt she would say: 'The answer's no as far as I'm concerned, but you can go and ask your father if you like and see what he says.' However, Beria was sometimes thoughtless in her comments, and 'Make sure you get what you can out of the old bastard!' was invariably one of the last things she said to Nita before we went to see him on Saturday morning.

Bob Howard's taxi bus left from the State Hotel. It was five minutes to the main street in Leonora, from where we walked to my father's house. After Nita went away to school I sometimes stayed until Monday. He took me on his bike, sitting on the crossbar, dropping me off at the base of Staff Hill for the short walk home while he went on to work.

My father was a light sleeper, waking up during the night for a cigarette. The cotton sheets were yellow with age and the blankets, the kapok-filled pillows and mattress all smelt of tobacco smoke. The bedroom I shared with him on weekends was the size of two rooms. Its curtains were rotted from the sun and hung precariously in tattered and fraying strips from the rods. The room was furnished with a 1920s oak dressing table and a stained plywood wardrobe. He always stored my pile of Christmas presents in the bottom of the wardrobe, and once I stumbled on his hideaway it was impossible to resist the temptation.

According to Beria, Ginger was quite handy around the house. When they were living in Agnew he made her a cake tin from a cut-down kerosene tin. It even had envelope ends with rivets and Beria said it was the best cake tin she ever had: 'I think the thickness of the tin helped spread the heat more even like.' He also made a cheese grater from a piece of galvanised iron. He used a house nail to form a grating surface, shaped it on a beer bottle and then fixed it to a piece of pine. The large Coolgardie cooler was constructed from a double layer of chicken wire filled with charcoal. When you wet the charcoal, it was so cold inside that even in the summer it kept the butter hard and you could set a jelly. The cooler stood in the shade on the open verandah next to the front door and although my father was at work during the day and the house was empty, no one stole any food.

The eating area was separate from the kitchen, and was furnished with a simple slat wooden table and four chairs. My father was clean but not fastidious, and when he wiped down the table with the dishcloth, breadcrumbs got caught in the grooved joins between the timbers. Scraping it out with the blade of a bone-handled knife was one of my favourite pastimes. Tucked into the top of the doorjamb which led through to the rear landing and the kitchen were hundreds of wishbones. Whenever my father had a chicken he dried and added another one to his collection. I wondered why. 'I don't know. Maybe they'll bring me some good luck.'

The cramped kitchen was barely large enough for the open-fronted kitchenette in which he stacked his crockery and cutlery and stored his dry and tinned food, the small wooden table covered by a discoloured plastic tablecloth, two odd upright wooden chairs and his battered armchair near the fire. My father kept changes of clothes for me and during the winter the kitchen was the only warm room in the house. After my bath, dressed in blue and white striped flannelette pyjamas buttoned up to the neck, I sat to the side of the fire in his armchair, with the oven door open for added heat. Just like him, I slurped my tea from the saucer.

The Saturday routine never changed. After breakfast we followed the beaten track past the disused corral of rusting and disintegrating metal pipes to collect his washing and ironing from Mrs Saunders. Her yard was sheltered from the street and her garden was a thick tangled undergrowth of scarlet bougainvillea and morning glory. I held my father's hand, afraid there was someone lurking in the undergrowth, about to jump out.

Mrs Saunders was meticulous. My father's laundry was carefully folded, neatly wrapped in new brown paper and tied with string caught in a bow. He always wore muted multi-coloured fine cotton Oxford pinstriped shirts, with the sleeves rolled to the elbow and held in place by elasticised steel armbands. His woollen trousers were dark brown or navy blue, and for years he wore Italian elastic-sided slip-on dark brown shoes with black knee-length woollen socks.

When everything was done in the house, we went 'up town' for the morning. The first stop was always at the newsagency to collect my weekly copies of the English children's papers, *Jack and Jill* and *Play Hour*. They were on permanent order and kept me entertained throughout the weekend. I read them over and over again. While he talked with friends I played in the main street outside the shops and the hotels, walking up and down and listening in to other people's conversations, which I repeated to Beria when I got home. Regularly during the morning my father brought me an icy cold drink mixed from lemonade and a raspberry essence which was only available from hotels and had a unique taste and smell.

On each of these Saturdays my father gave me two shillings to spend on sweets. Priced at four for a penny, the white paper bag of black cats, ripe raspberries, mint leaves, Scotty jellies, conversation lollies and boiled and satin sweets was a feast. He sometimes gave me a second two shillings, which I saved. Without fail he gave me a ten-shilling note to take home and deposit into my Commonwealth Bank post office savings account. School banking day was exciting and I stared at the stamped entry and the growing balance. Sometimes I had as much as £10 in my account. However, Steve's gambling left Beria with no money and, without saying, she withdrew all but one shilling of my savings, the balance required to keep open the account. The money was never mentioned, and I dared not ask. I told my father, who listened without making comment. After a couple of years I stopped saving.

The ringing of the angelus at midday brought the town to a standstill – a sign for the shops to shut and for me and my father to head for home. Sometimes we were invited for midday dinner by Nita and Mal Mackay, who had been friends of my father since they met in Laverton in 1938. Macka was a rough diamond shearer and Nita – after whom my sister was named – was a thin woman who liked to joke. She would blacken her eye with boot polish and tell anyone who enquired: 'Macka punched me!' I loved being with my father and, although Nita and Macka made a huge fuss, I resented the interruption to our routine. Nita always cooked a wonderful dinner, but I wanted to be at home with my father.

Although I had no friends in Leonora, I was never bored, nor did I look to my father to be entertained. He bought me books and glossy Classic comics. I spent the weekend reading, fossicking around on the flat looking for centipedes and lizards, and turning over bits of rusting tin in the disused chookhouse. Sometimes in the afternoon we returned to the main street. More often than not my father took me to the Saturday night pictures but it was a waste of his time. I usually fell asleep immediately the picture began and he carried me home at the end of the night.

Three or four hundred yards across the flat from the house was a dirt road which led to the Leonora railway station. There were four houses along this stretch. Old man Mr Leaney and his daughter lived closest to the railway station, in a house almost covered by a lush creeper. Mr Leaney rode around town on his old battered bicycle, the bottom of his trousers secured by sprung steel clips. He sat high on the seat, his back straight, his knees and elbows turned out, steering the horn-shaped handlebars and pedalling at a measured pace. For an hour on Sunday morning I sat on the front verandah, listening, while his daughter played hymns on an American organ. The music floated across the paddock and the sonorous tones of the reed organ swirled around the house and filled the air.

For two or three years my father was honorary first-aid man for the Leonora and Gwalia football teams. Before the match he was kept busy massaging players' legs and when someone broke down with cramp during the match he sprinted onto the field and administered one of his magic oils. The wooden medicine box opened out like a motor mechanic's tool box and was packed with bandages, sticking plasters and bottles of strong smelling potions. During the week it sat on the floor under his bedroom window, next to the dressing table. My father knew I was inquisitive and made it clear the box was not to be touched. Although I fiddled with the hooks, I never dared open it.

Almost the entire town turned out in support of their team and games were hard fought to the death. Steve had no interest and, consequently, never once went to the football. The matches were played week about in each town and the rivalry between Gwalia and Leonora was fierce. It started in primary school and continued, unabated, forever. Men who were friends and workmates on the mine became the bitterest of rivals when they walked through the gate of the oval.

At three-quarter time the players dispensed with the traditional oranges and my father handed around a bottle of sweet sherry from which they all took a healthy swig. On the biting cold Sunday afternoons the warmth of the alcohol guaranteed a spirited final quarter. It was customary for the two teams to get together around a keg at the end of the match. When the policeman Tom Clews joined the Gwalia team, even though he had never played before arriving in the town, he found himself in a unique situation. At the end of the game, the players (some of whom were underage) adjourned to the State Hotel. Tom made it clear: 'When I walk through the bar, I don't want to see any of you with a beer in your hand.' They always kept a glass of lemon squash on stand-by. Upholding the law and being a member of a small community was sometimes a delicate balancing act. Even though it placed him in a difficult situation with his team-mates, he charged Mr Chomley, the publican at the Commercial Hotel, when he sold the football teams a keg of beer on a Sunday. The irony of Tom Clews winning the end-of-year Chomley trophy for the most improved player was not lost on him.

The football matches were played on a graded gravel oval which, in the wet weather, instantly turned to mud and a player in full flight skidded for up to sixty feet. In the dry it was agonising; skin vaporised on impact with the compacted red earth, exposing oozing flesh; blood trickled from knees and elbows. Cuts and abrasions took weeks to heal. In the dressing sheds at the end of the match I watched as my father helped tend the wounded. Men, some with tears in their eyes, swore and moaned in agony as he swabbed injuries and with tweezers picked out the hundreds of tiny fragments of gravel caught in the exposed flesh.

In the second week of the Christmas school holidays, 1952, soon after I got my bike, I was riding down the hill at full speed when my towel got caught in the wheel. I landed face down with my arms outstretched and skidded through the gravel. I was wearing only bathers. I left my bike where it fell and ran home, covered in blood and screaming in pain. Even Beria, who was not a sympathetic nurse, was shaken by the sight. She put me into a warm bath and splashed me, using the movement of the water to dislodged the gravel embedded in the bare flesh. She borrowed a bottle of mercurochrome from Joan Gray, painted me red from top to bottom and bandaged me in strips of a torn-up sheet. The next morning Beria took me to the hospital and Matron Corner finished the job of picking out the gravel. The healing was agony, and for a couple of months my legs, arms and ribcage were covered in thick scabs which cracked and bled when I walked.

It was around about the same time that Patchy, my dog, barked and growled for three days and nothing would quiet him. He started on Friday night, barking incessantly at the bottom of the kitchenette and refrigerator. Each time Beria chased him outside, he came back and barked. She crouched on her hands and knees and investigated by torch light. There was nothing. 'You stupid bloody dog. What's wrong with you? There's nothing there.' Finally late on Monday afternoon all was revealed.

As I came through the back door onto the verandah I was met in the passageway by a four-foot green tree snake. It was my first encounter and I was frightened witless.

'Mum, quick!' I shouted. 'There's a snake.'

Beria was in the kitchen talking to Joan Gray. After telling me to get outside, and declining Mrs Gray's offer to get Harry's shotgun, the two of them stood behind the snake, watching and waiting until it managed to get off the polished floor and onto the cement verandah. At the door the snake turned left and slid behind a hurricane lamp resting against the wall. Beria grabbed the nearby tomahawk, and as it emerged she chopped off its head. For good measure she chopped the body into pieces. The snake's remains were gathered and placed inside a sugarbag, which Beria held out for me to take. 'Go and dump it down the flat,' she said.

My mouth dropped and I reeled in horror. Not for all the tea in China was I going to touch the sugarbag.

'Come on, don't be stupid,' she said impatiently. 'The bloody thing's dead, now take it.'

'No,' I said defiantly. 'The snake might come back to life.'

Even Beria was forced to laugh at the power of my imagination. 'Come on, come with me,' she said. Holding hands, we happily headed off down to the flat, with me on one side of Beria and the snake on the other.

∞

I can't remember a time when Beria didn't have chooks, and most Sundays we had one for midday dinner. When I was old enough it became my job to chop off its head. It was a Sunday morning ritual. Beria selected the chook and, once caught, it was carried to the woodheap, held by its wings and legs, and with one short, sharp swing of the axe it became Sunday midday dinner.

The chook was made into risotto, or baked in the camp oven and served with baked potatoes, baked onion, fresh green beans, Edgell's tinned peas, and smothered in gravy. Beria swore blind she could taste the difference, and there would be a guaranteed return trip to the Co-Op store for an exchange if I brought home a tin of Plaistow's peas instead of Edgell's.

During the summer months, some houses used a single or double Primus stove, a form of Tilley lamp, in which air pressure is used to supply the burner with methylated spirits. Beria cooked all year round on a wood stove. During the hot months it was lit morning and evening. In the winter it burned all day.

There was the running gag from men standing with their arses close to the fire. 'I'm just warming the whole of my body.'

Beria couldn't believe it when her closest friend confessed her husband belted her. She thought they were the perfect couple. Once he punched her in the head so hard he knocked her out. Steve hit Beria when he was drunk. The next day was a repeat conversation: he was always sorry and he didn't mean to hurt her.

'You should have thought of that last night when you hit me.'

Steve put the blame back on to Beria. 'You make me wild when you argue all the time.'

She wouldn't give an inch. 'Too bad, and anyway, it still doesn't give you the right to hit me.'

Beria never talked about it with anyone, not even Lewie. One day, after an especially unpleasant incident, I daringly broached the subject. 'Now you listen to me, sweetheart. You mind your own business, and stop worrying about things which don't concern you.'

Steve bragged about his physical prowess, fancying himself as the town's strongman. He insisted on working alone underground because, according to him, no one else was smart enough, or strong enough, to match him.

It was a different story when Lewie was living with us. One Saturday Steve came home with a face like thunder and a mood to match after losing his wages in a couple of hours at the betting shop. I was sitting with Lewie and Beria at the kitchen table. Beria had a

And be home before dark

go at Steve for his stupidity. 'You're a mug,' she said, 'giving all your money to Dickie Bates like that. I don't know why you bother to bet – you don't know one horse from another. You might just as well give him your money, because he's going to get it anyway.' With that, Steve leapt to his feet, picked up his plate and hurled his meal against the kitchen wall. In an instant Lewie grabbed him by the shirt front, threw him on the floor and started belting into him.

Beria was taken aback by Lewie's reaction and strength. 'Don't hurt him!' she called out. 'Don't hurt him!'

Lewie continued to thump him. 'I'll more than bloody well hurt him!'

When Lewie let go, Steve abused them both in Slav and stormed out of the house. Beria and Lewie sat at the kitchen table, discussing Steve in the plainest language, neither realising he was crouching outside under the open window, eavesdropping. Hearing more than enough, he burst into the kitchen, threatening Beria. After Lewie manhandled him out of the house, Steve went back to the State Hotel. Beria was wild. 'That's it. I'm not putting up with any more of his bloody shenanigans. He can go and find someone else to do his washing and ironing.' She packed his clothes into a suitcase, lugged it to the State Hotel, walked into the public bar and, in front of his mates, threw the case at him. 'And bloody well don't come back because you're not welcome!' Steve waited till the pub closed at eleven o'clock and came creeping back to the house. When I woke up the next morning everything was back to normal, although Steve remained cautious and only bashed Beria when Lewie wasn't around.

∾

Once Lewie was married everything at home changed. Although Beria and Steve weren't yet married, he told her not to visit anyone, and I was not to have any kids in the house. My friend, Jan Quarti, was the only friend who came inside. Steve expected Beria to be waiting when he got home from work, and the kitchen fire had to be alight. He was dangerously jealous of Beria. 'If he saw me talking to another bloke,' she said, 'he accused me of being on with him.'

Steve went to the pub every afternoon, and if Beria asked what time he would be back for tea he sneered, refusing to give any indication: 'I don't know. When I get here.'

Steve spoke broken English and my sister-in-law, Jean, was convinced that back in his own country he'd be considered a slow learner. She eyed him suspiciously and said you could see the hate in his eyes when he looked at me. She was adamant: 'Given the chance, I reckon Steve'd do Ronnie a mischief.' He hated kids with white hair and I was the only white-haired kid in the town. Beria was aware of his antipathy: 'Steve was always jealous of my kids, but he hated Ronnie the most. He used to threaten to blacken his hair with the bottom of the frying pan.'

With Lewie gone, Steve was no longer afraid to threaten me. I developed a fear which quickly reduced me to tears, especially when he started taking the frying pan off the stove and moving towards me brandishing the blackened bottom. When Beria intervened – 'Steve, that's enough. Now leave him alone' – it ended in an argument. It was because of Steve, and Beria had no say in the matter, that I was forced on numerous occasions to go and live with other people. When she was pregnant with my sister Joan, Steve often told her not to bring the baby home if it had fair hair: 'And he meant it!'

One night I was dressed for the pictures and sitting on the kitchen floor eating a buttered crunchy potato, which Beria cooked on the oven slide, and reading an illustrated comic of *The Children of the*

New Forest in *Playhour*, when Steve arrived home late for tea. He was drunk, he had lost all his money, he was spoiling for a fight. Beria was irritated and it was only a matter of minutes before an argument started and Steve threatened her. 'Shut up or I hit you.' Beria didn't care and wouldn't be silenced. 'No, I won't shut up. And anyway, why should I? Just because you say so. You can go to buggery as far as I'm concerned. You're not my boss, you know!' With that, all hell broke loose. There was a lot of shouting, and pushing and shoving. Their bedroom was off the kitchen and in seconds Steve had Beria pinned to the bed by her throat, threatening to kill her. Screaming, I ran back to the kitchen table, grabbed the large butcher's knife and carried it into the bedroom. I leaned across the double bed, trying to cut Steve's head. Beria caught sight and shouted at me: 'Push it in, Ronnie, push it in!' The knife was enough to make Steve release his grip. There was a tirade of abuse and in minutes things settled down. Steve left the house and went back to the hotel until closing time. Once again Beria started to pack our cases to leave. I can't remember how many times she packed and unpacked. When anyone asked Beria why she didn't leave him, she said: 'I've got no money, and anyway, where would I go?'

Whenever Steve got drunk he threatened to cut Beria's throat. A couple of times I thought he was actually going to do it. My sister Joan was so scared she would get up after they had gone to bed and hide all the kitchen knives under the fridge. After one fight, Beria walked out of the house. She was gone for a few hours but it got so cold she had to come home, by which time Steve had gone to bed, leaving the loaded double-barrelled shotgun leaning against the door. Beria was unusually apprehensive. 'I wasn't sure whether he meant for me to shoot myself, or he was going to shoot me. I slept on a chair in the kitchen that night, with my shoes on, ready to run if Steve came out of the bedroom.'

Steve was cunning and tried to hit Beria where the bruises wouldn't show – smacking her across the face but punching her in the back and chest. Once he misfired and gave her a real black eye. 'I thought he had broken every bone in my face.' When anyone asked, Beria told them: 'Steve hit me.' For some reason, he hated anyone knowing he hit Beria. 'Is no their business. Why you say I hit you?' Beria couldn't believe he would ask such a stupid question. 'Well, you did. What do you want me to say? I did it in my sleep?'

Beria bought her clothes, and sometimes mine, by catalogue from Rockman's, Foy's and Winn's department stores in the eastern states. Whenever they had a fight and Steve hit her, Beria would send away for a COD (cash on delivery) order. When he complained, Beria told him: 'Well, if you learned to keep your hands to yourself, I wouldn't be sending off for them, would I?' That shut him up. Steve had to pay and it left him less money to gamble. In the early 1950s he was the highest paid underground driller on the North-eastern Goldfields. The basic wage was £22 a fortnight. Steve brought home £250 a fortnight. He gambled and lost the lot, even raiding the jar Beria used to save her threepenny pieces. When she suggested saving some for a rainy day, he thought she was talking about the weather. 'It's just an expression, Steve. It means to save some for later.' He curled his lip and scoffed at the idea. 'Why? No one else she's gunna spend my money.'

One of Steve's favourite meals was a stew made from potatoes and baccalà, a salt-dried fish which came wrapped in cheesecloth and tied with string. You had to soak it overnight before cooking. Beria used the tin tub in the washhouse. One night Moggie the cat stole and ate it. I wasn't a fussy eater except for this foul dish which stank out the house. I ate the potatoes, but no matter how much Steve glared and muttered, I pushed the baccalà around the plate. The longer I dawdled the more edgy he became – glowering at me. As a torment, he placed a bottle of Scott's Emulsion Cod Liver Oil in the centre of the kitchen table, offering me a choice. As it was touted as a general cure-all for children's wellbeing, Beria once forced me to take a tablespoon of this off-white slimy mixture; she held my nose and poured it down my throat. I heaved and vomited down the front of her dress.

I sat, refusing to eat. Fuming at my stubbornness, Steve left for the hotel. Having feigned his departure he burst into the room as Beria was removing the plate of cold stew from in front of me. There was a fiery exchange and Beria turned on him: 'Listen, Steve. He's not yours, so mind your own business and leave him alone.' Steve walked out, hurling a tirade of abuse. Beria put the stew back in the pot and went and dumped the half-full bottle of Scott's Emulsion, which had sat in the kitchenette for a couple of years, in the bin outside the back gate.

Without exception, even when he was broke, Steve spent the whole of Saturday drinking, and gambling at the local SP betting shop, which was directly opposite the hotel. From the moment she climbed out of bed on a Saturday morning, and for the next three hours, Beria prepared Steve for the day. Every week I watched the ritual unfold. I knew to keep well out of the way because nothing was allowed to hinder its progress. Regardless of the state of their relationship, Beria was expected to dance attendance upon him.

During the working week Steve's breakfast was a raw egg, which he drank from the shell and washed down with a cup of tea. Saturday and Sunday mornings were different. Beria cooked him two big, thick slices of ham, turned once and browned to perfection, a pan-fried soft-yolk egg cooked in dripping, and a slice of unbuttered white bread – it had to be a pipe loaf or Steve wouldn't eat it. Beria went every day, without fail, to collect a fresh loaf. As soon as he came home from work and before he went down the pub, he had something to eat. He cut himself a fresh crust of bread, a thick slice of ham and he picked a tomato from the garden. 'I was a bit late collecting the bread one day, and you wouldn't believe it,' Beria said. 'That bloody Vic Mazza! He went and sold my pipe loaf on me. I can tell you right now, he won't do that again in a hurry.'

On Sunday morning Steve had a two-egg omelette cooked with finely diced rump steak and the giblets from a freshly killed chicken. He sat at the kitchen table eating his breakfast in silence, listening intently to the ABC racing programme, 'Two Way Turf Talk', which went to air at eight-thirty every Saturday morning.

Steve had a flair for clothes, and Beria took great pride in his appearance. He owned half a dozen European-cut, double-breasted navy suits, fifteen pairs of hand-tailored trousers – he only wore brown or navy – a pure wool brown English double-breasted herringbone overcoat, several dozen white shirts – long-sleeved in winter and short in summer – and square-toed black lace-up Marshall shoes, which Beria polished to parade-ground standard. His trousers, underpants, singlet and black knee-length woollen socks were laid out in readiness on the bed. The impeccably ironed shirt was on a wooden hanger. To make it easier, his socks were folded back from the heel, and the shoes set on the floor.

After breakfast, Steve shaved using a safety razor, a stick of green Palmolive shaving cream wrapped in silver paper and a badger-hair shaving brush. The same discoloured styptic stick for shaving nicks lasted for years. He used California Poppy hair oil and brushed his teeth only on Saturday morning, and always with Ipana toothpaste. He only had a wash on the weekend.

Steve left the house at around ten o'clock and returned for midday dinner, after which they went into the bedroom and closed the door. Oftentimes he would change his shirt if it were slightly marked. He returned from the pub in time for tea and, providing peace prevailed, went with Beria to the pictures, leaving her at half-time and returning to the pub, where he stayed until closing time.

Three or four times in the summer we had a pig or nanny on the spit. Steve would set and light the fire, prepare the animal and start the cooking. As soon as the pub opened at ten for the two-hour session, he disappeared, leaving the tedious and hot hand-turning of the stick to Beria. He came home in time for midday dinner, after which he called Beria into the bedroom and closed the door.

Every second Sunday afternoon Steve and a mate, Frank Keane, ran the illegal two-up school down behind the solidified ash heaps, or the purple dumps as they were known because of their colour. Steve and Frank were the dealers, and not beyond stealing from the punters. Steve came home with his pockets bulging with never fewer than thirty or forty one-pound notes – the dealer's percentage of the ring. He skited blatantly to Beria, demonstrating the art of holding the cash and, with an ingenious sleight of hand, pocketing part of the proceeds. He kept, and gambled, all the money. When he dropped a pound note on the kitchen floor, Beria used her foot to flick it under the refrigerator. When he was drunk she stole his money and hid it in a suit jacket, reckoning it would be the last place he would look. Once when they were holidaying in Perth he found a £10 note tucked into an inside pocket and was puzzled how it came to be there. Beria was ropeable.

Two-up was illegal, but on instruction from high command in Perth the policeman in Gwalia turned a blind eye. When Tom Clews arrived in town Steve and Frank Keane handed him an envelope containing £5. 'What's this?' he asked. When they explained it was a well-established weekly practice, Tom Clews set them straight. 'Not with me it isn't. You can donate the money to the Police Boys' Club. There's a chamber pot on the bar, put the money in there.' And they did, every week.

Steve was a chain smoker and the dark green marbled plastic ashtray on the kitchen table was filled with roll-your-own butts. They were so small I could never understand how he didn't burn his lips. He smelt strongly of tobacco and two fingers on his right hand were permanently stained with nicotine.

Steve constantly borrowed money from the hotel bar, from the neighbours – which he always repaid – and, after she went to work, from Nita. He made Beria do the asking, or demanding, on his behalf. He borrowed £30 from Nita while she was working on a sheep station outside of Leonora. She earned £6 a fortnight, plus her board and lodgings. The owner of the station, concerned at the amount of the loan, contacted my father lest it be thought they were withholding her money. My father listened but made no comment.

On Steve's whim, Beria told Nita and me we were not allowed to walk past the front of the State Hotel, for any reason. When he came home Saturday midday he was in a fury, convinced he had seen us walking past the hotel that morning. Nita protested her innocence but Beria didn't believe her. She got a belting and was grounded from the pool for a week. A couple of weeks later Beria discovered Steve was wrong – it was Sally and Johnny Williams. As usual, Beria used her old excuse: 'Well, I didn't know, did I?' While Sally and Nita did look similar, Steve, with his poor eyesight, couldn't tell the boy didn't have white hair.

Beria called Steve a 'street angel and a home devil'. She said he was two people, in both personality and appearance. Sober, he was introverted and reasonable; drunk, he was warped and cruel. There was a physical transmogrification. Under the influence of drink his face became ugly and menacing. His flawless olive skin turned to dark purple, and the lambent brown eyes became as black as coal and filled with hatred. Beria said it was his 'raging-bull' look. If he made eye contact, he curled his lip, sneered audibly and half-closed his eyes as he turned his face away in scorn. He threatened to shoot anyone who disagreed or dared to argue with him. He said he was more clever than anyone else and that Beria was stupid – the one thing guaranteed to get Beria's back up.

I hated Saturday nights when I was not visiting my father in Leonora, and I felt sick to the pit of my stomach when Steve bashed Beria. When he came home from the hotel, you could tell what was going to happen from the way he sat at the kitchen table. If he sat sideways in his chair, legs crossed and threatening, it required extreme caution. Beria only had to give me a look – the slightest tilt of her head – and I knew it was time to disappear. I'd go to my room, climb into bed, and try to hide from the awfulness. However, there was no door on my room and I could hear everything he said, and did.

Sometimes after Steve hit Beria, she would go for weeks without saying a word to him, and answering only if it were absolutely essential, and then in the most perfunctory manner. Steve would try to make up by bringing her a cup of tea in bed. Beria would ignore the gesture, leaving the tea until it was cold, and then, if he were still around, make much of throwing it out. Even when they weren't talking, Steve still forced her to go with him. He nudged her every morning at five o'clock – 'Eh' – without fail.

Every night during the winter months Steve sat at the kitchen table and drank a large beer bottle of muscat which Beria ordered from Vidakovich, a Slav vigneron in the Swan Valley. It arrived by train in ten-gallon oak barrels. It was Beria's job to keep up his supply – siphoning it off into beer bottles. When I was old enough she gave me the job, which had a certain benefit. Using a length of clear rubber hosing, I filled ten beer bottles; however, the continual suck-starting of the sweet fortified amber liquid made me tipsy, which made Beria laugh. From time to time, Steve gave me a quarter of a glass of muscat diluted with water and a sweetened with a teaspoon of sugar, which settled on the bottom and which I ate with a spoon.

The tongue-and-groove muscat casks were made from recycled English oak Scotch whisky barrels and held firm by three evenly placed steel bands. When Steve collected a barrel from the train he insisted the stationmaster watch while he inspected it. It was well known that railway employees helped themselves to a couple of bottles by moving the middle band and drilling a small hole which they plugged with a piece of sharpened dowelling before returning the band to its original position.

Soon after nine o'clock Steve went to bed. He kept a bottle of Chateau Tanunda Five Star Hospital brandy kept under the bed. When he woke up during the night he took a swig. He drank a bottle a week, which Beria said pickled his brain.

Lewie married Jean Ryan at the Sacred Heart Catholic Church, Leonora, on 17 December 1953. The temperature was 117 degrees. They were both twenty. Jean's sister Peggy was bridesmaid and Steve was the best man, which left Beria without a partner at the church and at the wedding breakfast.

In the weeks leading up to the wedding there was an ongoing flurry of activity and stern whispered conversations after Lewie obtained a full copy of his birth certificate. Even Father Moffatt became involved. One evening Beria and I were walking home from the park. As we passed in front of the State Hotel Father Moffatt pulled up in his car and he and Beria talked, animatedly. I was told to stand away so that I couldn't hear what was being discussed. When he left, we walked home in silence – a sure sign of Beria's unhappiness.

Lewie's certificate was stamped illegitimate. Sergio Gherardi and Beria weren't married when he was born. There was also confusion about his date of birth. Lewie's name was Stammers, Beria's maiden name. It was changed by deed poll on his wedding day to Rocchecioli, the name by which he had always been known but with a different spelling from that of my father. The name change cost £25, an amount which caused continuing acrimony.

Lewie worked at Sullivan's garage in Leonora, a job he took with the promise of an apprenticeship. When Mr Sullivan gave the apprenticeship to his son, Lewie went to work for Tommy White, driving the mail truck twice a week to Wiluna, a distance of 188 miles over corrugated dirt roads. Jean worked in the Leonora greengrocery owned by her mother Mary and her husband, George Edward Le Feuvre. A smidgeon under five foot one, Jean wore fashionable high-heeled platform-soled shoes to compensate. She had an ample bosom, a glorious head of thick dark wavy hair, clear skin and protruding front teeth about which she was self-conscious, never allowing them to show when she smiled. Lewie was good-looking, six foot tall, and had inherited Beria's flawless pale skin, bright blue eyes and dark hair. His ears were large and stuck out.

Beria had no inkling of the romance and when Lewie broke the news she was taken aback, and lukewarm to the idea of his going out with Jean Ryan. Beria and Lewie were close and she harboured a secret yearning he would marry Val Parkinson, who lived around the corner from us and whom Beria considered to be the right girl for him. Beria's antipathy towards Jean never abated and the pair maintained an uneasy relationship.

I was six, and this was my first family wedding. I could hardly contain my excitement, listening to every detail.

Jean wore a simple self-patterned white satin dress with scalloped elbow-length sleeves and nylon diamond-patterned elbow-length mittens. The fingertip net veil hung flat against her back and was anchored to her head by a weighty traditional headdress of wax orange blossoms and lilies, which softened in the heat. Peggy, her sister, was matron of honour and wore a long blue organdie dress with a shoulder-length tulle headdress, which sat on the top of her head like a cocky's crest. The sheaf bouquets of white gladioli and pink carnations, with trailing satin ribbons, were stored in a shop refrigerator until the last moment. Beria and Mary both carried posies of blood-red rosebuds, something I had never before seen or smelt. Outside the church a crowd of women who knew the couple, but were not invited to the wedding, waited to see them and join the guests in throwing confetti. Most of the women considered it an appropriate occasion to wear a hat.

Beria made for me a pair of brown woollen pin-striped short trousers, which I wore with elastic braces, an oatmeal gabardine shirt, and sandals with short white socks. My hair was combed with Californian Poppy Oil.

Beria's heavy rayon burgundy and white dress came from Rockman's in Melbourne and was boldly patterned with twisted nautical ropes. She accidentally chipped one of the four ornamental ceramic burgundy bodice buttons. Beria didn't own a hat and borrowed a black felt creation with a turned-back brim, no crown, and secured at the back with a half-inch felt strap decorated with silver studded daisies. Her shoes were fine-soled, high-heeled black patent leather, with a peep toe and an open basket-weave front. Beria never wore stockings. Nita, who was home from Dongara for the Christmas school holidays, wore her white speech-night dress and white and brown Chanel-style shoes. They both had their hair permed specially.

Inside the stifling galvanised-iron church, I sat with my father, Beria and Nita. All the ladies in the congregation had their heads covered by a hat or scarf, and some fanned themselves with spade-shaped woven palmetto fans, which they carried and used everywhere – even in the street. It was Father Moffatt's first wedding in Leonora. Steve paid him for his services, increasing the payment at the last minute from £5 to £11 when he had a win on the races.

The church had a centre aisle with about ten wooden pews on either side; the tin walls were painted pale lime and hung with European-style stations of the cross. The polished wooden communion rail separated the altar from the congregation. Three steps led up to the altar, which was draped in white deep-lace and cotton altar cloths, washed and starched by the women of the parish. They had a roster for the cleaning of the church.

On either side of the tabernacle, which was hidden behind a satin curtain embroidered with IHS, were matching single and nine-prong brass candleholders. Two three-foot statues – the Sacred Heart of Jesus and Our Lady of Fatima – were on either side of the altar. Sylvia Poletti played the organ, which was on a rostrum in the corner at the back of the church. A large coloured portrait of Pope Pius XII hung in the portico. The interior of the church smelled of dry heat, red dust and the residue of burnt sandalwood from the thurible used at benediction and other services – the fragrant smoke symbolising our prayers rising to heaven and purifying what it touches. A door on the right-hand side led through to the presbytery, where the priest prepared and also heard confession.

Before the wedding breakfast, everyone went to the White House Hotel for a celebratory drink. By mistake, Beria was left behind. When it was noticed, Lewie went back to the house to collect her. He found her sitting alone on the back verandah, crying. She later commented: 'It should have been the happiest day of my life, but it wasn't. It was the worst.'

As the sun was setting, Lewie and Jean went outside to have some photographs taken, standing next to the bridal car. I followed and stood a short distance away, staring, not saying a word. I was fascinated by the glamour of it all and not quite sure what to make of it.

The wedding breakfast for about twenty guests, including Father Moffatt, was held on the back verandah of Mary and George's house in Leonora. The semi-enclosed verandah, with a bare overhead light bulb, two washing troughs in the corner and a cement floor, was emptied of stored debris and car parts and set with borrowed mismatching kitchen chairs, and several tables pushed together and covered with white damask tablecloths. The troughs were filled with ice and used to keep the beer cold. Beria felt excluded. 'Mary and George sat with the bride and groom. I was down the far end of the table with policeman Roy Patterson, who drove the bridal car.' I sat with the other children at a table set up outside the bathroom door.

Mary was an excellent cook and did all the catering for the wedding breakfast, as well as the full supper for the eighty or so guests at the reception. Beria left the wedding costs to the bride's parents and she did nothing to help with the preparations. Steve paid for a keg of beer. The wedding breakfast was simple fare: cold chicken, ham, lamb, salads, home-made fruit salad and ice-cream, and wine trifle, my favourite, in a large crystal bowl. It was normal in the town for a group of volunteer ladies to help on the day; they arrived, served the meal and cleared away the mess. When it came time to serve supper at the wedding reception, the married ladies helped out, heating and serving the food and cleaning up the kitchen. For Mary it was a day of hard work while Beria sat on the sidelines and watched, with little pleasure.

The reception was in the Federal Hall, which was considered to be a bit more posh. Jean and her sister Peggy spent a lot of time unwrapping wedding presents, which were put on display. Beria was livid when her dinner service was missing. When she asked, Jean said, 'Oh, I forgot. It's at home behind the bathroom door.' That was the final straw for Beria. She was already upset by a series of what she said were intentional slights. None of her friends from her guest list had been invited, and she was not included in any of the wedding photographs. We left the reception as supper was being served and before the bride had changed into her going-away outfit.

Mary made the wedding cake, a two-tiered design crowned with a traditional sugar bride and groom. Jean kept the top tier for the christening of their first child. It was stored in a cake tin on top of the kitchenette and was an object of my constant attraction. When Lewie and Jean were first married they lived in a house opposite the state school. I used to go and stay some weekends. Whenever I was taken to see them I asked if I could look at the cake. One day when I asked, Jean said, 'I haven't got it any more. It went off, so I threw it out.' I was devastated and harped on it for months, to the point of irritating Beria. 'Ronnie, will you stop talking about that bloody wedding cake. It's gone.'

The next morning, Lewie and Jean left by train for Kalgoorlie. The train stopped at the Gwalia station for about fifteen minutes, but Beria didn't bother to walk the short distance to the station to see them on their way. They returned a week later, and Beria was peeved that Jean brought back a cup and saucer for her mother, by way of a thank you for the wedding. 'I didn't get anything, did I?' Beria never forgave Jean for the cup-and-saucer incident and it set the tone for their relationship. Every time there was an argument Beria mentioned it.

∞

Queen Elizabeth II was crowned at Westminster Abbey on 2 June 1953, one of the coldest months on the goldfields. Steve was on afternoon shift and Beria and I listened on the wireless to the live broadcast. It was five o'clock in the afternoon. As Elizabeth was crowned, Beria was sewing. I marched back and forth in the kitchen keeping time to the band music.

The following Christmas Beria bought me *The Queen's Coronation Book*, filled with colour plates. Spread across the two inside cover pages was a route map of the procession, with arrows indicating the direction of the procession to and from the abbey. With my finger I traced the journey of the Queen's gold coronation coach. At school we were given a specially minted copper coronation medal hanging from a patriotic red white and blue grosgrain ribbon, and disk badges of the smiling Queen, swathed in white fox fur and carrying a huge bouquet of pastel roses, and of the Duke of Edinburgh dressed in a naval uniform.

To mark the coronation, London chefs Constance Spry and Rosemary Hume created Coronation Chicken, a delicious cream chicken curry, served with steamed or boiled rice. Lewie's mother-in-law, whom I adored and called Auntie Mary, was an exceptional cook and sometimes served Coronation Chicken when we went to see her.

The royal couple flew into the west the following year, landing first at Kalgoorlie. In her speech at the Kalgoorlie Oval the Queen told 5000 people: 'We know well what the Eastern Goldfields have achieved in peace and war. We trust that you will all enjoy the lasting happiness and prosperity that you so richly deserve.' Her presence on the goldfields meant little to the locals and they weren't particularly demonstrative. The children were more enthusiastic, running up to the Land Rover as the standing Queen and Duke slowly circled the Kalgoorlie football oval.

It was reported: 'Before going by air to Perth, the royal couple drove to nearby Boulder, where Her Majesty was offered a bouquet by a five-year-old Aboriginal girl, who had been learning not only how to speak English, but to enjoy the taste of fruit and vegetables. Just a short while earlier her diet out in the bush had been lizards, grubs, goanna and possums. The Queen didn't touch the dusky little tot's flower offering. It was left on the table because of the poliomyelitis precautions, but she asked her equerry if he could get one of the press photographs taken of the presentation.'

Beria laughed when it was announced on the wireless that everyone had to stand six feet away from the Queen and no one was allowed to shake her by the hand.

Even though we were isolated, Gwalia didn't go untouched by the polio epidemic. With fewer than a hundred kids, three of them 'got the polio' – Lorraine Loftus, Helen Hilary and Johnny Turich. Johnny Turich was away at Christian Brothers' College in Kalgoorlie. With the initials CBC, the students were known as the 'corn beef and cabbage' boys. The Catholic brothers rang the policeman early in the morning and he went to see Mrs Turich. She didn't speak much English and Beria was her only friend. 'Steve had only just gone to work, so it was a bit after seven o'clock when I heard this terrible screaming. Naturally, I flew outside to see what was wrong. Next thing, Mrs Turich comes running into the yard, wailing. She was crying so much I couldn't make any sense, so I brought her inside and we sat down in front of the fire. She was shaking like a leaf and I put a rug over her legs. In the end I had to grab her by the shoulder and shake her. When she told me the terrible news, my heart sank. Johnny was a teenager. He was a really fast runner and we used to kid him about being in the Olympic Games one day.' I loved Johnny Turich – he taught me how to swim. They brought him home in a wheelchair and no matter how much Beria tried, I wouldn't go near him.

Lorraine Loftus and her brother, Barry, were Joan Tagliaferri's children from her first marriage. When Lorraine got the polio, Joan took her first to Perth, and then for eight years to a children's hospital in Mount Eliza, just outside of Melbourne. Lorraine was away for nine months of the year, and underwent twenty bone-graft operations, moving a bit from here and a bit from there. Every year Joan took the Trans-Continental train across the Nullarbor to collect Lorraine and bring her back to Gwalia; it took five days each way.

After learning how to walk and talk, Lorraine ended up with 50 per cent use of her arms, and walked with callipers and crutches. I watched as she lurched along, dragging her feet on the ground and wearing out a pair of surgical boots every three months. They cost £16 a pair. Her cumbersome wheelchair, a design of connecting chains and wheels, was stored on the front verandah. Try as I might, I was too scared to touch it.

There was no government help available and it cost Joan and Bob fourteen guineas a week for Lorraine's hospitalisation. Bob had to work two jobs – underground on the mine and as a barman at the State Hotel – while Joan was in the Leonora hospital laundry. They did it really hard, living on anything Bob could shoot. He used to set rabbit traps, then get up at 4 am and ride his pushbike to see what he'd caught. He'd come home, have some breakfast and go to work. He didn't finish at the pub until midnight. He did that for years.

Joan and Bob lived down near the convent and occasionally, when Steve was on afternoon shift, Beria and I would go there for tea. Between them, Joan and Beria sometimes knocked up a pot of home-made gnocchi and napolitano sauce, my favourite. My father taught Beria to make gnocchi and, according to her, it was the same recipe my grandmother used in Italy. Beria made sure we were home and in bed before Steve finished work. When he was on the afternoon shift, Beria went to bed early and read – usually a *True Romance* – but the light was out a quarter of an hour before he was due home, and then Beria pretended to be asleep: 'It got to the stage where I hated going to bed with him.'

A couple of years before, in 1952, Helen Hilary caught the polio. She was a one-off case in Gwalia. Beria and her mother, Edie, were friends. Beria used to make pastry for her, using butter and not lard.

Helen Hilary said: 'It was Saturday morning, and I had a bad headache, which was unusual for me. As I did every week, I walked two miles into Leonora to do the messages for Mum. I remember I was wearing my brown sandals. When I'd finished the chores I walked home again.

'Mum thought I had the flu, and in the afternoon she made me lie down because we were going to the pictures that night. When I got out of bed at teatime she said, "You are not allowed to tell anyone you have the flu." As soon as I got to the pictures I told everyone; it was a form of status symbol.

'The next morning Dad and I walked the eighteen holes around the golf course, which is the worst thing to do with polio. I was so tired Dad had to carry me home. Before tea, I went to visit the Elliotts. I was lying on the floor reading a comic, but then I couldn't get up. I can't remember but I guess one of the Elliott girls helped me.

'On Monday, Mum said I didn't have to go to school. She had to help me to my feet so I could go to the toilet. I fell down, twice. Mum said it was because I had been in bed for a while, and not to worry. Then I fell down again. I was so frightened, and we were both crying.

'Mum called the ambulance. On the way to Leonora hospital we went past the state school just as they were ringing the bell for the end of lunchtime. The last person I saw in the school yard was Kay Quarti, my best friend. I didn't see her again until I was twelve – three years later.

'Both Mum and Dad wrote to me every week, and they came to see me whenever they could. Dad always told me to be a good girl, and do what the physiotherapist said. So that I wouldn't feel like I was missing out, Mum used to tell me everything they were doing, even what they were having for tea. One letter from Dad really made me cry. He said: "The cat sends a miaow."'

It was Sunday afternoon, the summer of 1954, a month or so after Lewie's wedding. The atmosphere between Beria and Steve was tense and Beria was not talking. The night before, Steve came home drunk; they argued and he belted her. Having finished his dinner, he called her into the bedroom and closed the door. When they re-emerged a short time later, Beria was agitated. They began arguing again. I was standing in the passage, watching. Beria said she couldn't stand it anymore: 'I'm sick and tired of all this fighting and arguing. I'm going to get rid of myself.' Steve sniggered at her. 'Go on, do it.'

It all happened so quickly. Beria removed the long cotton tie from the waist of her dress, tied it around her neck and pulled it tight. In a matter of seconds she fainted and fell on the floor. I started screaming and Steve, stunned by her action, rushed to undo the tie, patting Beria's face to bring her around. After a minute or so she opened her eyes, stood up, went outside and sat on the bed against the front wall of the house. Steve tried to apologise but Beria was having none of it. 'Just go away and leave me alone, will you. You've caused enough bloody trouble for one day.' The more he tried the more agitated she became. Eventually he went back down the pub. After that, things quietened down, and for a time Steve was less violent. He promised Beria if she had a baby he would give up gambling.

About a month later Beria announced we were going to Perth for a holiday. She insisted on travelling first class. When Steve complained about the cost, she gave him a piece of her mind. 'Why should I travel second class? You don't. I go first or not at all!'

We travelled all day by steam train from Gwalia to Kalgoorlie, and overnight on the Kalgoorlie Express to Perth, sharing a two-berth cabin with our own shower and lavatory. I slept in the top bunk, and was rocked to sleep listening to the clickety-clack as we thundered through the night, leaving a plume of white smoke trailing in the sky. An hour before our arrival in Perth, the conductor brought us a cup of tea and two McVittie's digestive biscuits. A few miles out the train went through the Darling Range escarpment tunnel. The conductor warned us, and I waited, not knowing what to expect. A lot of squealing and laughing could be heard when the carriage plunged into darkness and the smell of smoke filled the air. A minute or so later we emerged into bright sunshine and sweeping views of Italian market gardens, all hazy through a mist of water swirling on the breeze as the pressure of the spume turned the heads of the sprinklers and created a sequence of mini-rainbows.

Overnight in the carriage I had been playing with Beria's new pair of white high-heeled shoes. I put them in the bottom of the wardrobe and they were left behind when we got off. Beria was ropeable.

We stayed with Nana McGregor, my aunt Silvia's mother-in-law, in North Perth, within walking distance of the city centre. The house was a solid brick Victorian terrace, with a tessellated-tiled front verandah, a side walkway, and a lawn and garden at the rear. Inside was fussily maintained; the chairs had antimacassars and the pillowcases and sheets were starched and ironed.

It was my first meeting with Nana and we liked each other from the start. Nana, whose name was Lillian, was the family matriarch. Nana was born in 1879. She was a statuesque, formidable, upper-working-class woman who carried her size with style. She wore black kid leather shoes and socks, and a dark skirt and blouse with a wraparound pinafore. Nana knew the value of a shilling and kept her housekeeping money in a clip purse, which was tucked into her generous bosom. She always paid cash, delving inside her brassiere to find the required sum, then putting the purse back where she knew it to be safe.

Nana slept in the front bedroom while her husband, whom we all called Father, had been relegated to the back verandah sleep-out. A gentle soul, Father had retired after years of working on the Fremantle wharf. Nana and Father had one child, Jack, who was married for a short time to my Aunt Silvia. They referred to him as a 'wanderer' or a 'no-hoper'. Jack worked for the government and was involved in a financial incident which came to the attention of the police. One step ahead, Nana shipped Jack off to South Australia.

There was no arguing with Nana. She carried a grudge and thought nothing of going out of her way to be hurtful. When Uncle Jack and Aunt Silvia divorced, Nana was determined she would raise her only grandson, Don, insisting mother and son move in with her. Aunt Silvia went to work as a cook for a Mrs Oliphant and Nana took care of Don. In return, she took Silvia's pay packet and gave her a small allowance. Many a time when Silvia came home on her half-day off, planning to spend time with her son, Nana would say: 'Oh, what a shame. He has gone to spend the day with his auntie Martha.' It broke Silvia's heart but she never complained. When Silvia met and began courting Les Watkins, a cobbler, Nana wouldn't allow him into the house until they were married. They had to meet on the corner.

Meals with Nana were a formal affair. It was always a two-course meal; soup in the winter and a pudding in the summer. A pumped leg of mutton with white sauce and boiled potatoes was a particular favourite. Supper was tea or hot chocolate and home-made cake, which was served at precisely the same time, and anyone who failed to wash their cup and saucer missed out the following night.

Saturday afternoon was devoted to cooking a steamed bread pudding for Sunday midday dinner. The taste was made more agreeable by the silver threepenny pieces liberally sprinkled through the mixture. To my joy, most of them seemed to end up in my serving. Made from stale bread, the recipe was created during the Depression as a poor man's plum pudding. Its aroma filled the air, making your mouth water as Nana cut thick slices and served it with steaming yellow custard. The leftovers were eaten cold for supper.

The underside of Nana's upper arms hung heavy and pendulous. Always looking for something to amuse myself, I said, 'Nana, can I play with your fat arms?' She obliged, allowing me to bounce the loose skin in my hands.

Nana McGregor's grandson, Don, also lived with her, together with his wife Linda and their two children. Don was a brilliant accounts clerk. Unfortunately, he loved the drink and couldn't be entrusted with any personal cash. His mother, Aunt Silvia, went every week to collect his pay from where he worked. Beria had her views but she never discussed them with Silvia. 'The problem was Don was never allowed to stand on his own two feet. I know Nana McGregor meant well, but she ruined him; she always treated him like a child. They had no life with Nana. He wasn't allowed to make any decision and Linda was like a servant. She was there at Nana's beck and call. It's no wonder Don drank.'

Don was working at a bakery and within walking distance of the house. Each day he came home at midday. I adored him, and ten minutes or so before he was due I went more than halfway to meet him. He would hold my hand as we walked back together. Don was a tall, good-looking, charming young man with a serious problem. He hid bottles of sherry and muscat in the garden and during the evening, while they were playing cards, he would slip out regularly for a nip. Everyone except Nana laughed about it. While Don was at work we searched the garden, hiding the bottles in unlikely places all over the house. Nana McGregor idolised Don and did everything humanly possible to get him off the drink. Sadly, it worsened with time.

For a couple of months, Don came to Gwalia and worked in the mine's pay office. He boarded with Beria and Steve, who encouraged him to drink with him at the hotel. Somehow, Don met and became friendly with a neighbouring couple who were also drinkers, and joined them in a four- or five-day binge for which he paid. When Don didn't come home Beria suspected where he was and went knocking on the door. They denied any knowledge, even though Beria was sure she caught a glimpse of Don lurking in the shadows. The next day when Beria went to collect the bread, Vic Mazza told her Don had been to the shop buying food and was 'a bit worse for wear'. Immediately, Beria went to the policeman and together they went and brought him out. Don kept apologising to Beria, his favourite aunt, and after days of drinking was desperate to take a bath.

Later, in a heart-to-heart with Beria, Don explained he missed his children and was going back to Perth. Reg Barden said he had been one of their best workers. That was the last time Beria and Don saw each other. He died soon afterwards from a combination of drink and prescription drugs.

Around every corner in Perth was a new discovery. I was wide-eyed at the sight of the shops, the streets, and the height of the buildings. In Gwalia we walked; here we took the tram and the trolley bus. Each morning I took stale bread to feed the ducks, which in Gwalia we shot and ate with polenta. The pond on which the ducks swam was bigger than our pool and, compared to the Gwalia park, Hyde Park was a forest. Boans department store was a visual paradise – an Aladdin's cave of sights, sounds and smells. I rode up and down, endlessly, on the wooden and brass-inlaid escalators. While Beria went shopping I stood in the corner of the lift – listening and watching, and travelling between the floors. I had never seen a shop dummy and caused some merriment with other shoppers when I lifted up a skirt to investigate. I was shocked and called loudly across the floor to Beria: 'Mum, she's got no pants on!'

Beria made it quite clear: 'If you get lost, stand still and I'll find you.' It happened and I panicked. Disoriented, I wandered off and began to cry. A small crowd gathered and eventually Beria pushed her way through. I was so relieved; however, she had a face like thunder. She grabbed me by the arm. 'Didn't I tell you to stand still?'

'Yes,' I replied, with tears streaming down my face.

'Next time do as you are bloody well told!' and with that she gave me a wallop on the backside.

A gentleman in the crowd sprang to my defence.

'Don't hit him, lady', he protested. 'He's upset!'

Beria was in no mood for any interference. 'Mind your own bloody business, or I'll give you one as well!'

I spotted a bride doll in a shop window and for a week I pestered. It stood about six inches high and cost two shillings and sixpence. The more Beria said no, the more I asked why.

'Ronnie, you can stop that whining right now. You just can't have it. Alright?'

'Why?'

'Because little boys don't have dolls.'

'Why?'

'Oh, for God's sake, Ronnie, I don't know. They just don't.'

But I kept harping and, in the end, for the sake of peace and quiet, she bought it for me.

'Now, will you give over? You've got your bloody bride doll, and you are not to tell anyone I bought it for you.'

'Why?'

'Because I bloody well said so, that's why, and I don't want to hear another word about it.'

We went into Harris, Scarfe and Sandovers at lunchtime; the shop was packed. I took the doll out of the paper bag, held it in the air for everyone to see, then said at the top of my voice to the girl behind the counter: 'Look what my mum bought me, a bride doll!'

Beria didn't know where to look.

∞

As luck would have it, Beria and I were in Perth at the same time as the Queen and the Duke of Edinburgh and for the six days of the royal tour Western Australia came to a standstill. People slept out, or arrived early in the morning, to gain the best vantage points. On the night of Perth's big royal progress, Beria and I joined the throng of thousands waiting to catch a glimpse of the Queen and the Duke of Edinburgh as they drove along St George's Terrace.

Buildings were decorated with coloured lights and draped with the Union flag. The royal cipher, ER II, and giant floodlit reproductions of the Dorothy Wilding portrait of the Queen hung from city buildings. The same picture of the Queen appeared on a stamp. She was dressed in a Norman Hartnell blue satin off-the-shoulder evening gown. Eight illuminated and decorated steel arches, topped with giant crowns and fitted with hundreds of coloured lights and various symbols of colonial devotion, spanned the St George's Terrace, lighting up the night sky and dwarfing the people below. Huge spot-lit globes of the world appeared to be suspended in mid-air. Giant boomerang-shaped banners proclaimed: 'GOD BLESS OUR QUEEN'.

As the Queen's motorcade drew closer I was overwhelmed by the rolling wave of noise. Everyone was cheering and brandishing flags. Moments before the Queen's car passed at a snail's pace I was lifted and seated on top of a taxi telephone box; I had a clear view over the heads in front. The motorcade was led by eight motorcycles and a contingent of twenty mounted police. Smiling and waving to the cheering crowd, the Queen and the Duke were sitting in the back of a gleaming car. I was dazzled by the light bouncing off her diamond tiara and three-strand diamond necklace. The waving hand was encased in a long white kid glove, reaching way past her elbow. The blue of the Garter riband was a bold slash of colour, running from her left shoulder; on the other shoulder was a large spray of Australia's wattle to complement the yellow tulle gown created especially by Norman Hartnell for the Australian tour. The full skirt was heavily beaded in a wattle motif.

As suddenly as she had appeared, the Queen was gone, but the thrill didn't abate. People were running along the street, chasing the car and cheering. The next morning, Beria took me to buy a gold-sprayed lead coronation coach, pulled by eight hand-painted Windsor Greys. When offered a choice I opted for the larger. It was

£5. 'I'm sorry,' Beria told me. 'I'd love to buy it for you, but I can't afford it.' I happily accepted the smaller of the two. Back at Nana's I sat on the floor in the bedroom, playing with the coach.

∞

About five months after our holiday in Perth, Beria and Steve were married at the Leonora Registry Office, at 7 pm on 13 September 1954. It was a quiet affair with two witnesses, Max and May Talbot. During the day Beria cooked a chook which she left on the table in readiness for their return. It was the first time I tasted tinned asparagus. There were olives and home-made cheese straws served in leaf-shaped china containers, with the stalk as the handle.

As a wedding present May gave Beria the latest in designer partyware – a twelve-inch diameter hardened plastic dish fitted with eight multi-coloured triangular serving containers, which Beria filled with salted peanuts and home-made potato chips.

Beria, who was five months pregnant, wore a white full-skirted Everglaze dress with a double-breasted bodice and a large stand-away collar. Even though Lewie and Jean lived across the road from the Registry Office, they were not invited. I waited with Nita, who was home for the August school holidays. No one took any photographs and the next morning Steve went off to work on the mine as usual.

∞

Some nights after the evening meal, for about half an hour before I went off to bed, we played the card game of grab or snap. Time and again it followed the same pattern. Beria and Steve would allow me to win a couple of hands and then subject me to a continuing losing streak. Frustrated, I ran off to bed, crying. Laughing uproariously, they called to me: 'Come back, we'll let you win.'

After four or five repeats of the same routine the torture of it upset me deeply. One night I was so distressed, when Beria came into the bedroom to say goodnight I ignored her. She waited for a moment, then turned and left.

Beria's and Steve's antics played on my mind and I developed a phobia about losing, and a reluctance to participate in any competitive sport, bursting into floods of tears at the prospect; I wouldn't be cajoled. The dread lasted for some years. During a holiday in Perth, my father took me to *Jack and the Beanstalk*, playing at His Majesty's Theatre. When a cast member tried to involve me with other children in an on-stage apple-eating competition, I cried. My father, and the cast member, didn't understand my reaction.

A week after Christmas 1954 I was sent off to stay with Wint as a preparation for the arrival of Beria's new baby. Joan Anne Salinovich was born on 14 January 1955, in the Leonora District Hospital. Beria was almost forty-four and stayed in hospital for the usual fortnight. It was about a week after she returned home before Wint took me to meet my new sister. She was sleeping in a cane bassinette and swamped in nylon frills, mosquito netting, gathered lace and a shell-patterned crocheted rug made from the finest baby wool. Joan, who was wearing a nappy and singlet, was bright yellow. I stared for a bit, wondering. 'Mum,' I said. 'She's not white, is she?'

Beria looked to Steve for his reaction to my comment. 'Don't be so bloody ridiculous; of course she is!' Steve glared, while Wint, sensing I was skating on thin ice, pushed me outside to play. I stayed with Wint for another month or so while Beria and Joan, who was a bad sleeper, established a routine, and it was several weeks before the jaundice faded.

Steve went to visit Beria in the hospital only once after the baby was born, and it was Lewie who brought her and Joan home. Beria was hurt by Steve's neglect: 'He made a big man of himself buying champagne for the doctor and chocolates for the nurses. I got nothing.'

Joan was about eight weeks old and Steve had just left for work at the mine. Beria was sitting at the kitchen table, breast feeding, when Joan slipped from Beria's grip and landed on her head. Beria got a hell of a fright. She scooped up the screaming baby and ran next door to Harry Gray, who drove her to the hospital. Joan was thoroughly examined and sent home with a clean bill of health. Several months passed before Beria was brave enough to mention the incident to Steve.

It was about the same time that the teenage son of Beria's friend, and his mate, took advantage when I went to visit. It happened twice. The son's bedroom was separate from the house and, while Beria was inside talking, they took me into the bedroom and had me perform oral sex on both of them while they sat on the side of the bed.

Ben Poole lived in a two-room camp behind Mrs Patroni's. He was the only amateur photographer in the town. The corner of his tiny kitchen was converted into a darkroom. Mr Poole was a Scot with a black dagger tattooed onto his leg at the exact spot his sock would reach when he wore a kilt. He played chess by mail, sending his move once a week to a friend in Perth.

The night of Joan's christening at the St Francis of Assisi Catholic Church, Mr Poole came to the house and set up in the kitchen. Joan was almost six months old and the christening was a quiet affair but not without incident. When I moved too close to the font, Steve sent me to the back of the church.

Joan's arrival complicated my life with Beria. I was eight, and at an age when Steve resented my presence. The sight of me made him irritable and Beria anxious. She kept us apart as much as possible, sending me out to play, or to my room to read, when he came home. She even fed me early to avoid any unpleasant encounters. My inclination to argue and interrupt landed Beria into trouble. Steve never once raised his hand to me, hitting Beria instead. She warned him, meaningfully: 'I don't care what you do to me, but if you ever touch Ronnie, I'll get you when you're asleep.' Steve told her I was not allowed to nurse the baby, or even come too close to the bassinette. To keep the peace, Beria always took his side and in the first twelve months of Joan's life I held her only once – for the christening photo – and at Ben Poole's insistence.

For the five years I lived with Beria and Steve in Grinning Joe's house, Christmas was a magical time. The preceding weeks were filled with anticipation, and everyone looked forward to being part of it. The celebrations began on Christmas Eve with the Christmas tree and presents in the park, followed by midnight Mass for the adults. The festivities continued through to New Year when families headed off for their annual two-week holiday. I was curious about the Fresh Air League holiday camp in Esperance but was too embarrassed to ask why the air was so fresh, and whether it came in a bottle.

For the Italians in Gwalia, European food and traditions formed an important part of Buon Natale – a link with the old country. There was no roast turkey or plum pudding with brandy sauce. Instead, Beria cooked a leg of ham in the copper, which she scrubbed with salt and vinegar until you could see your face in it. She added a bottle of beer or red wine, a handful of peppercorns and a pound of sugar to the water. She boiled the ham for an hour, removed the hot coals from the fire, covered the copper with a pile of old towels and blankets, leaving the ham to cook in its own heat and lifting it from the water the following morning. She carefully removed the flap of skin and covered the remaining layer of white fat with breadcrumbs. The skin was used to seal in the freshness.

On Christmas morning Steve killed a rooster to make risotto, which we ate late morning, following which we joined a crowd of between thirty and forty adults and a swarm of kids going from house to house, eating and drinking and travelling around the town on the back of Ike Nye's old delivery truck. Isabella Pennefather was a large woman, and everyone knew she had to travel in the front. The rest of us clambered onto the open timber tray and we chugged from one location to the next. Beria and Steve always walked.

Wherever we went on Christmas Day, kitchen and dining-room tables were weighed down with roast chooks and roosters, legs of ham and pork, potato and pea salad, traditional Italian cakes and panforte, glacé and marzipan fruit, tiramisu, lasagne, spaghetti and bowls of home-made cheese straws and potato chips. Beria made ice-cream from powdered and sweetened condensed milk. Once a year she bought a tin of SPC fruit salad – her favourite – which never tasted as good as it looked in the cut-glass bowl. I picked out the maraschino cherries and grapes, leaving the small pineapple triangles, still spotted with remnants of the tough outside skin which stuck into your tongue.

Beria's rich Christmas cake took several weeks of preparation. First the loose currants, raisins and sultanas were picked over, washed and then left in a bowl for a couple of days on the back verandah to soak in lashings of brandy and muscat. They were stirred regularly and finally the spices were added in preparation for baking day. I stood at the end of the kitchen table, watching and asking the same questions.

Beria knew the recipe by heart: a pound of butter, a dozen freshly laid eggs, which I collected from the chookhouse on the day, a pound of brown sugar, four or five cups of self-raising flour, a cup of plain flour, two heaped serving spoons each of golden syrup and treacle, cinnamon and allspice. She had the same nutmeg seed for years and it was my job to grate it for the cake. Beria stirred it with a large wooden spoon, allowing me several tastes along the way. However, the best bit was licking the yellow English mixing bowl because Beria always left me two big spoonfuls of the thick brown mixture.

Using my father's cake tin, she let it cook for about three hours, keeping the temperature constant with a supply of kindling wood Steve cut for her especially. The smell floated through the house and hung on the air outside. Beria checked its progress, opening the oven door just enough to allow her to gently push the kitchen knitting needle into the centre of the cake. Only when it came out as clean as a whistle was the cake taken from the oven, left to cool in the tin, and wrapped for four weeks in an Irish linen tea towel. With a sigh of relief, she remarked: 'I'm happy it's not cracked.' The cake was never iced and my fingers itched to pick out and eat any fruit which had broken through the surface. With great anticipation, the cake was removed from the tin on Christmas and decorated every year with the same sugar Father Christmas, which belonged to me. Beria bought it for me from the chemist in 1951. It cost two and sixpence.

Every year after we had finished the cake I asked her the same question: 'Mum, can I eat Father Christmas?'

And every year she gave me the same answer: 'No, Ronnie, you cannot eat Father Christmas. Now put him back in the kitchenette and leave him there.' And that's where he sat for another year.

One year as I was putting him away, Beria commented: 'Ronnie, I think a little two-legged mouse has been having a bit of a nibble at Father Christmas.'

Beria and my father made sure that Father Christmas left a pile of presents at the end of my bed; however, Beria made it clear: 'You have to pay Father Christmas for all the presents. He doesn't bring them for nothing, you know.'

Christmas for Beria in the Salvation Army children's home had been miserable. She was determined things would be different for her children, scrubbing floors on her hands and knees to make sure her kids had a decent present. Between Beria and my father I was given a cowboy suit with leather chaps, a traditional Indian costume with a feathered headdress, a gleaming blue and white twenty-inch Swansea bicycle and a battery-operated train set. One Christmas Eve, Beria and Lewie were so excited, and made so much noise playing with my new toys, they woke me. 'Go back to sleep,' Beria whispered. 'Father Christmas has just been.'

Most of my toys never left my bedroom and were as good as new. I didn't ask when my battery train set mysteriously vanished. My 24-inch golden, imported English teddy bear had brown glass eyes and an embroidered black woollen nose. He was a present from Beria after she went to Perth for a holiday with Steve and Lewie and left me behind with Wint. Teddy was a good-looking bear and in pristine condition, except for a single broken strand of wool on his paw. He was treated with care and never once removed from my bedroom. Without asking, Beria gave him to my nephews who pulled and tugged at his head, ripping it from the body. He ended up in the rubbish bin.

The present I loved most was a tin replica of a Victorian kaleidoscope, the outside of which was elaborately hand-decorated. I spent hours holding it up to the sun and gazing at the dazzling coloured patterns. It was a constantly moving stained-glass window, whose mechanism was a puzzlement. Try as I did, I couldn't work out how the patterns were formed. To satisfy my curiosity I pulled it apart, only to discover it contained small pieces of coloured glass and a series of mirrors. Beria was livid and gave me a real telling-off. 'There's no point in crying and saying you're sorry,' she said sternly. 'It's too late. You shouldn't have bloody well pulled it apart.'

From about the time I turned seven my father never bothered with Christmas or birthday presents for me, and when Steve's big earning days on the mine came to an end Beria had less money to spend on presents. I was happy with a new pair of bathers and, on one occasion, a fringed beach towel. Royal Family books and the English children's annuals – *Jack and Jill*, *Play Hour*, *School Friend* and *Girls' Crystal* – remained favourites. But there was one special Christmas treat. Beria always gave me muscatels and almonds which came in a cellophane-wrapped blue oblong box. On the front was a cut-out of a bunch of grapes through which you could see the almonds and the big juicy muscatels still on their stalks. They were my favourite thing in the world and I was not expected to share them with anyone. Invariably, I sat and ate them in one go.

The first Christmas I recall with clarity was in 1952. Lewie was working day shift on the mine and his fiancée Jean arrived to spend the day. At midday she and I set off for the short walk to the mine, carefully carrying Lewie's hot Christmas dinner. He worked as a stoker on the producers, which was considered one of the best jobs there, and spent the eight-hour shift throwing mulga logs into seven open-topped roaring fires contained in huge steel furnaces which were ten feet in diameter and twenty feet high. The fires burned constantly and the internal hand-made bricks created such an intense heat the logs burst into flames almost instantly. I was terrified by the constant roar. The furnaces were surrounded with decking and a large ramp and railway track for the wood-line train. There was no safety rail, and to check the intensity of the fire the stoker stood on the side of the furnace, peering into the inferno. I was dumbstruck when I heard Beria talking of how Lewie slipped and managed, somehow, to save himself from falling headlong into the flames.

On one side of the work ramp was a small open-fronted corrugated-iron enclosure where the men took shelter from the sun and rain. Yards away, the chimneystack rose like a sentinel.

From years of use, the fitted wooden bench was worn smooth. I sat and watched as Lewie and Jean ate Christmas dinner together. They were in love.

The following Christmas was my first without Lewie living with us in Grinning Joe's house. He and Jean returned by train from their honeymoon the night before and came to visit on Christmas Day. They gave me a children's illustrated dictionary. It was also the year my father gave me the Swansea bicycle. It was ordered from Kalgoorlie and delivered to Auntie Mary's greengrocery in Leonora. I saw the wrapped bicycle resting against the entrance wall to the shop and when I checked the delivery tag I knew it was mine.

Although I didn't know it at the time, Christmas 1956 was my last one living with Beria. Nita and her boyfriend, Italo Cher, were in town from the sheep station where they worked and were staying at the house. Nita gave me my first watch and her old box Brownie camera. Later that morning, Joan Tagliaferri arrived unexpectedly with a present. Beria disappeared into her bedroom and reappeared with one for Joan hastily wrapped – a pair of ornamental china ladies, which had been Nita's Christmas present to Beria.

I spent Christmas 1957 with my father, Nita and Italo. I was delighted when, mid-morning, my piano teacher Kay Quarti called in with a beautifully wrapped present for me. She had attached a single white frangipani, the perfume of which was strong and exquisite. Later in the day I went with my father to visit a friend whose dog had a litter of pups. I was given an eight-week-old black cocker spaniel with a white flash on his long tail. I named him Tippy. Whenever I called, he came running across the flat, his huge ears flapping as though he would become airborne. He was the most affectionate dog and followed me everywhere.

By nine o'clock on Christmas morning, 1958, I had opened my present and eaten my breakfast. On the front verandah the temperature was 90 degrees, rising to a forecast of 104 degrees, and the pool didn't open on Christmas Day. My father, Nita and Italo had gone to visit their friends, leaving me with nothing to do. To help pass the time I was lying on the bed, daydreaming and half listening to the Australian Broadcasting Commission on Nita's portable battery-operated wireless. The playing of the national anthem caught my attention. There was a brief pause, and then a woman's voice. I listened, captivated by the cadence and the timbre of the voice. The tone of the delivery was unlike anything I had heard or known. I was used to a coarser, more strident note. As I listened, I guessed it must be the Queen and at that moment I knew there was something for me beyond Gwalia's claustrophobic horizons.

When the speech was over I waited for a moment, then reached across and turned off the wireless. I lay there facing the wall and staring at the home-made galvanised-iron shutters and thought about the Queen's message. Through the green latticework I could see the tall gum trees at the front of the house and, through the branches, the cloudless blue sky. The house was totally silent except for the frantic drone of the huge black blowflies caught against the flywire and struggling to escape, just inches from my face.

The temperature continued to rise.

∞

By the Christmas of 1956 Joan was almost two, and had reached an age where she was able to join in the preparations. Despite the eight-year age difference we got along without fighting and on cake-baking day we were a happy trio gathered around the kitchen table. The bowl of mixed fruit had been soaking for several days and the smell of spices filled the room. Moments before Beria poured the rich, fruit-laden mixture into the cake tin she sent me running to collect the eggs. I ran there and back but when I returned it was all over. The mixture had been poured, the cake was already in the oven, and Joan had scraped clean the bowl.

I couldn't work it out. There were so few moments in my childhood which belonged to me, and I would have been happy to share the bowl. I felt the tears well in my eyes, my throat constricted, and it hurt. I went back to the chookhouse where I sat quietly in the corner and cried. I convinced myself it would be different next year, but it wasn't. My heart sank when, just as she was about to pour the cake mixture, Beria told me to go and collect the eggs. This time I didn't run. I knew the joy of scraping the Christmas cake mixing bowl was no longer mine. As much as I loved Beria's Christmas cake, I didn't eat it again, ever. Beria didn't notice.

∞

When Nita was home from school in Dongara one May she went to spend the day with Jean in Leonora. When she arrived home she told Beria they had gone shopping to buy her birthday present – a box of handkerchiefs. Beria was disgusted at the thought of such a measly present. As it happens, Beria and Jean shared the same birthday, 6 May. On the evening of their birthdays Lewie and Jean came to visit. Beria handed Jean a wrapped box of handkerchiefs and was not the slightest bit sheepish when she opened her own present to discover it contained not only a box of embroidered pure Irish linen handkerchiefs, but also an expensive paste brooch.

If anyone gave Beria a bottle of eau de toilette and not concentrate perfume, she didn't hesitate to comment. 'What, too mean to buy me the perfume? You know I don't like eau de cologne.'

Lewie worked on the mine for wages, which didn't leave them with a lot of money to spare. Jean didn't know what to buy Steve for Christmas so she asked Beria, who suggested they finalise his outstanding account with Steve the tailor. Once it had been mentioned, Beria considered it a done deal and the debt was now their responsibility. Lewie and Jean were left to make regular payments on a bill which almost equalled Lewie's wages for a week.

⁂

Beria made no secret of the tension between her and Jean. After she and Lewie were married, Jean would come to spend the day with Beria. Lewie would drop her off at seven in the morning and collect her after work at about four o'clock. If Beria was in 'one of her moods' she'd go the whole day without speaking a word to Jean, answering any questions in the most cursory fashion. Beria had convinced herself Lewie favoured his mother-in-law Mary over her: 'It's all Jean's doing!' They argued a number of times and there were months of silence when they didn't see each other. Beria was not one to mince her words, but Jean eventually learned to stand up for herself.

'You've never liked me,' she told Beria, 'not from the moment I started going out with Lewie.'

'Got your claws into him, more like it.'

'That's lovely, that is.'

'Well, it's true. No one else was going to marry you.'

When Jean told her she didn't have to put up with this and announced she was leaving, Beria couldn't resist one last parting jibe. 'What do they say? Good riddance to bad rubbish.'

It was always Lewie who brokered the peace and convinced Jean to patch up their differences. Beria never apologised for her behaviour, nor would she admit to any part of the fault.

⁂

Hardly a day passed without Beria saying to me: 'Stop your star gazing!' Often, she asked why I didn't play with other kids. 'I don't want to,' I'd tell her. My favourite game was schools, with me being the teacher. Not surprisingly, the other kids hated that, so they went home. I dressed up in anything I could find, including Beria's old clothes and Nita's discarded unbleached calico petticoats. Beria even dressed me in Nita's confirmation outfit, a white dress with a red cloak. When I came back from the shop Beria always wanted to know who I had seen and what they were wearing. I told her in detail. 'I saw Mrs Little. She was wearing that dark blue dress with the little white flowers. She wears that a lot, doesn't she, Mum?'

I wasn't sure what Vic Mazza meant when he said to me, 'You're a funny sort of kid. Always on your own and always looking to have a chat.' I had a bike, a dog, and I was quite happy exploring the surrounding scrub catching brown lizards. I carefully dug them out of the hot ground with a stick, laid one on its back on the palm of my hand and watched as its little heart beat so fast in terror it almost leapt out of its chest cavity. You could see their veins through the fine white skin of their underbellies. I carried them around inside my shirt, setting them free at the end of the day. In the winter I went mushrooming in the flat behind the purple dumps and walked into the bush to pick the wildflowers – everlastings, yellow belly buttons and Sturt peas.

I preferred to talk to adults, and I was happy on my own, reading. I enjoyed some group activities. A young Dutchman who had been a scoutmaster in Holland arrived in town and set about establishing the 1st Gwalia Scout troupe. We were so keen we took to arriving at his house after he finished work at the mine, which didn't seem to bother him or his wife. With only one copy of the Scouting rule book, we sat patiently transcribing the Scout pledge until we knew it by heart: 'On my honour, I promise that I will do my best, to do my duty to God and Queen, to help other people at all times, and to obey the Scout Law.'

The Cobbers' Club met in the Workers' Union Hall. An English club, it was established to get boys off street corners and encourage them to become good citizens. It also set up a network of overseas pen pals. Mine was Ethne O'Hanlon from Sunniside, Carlow, County Carlow, Ireland. We wrote for several years and suddenly, for no reason, the letters stopped. The Cobbers' Club published its own monthly newspaper which arrived by post from Perth, addressed to Master Rocchiccioli. In the beginning the club was well attended, but most kids were bored by the educational aspect and the numbers dwindled.

Left alone, I sat in the dilapidated lounge chair in the washhouse for hours reading old copies of the *Daily Sketch*, a collated weekly version of the London tabloid filled with stories about Debbie Reynolds, Elizabeth Taylor, the glamorous Gabor sisters and London society. Poking around in a pile of rubbish to be burnt in the backyard, I found a discarded book of English poetry. 'The Inchcape Bell', with the sinking of the ship, was my favourite.

I enjoyed going shooting with Lewie, and became a crack shot with a .22 telescopic rifle. Beria was not surprised Lewie enjoyed shooting. 'He takes after his father. Sergio loved shooting as well. The two of us used to go out at dusk. I was six months pregnant with Lewie, and traipsing through the bush with his shotgun slung over my shoulder. Both barrels went off when I stumbled in a gully and went arse over head. One night we shot seventy little Jarvis sparrows. I plucked and I cleaned them, and I made spaghetti. God, it was beautiful.'

Once a year, Father Spain, Lewie and Stefano Fanetti went shooting for wild donkey to make twenty or thirty dozen Italian sausages. The Leonora butcher, Mr Newbon, donated the pork, and they mixed equal quantities of donkey with several pounds of crushed garlic as a preservative, and mixed herbs. Mr Newbon put the meat through his sausage machine, feeding the raw mixture into pigs' intestine, which they twisted and tied with string at sausage-length intervals. The sausages lasted for months and were especially popular with the Italians. They sold for ten shillings a pound and the proceeds helped finance the convent. We ate them raw, boiled, or pan-fried and wrapped in fresh bread. Men took them underground for their crib.

The freshly made sausages were festooned across the back of the verandah of the Dominican convent and left for several weeks to air-dry in the heat. After a couple of days they started to smell, and the sisters complained, insisting they be moved. In the heat, the dozens of garlic-laced sausages, all oozing and dripping fat onto the ground, were smelling out the convent.

When I was old enough I joined in with the gutting of the kangaroos, done where they fell in the bush. Lewie was an expert. With the carcass hanging from a tree, it took one quick slash to open the stomach from top to bottom. If the dead kangaroo was left for a time before being gutted, the stomach filled with air, and swelled. There was a loud *phoosh* as the point of the knife pierced the stomach and released a fetid rush. The air was thick with the choking bowel smell as the warm guts, blood and dark green entrails tumbled out and landed with a dull splat, spraying your feet. Lewie thought it a great joke to squirt the warm urine of the dead animal over those unlucky enough to be within range. Without water to wash it away, the stench lingered.

It took Lewie a couple of minutes to skin a kangaroo. With someone holding the hind legs, he made a couple of strategically placed slits to loosen the skin and then, using both hands, ripped the skin from the hindquarters to the head with one vicious yank. The bloodied pelts were thrown onto the back of the jalopy, taken home and rubbed down with salt. The flattened skins with paws in place and tails missing were nailed to the ground in the corner of the front yard. The stink of them made you feel sick. In a couple of weeks they dried and stiffened in the sun and were ready for sale. Beria salted and dried a joey pelt, which she used as a door mat.

One year, during an abnormally wet winter, the kangaroo population exploded to plague proportions, prompting the Leonora Municipal Council to offer a bounty. Lewie and his mate Ian Jones took me along when they went shooting. It took only a few hours to shoot 150 kangaroos. They collected one and sixpence a pair for the ears and left the carcasses to rot in the bush. Between them they earned £11 5s.

The goldfields were overrun with rabbits, providing a constant source of meat. Beria made rabbit stew with peas and potatoes in a thick white gravy. At around sunset we set the steel-jawed rabbit traps at the entrance to the burrows. The traps were placed in a shallow hole scraped into the hard ground, covered with newspaper and sprinkled with dirt. On return at first light most of the trapped rabbits were still alive. If there was a rifle we shot them; otherwise we gave them a sharp blow to the back of the neck – a rabbit-killer – or smashed their heads into the ground or against the quartz rock. Harry Gray, the butcher, kept a couple of ferrets which he released into the burrows, trapping the rabbits in sugarbags as they dashed to escape the razor-sharp teeth of the intruders.

I soon became a skilful gutter and skinner, gripping the hind legs in my left hand and yanking sharply with the other to remove the fur from the carcass. If the force of the wrench didn't rip off the rabbit's head, you dropped it onto the ground, held it with your foot, and yanked. Rabbiting was an easy way to earn money. We once made £5 by catching, dressing and selling forty carcasses for two and sixpence a piece.

The Irish Dominicans first appeared in Leonora and Gwalia in 1903, and operated a convent school in each town. At the end of January the five sisters arrived from Dongara for the school year and returned to the priory for their holidays. Waiting to learn which sisters had been sent to teach for the year and who was the Mother Superior was a matter of some interest to students, past and present.

In winter the sisters wore a full-length white serge overgarment and a calico petticoat, a black leather belt to which their rosary beads were attached, white stockings, black leather lace-up shoes, a black veil pinned to a starched wimple, a scapular, which reached to their feet at front and back, and a black cape. In summer they wore a white cotton version of the habit.

The St Catherine of Siena Dominican convent was a tin and brick building in Leonora. Their private chapel had six pews and an altar. Students were sometimes taken there to say the rosary. The convent was surrounded by a high tin fence and the simple wooden cross over the entrance was the only indication it was a religious establishment. Two sets of double wooden doors opened onto the back bullnose verandah where the sisters had a double-door kerosene refrigerator. There was a lawn in front of the chapel, and rose bushes. At the rear and the side of the convent were giant pepper trees and a vegetable garden. Directly opposite the entrance was the schoolroom. Sister Mary Clement was the domestic, taking care of the convent and the cooking for the other sisters. She was profoundly deaf and very kind. She always made sure the Italian kids' bottles of coffee were warmed at lunchtime.

Two of the Punch girls were born in Leonora and entered the Dominican convent. The two former students came back to teach as

Sister Mary Bernadette and Sister Mary Philomena. Directly opposite the front gate of the grounds was their family home. Sister Mary Bernadette stood and watched as the funeral procession of her father passed by. She was not able to attend because the sisters only went outside the convent grounds for hospital visits, to attend Mass, and to teach at school.

To supplement their income, the sisters taught piano. It was also customary for the parishioners to give them provisions. The Gwalia convent school didn't have a refrigerator and at lunchtime in summer they sent one of the students to my father's house to collect two blocks of ice, which were wrapped in sheets of newspaper to stop them melting during the short trip back.

As a consequence of the Cold War in Europe, the success of the Communists in South-East Asia, and the war in Korea, the Robert Menzies Liberal government resorted to the 'reds under the bed' scare campaign as a means of staying in power. In 1951 they introduced compulsory national service and Lewie was one of the first to be called up to do his 176 days of training. On his return, we went to the railway station to meet him. I was almost five, and bursting with excitement. He and Ian Jones looked so handsome in their uniforms when they returned to a heroes' welcome. As a present, Lewie brought me two packets of plasticine.

I was disturbed by the Hungarian uprising in October 1956. It was the weekend of the annual Leonora racing meet, and the revolution was the topic of conversation at the track. I listened to snippets and struggled to make sense of what I was hearing. Mrs Grudniski, the nursing sister who lived next door to Beria, was Hungarian. They were friends, and I wondered if she and her husband would have to leave and fight.

For thirteen days Hungary took on the might of the Soviet Goliath, and for a time seemed to be winning. Freedom fighters, most of them working-class youth and their parents, confronted Russian tanks with rifles and home-made weapons, wanting independence from the Soviet Union, and the reinstatement of basic human freedoms. On 4 November, Russia responded with a brutal invasion of Budapest, killing thousands of civilians. Every night, Steve listened for developments on the ABC radio news, ranting against the Communists and the German collaborators from the Second World War. The priest talked about the invasion at Mass, and read from the encyclical, *Datis Nuperrime*, issued by Pope Pius XII, lamenting the sorrowful events in Hungary and condemning the ruthless use of force.

Frightened there was going to be a war, I went to see Mrs Grudniski. She was married to a Pole, but her maiden name was Zsapo. She told me what was happening to her family in Hungary. Her crying did nothing to allay my fears.

A few months before the Hungarian revolt, an international crisis had developed over control of the Suez Canal, part of the major sea route from Europe to Australia, and the one my father had taken to Fremantle. He talked often about the ports of Said and Aden at either end of the canal, and how he had gone ashore at each of them.

My teacher, Mr Reilly, was a returned soldier, and at school assembly he explained how President Nasser of Egypt had taken possession of British property, and it should be returned. In late October, Britain started bombing Cairo. Mr Reilly told us there could be another world war and Australia would have to fight. I was worried Lewie might have to join the Army. Beria was impatient when I questioned her. 'How the bloody hell would I know if there's going to be a war? We'll just have to wait and see what happens.'

The good news of a dance pinned on the hotel notice board was always cause for great excitement, and everyone helped with the preparations. The decorating of the AWU hall, and the polishing of the timber floor to a dangerously high sheen was the responsibility of the young men, helped by lots of eager kids. It took most of the day. The floor was thoroughly swept and sprinkled liberally with kerosene-soaked sawdust. The sheen was achieved by sitting a partner on a chaff or sugarbag, and dragging them back and forth. It was not uncommon for some poor woman wearing high heels to have her feet slip away from underneath her in the middle of a Pride of Erin and end up flat on her back, legs in the air.

The hall, with a stage and screen at one end, was decked with streamers made from bolts of crepe paper, which the girls and the younger children cut to width and laboriously twisted and folded over and under. Festoons of balloons, inflated by mouth or using a car hand pump, were hung from the ceiling and released during the evening. The dance card included the Progressive Barn Dance, Pride of Erin, Maxina Waltz, Gay Gordon's, Boston Two-Step, the Valetta, the Modern Waltz and the Foxtrot.

This was one of the rare occasions when children were excluded. The green tin doors at the top of the short flight of wooden steps opened at seven-thirty. It was a grand, but not formal, occasion, and everyone dressed accordingly. Some of the older women wore ball gowns, although by the mid-'50s most men had done away with dinner jackets.

My father bought Nita her first ballerina-length evening dress. It cost £15 and was made from tartan taffeta patterned with bottle green, aqua, yellow and turquoise. It had a deep-cut square neckline with a ruche inset, short puffed sleeves and a three-quarter skirt. The next morning I noticed she'd lost the yellow velvet rose attached to the waist. When I asked, she told me churlishly to 'mind your own business'. Nita borrowed Beria's cherry red 'topper' – a three-quarter coat which featured a broad shawl collar, jetted slant pockets, deep cuffs, padded shoulders, full satin lining, and an inverted back pleat which fell from a curved yoke. Without a front fastening it was cut to swing as you walked. She pinned Beria's large blue and white paste spray brooch to the collar.

I waited each month for the Education Department's travelling library, which arrived by train in an orange tin trunk. While most kids weren't interested in reading, I changed my book every couple of days. Beria made me a blue sailcloth library bag with a drawstring. The list of travelling book titles was almost entirely English.

Beria bought me my first Enid Blyton *Secret Seven* book from the newsagent in Leonora. I read it sitting on top of a chaff bag in the galvanised-iron shed where she stored the pollard and bran for feeding the chooks. I wondered if the pigeons cooing in the adjoining loft sounded like Enid Blyton's first cuckoo heralding the arrival of spring. She wrote of rose gardens and playing fields, and of sweeps of swallows circling overhead. Outside, in the giant gums, the cawing crows with glass-like white eyes shattered my silence.

My imagination was awash with images of the English countryside as I sat in the above-century temperatures. I hankered for the life of Christopher Robin. I was mystified by the adventures of Badger and Mole from *The Wind in the Willows* and I dreamed of currant buns and home-made lemonade. I wondered how Nita's midnight dormitory feasts at school compared with those at Malory Towers.

While the Secret Seven bounded through rolling fields of bright yellow buttercups and blue forget-me-nots, in Gwalia I wandered across the gravel flat where the pig melons grew in profusion, the roosters crowed, contented chooks clucked as they wandered free and scratched around in their sand baths and, under the scattered rocks and rusting tin, centipedes, spiders and lizards sheltered from the blistering heat of the day. I loved the adventures of *Shadow the Sheep Dog* and the perils of *Digit Dick in Black Swan Land* but they didn't provide me with the same escape.

I never tired of sitting at the kitchen table, looking at the ornate Arcadian landscapes of bucolic England transferred onto the lids of Beria's button and sewing tins. Nita fancy-worked doilies and supper clothes of thatched cottages with pocket-handkerchief gardens bursting with hollyhock, sweet peas and foxgloves, all sustained by a foreign breeze. On Arbor Day we planted English and European trees. British was best, and England was home, even though we had never been there. The Country Women's Association and the Golden Wattle cookbooks contained recipes for the uniquely British Eccles cake, and bubble and squeak – a pan fry of meat and vegetable leftovers, served on toast, usually on Sunday night and sometimes for breakfast. Italian food was represented by Macaroni Cheese.

Guy Fawkes Day was a big celebration imported from the Mother Country. Parents and kids spent weeks building bonfires and kids pinched branches from each other's bonfires. On 5 November the town was set ablaze. The boxes of crackers were on display on the counter in Mazza's and we stood around talking about the ones we wanted. The money came from collecting and selling bottles, and every last penny was spent on Catherine wheels, Roman candles, mines, fountains, golden showers, sky rockets, penny bombs, tom-thumbs, sparklers and throw-downs – explosive packages sealed in a waxed paper that made a noisy bang when thrown onto a hard surface. Sky rockets were launched from beer bottles, and the next day we scoured surrounding bush looking for the fizzog rockets.

Lorraine Loftus, who had the polio, was sitting in her wheelchair when a live stray cracker landed in the paper bag of crackers at her feet. Fortunately, Beria and Steve were standing just feet away, and had it not been for Steve's quick thinking, lifting her out of the chair just seconds before the bag exploded and sent crackers and sky rockets flying in all directions, she would have been burnt, if not killed.

About a dozen of the men in Gwalia lived in primitive camps scattered throughout the town, and on the fringes of the mine site. For me they were a source of endless imagining. They came from nowhere and disappeared into the Australian bush. Some of them never made contact with their families again. When they found a place they liked, they shifted into an existing camp, or built a new one on a bit of vacant land, and stayed forever – sometimes until they died. Apart from scrapping with a cheeky kid, they were rarely in any trouble with the law, except for Steve Rakich. He was a Slav, small, and one of the more colourful of the town's characters. At all hours of the day and night he wandered around, hauling his noisy handcart packed full of wood, empty bottles, sheets of tin, lengths of timber and junk, most of which he pinched from other people's backyards, or the mine. He was aged somewhere between fifty and sixty and earned a few extra shillings doing odd jobs around the town. Beria sometimes paid him to chop the wood, most of which he came back and pinched in the night. Old Steve Rakich charged a shilling an hour to hand-turn the lamb on the spit and Beria reckoned, in the middle of summer, he was worth it.

I was a bit wary of Steve Rakich. Most of the time he was drunk and abusive but when he was sober he was quite nimble, and not backward in hitting if you came within range. Several kids tormented him, running around his cart and grabbing things. He went mad, trying to give chase, or throwing stones and cursing in his native tongue. Sometimes he was so drunk he fell down on the ground. The kids danced around, laughing and shouting. For fun at night they threw stones on his roof, or shook the tin on the back of his camp. Safe in the darkness, they called out to him as he staggered from his camp, peering and cursing. I was too scared to tease him because I knew if Beria caught me she would have given me a clout. Besides, he was not so silly that he failed to recognise me, or too drunk, and he knew that Beria was my mother and married to Steve. They used to talk to each other in Slav.

For a couple of years Steve Rakich lived about thirty yards away from Beria and Steve's front door. It was so close to their front gate you could see into his dirt-floor humpy, a rusting structure put together from sheets of tin. He had no facilities, not even a lavatory, and the place was furnished with wooden crates and boxes, chaff bags and discarded furniture he picked up around the town. I was a real little stickybeak and occasionally on a Sunday afternoon when he was sober I went to see him. He was an animated character, although I never understood a word of the political gibberish he talked about Yugoslavia and Australia.

When he was drunk and melancholy, he sang Slavic folk songs, and talked and argued with himself at the top of his voice. Beria and Steve would listen from their front verandah, out of sight, and laughing, especially when he complained about Steve.

There was a regular pattern to Steve Rakich's life. Every twelve months or so he would be charged with providing alcohol to the Aborigines, thrown into the gaol, hauled before the magistrate, and sentenced to three months. To his delight, he would be packed off to the Fremantle gaol for what he called his 'holiday'. He returned home dried-out, and looking clean and smart in a new safari suit. It took only a couple of weeks before he was back to normal, and already preparing for his next holiday.

Soon after old Milano was knocked off his bike and killed outside the Cuginis' house in Tower Street, Joe Puselli moved into his camp on the lower incline of Mount Leonora. It was a typical two-room, rusting tin and wire shelter which looked out across the town. The camp was surrounded by scrub, a few stunted trees and a bowerbird collection of junk. Puselli wasn't dirty; he showered and did his washing on the mine. Like old Milano before him, Puselli used to ride past our house on his bike, followed by his two kangaroo dogs.

Puselli didn't bother with other people but he was friendly with Eugene and Mary Passeri, who lived nearby with their sons Gino and Peter. Joe Puselli and young Peter Passeri often went riding into the bush on hunting trips. Peter was with him when a kangaroo attacked and almost ripped apart one of the dogs. Puselli was devastated. He put the injured animal around his shoulders and carried it back to his camp. For weeks he hardly left the dog's side, and tenderly nursed it back to health.

When we stopped seeing Puselli riding around town, the policeman Tom Clews went to check. It was more serious than he expected. In a drunken state Puselli had fallen into his open fire and was badly burnt. Mr Clews took him to hospital but he died a few days later.

I can't remember why I called him Billy Woof-Woof. However, since I didn't know his real name, and he didn't bother to tell me, the nickname stuck. No one seemed to know how he came to be in Gwalia or where he came from. I learned his real name – Richard John Butler – after he died. He was buried in a pauper's grave.

Billy Woof-Woof never washed and wore the same clothes, day and night. He stank to high heaven. His unsmiling face was covered in moles and warts, and his hands and nails were caked thick with black dirt and grease. There was not a visible speck of clean skin. Billy was a recluse who spoke only to say 'Ta', and if you overstayed your welcome, loitering a moment too long at the door, he would mumble, 'I am going to bed now' and close the door.

Billy's squalid one-room humpy, directly behind the butcher's shop, was Gwalia's crudest. It had no flooring and the ground was covered with bags and strips of linoleum. The four-post frame was covered with various-sized sheets of rusting and painted tin, and built around the chimney and open fireplace. The shelter was a little over head height, and tied together with long strands of wire. The roof was weighted down with rocks and the camp rattled in the wind. To keep out animals and people, the lower part of the open doorway was blocked by a sheet of tin. I never saw Billy venture out, or anyone enter. The camp measured about eight by nine feet and I was itching to have a look inside. From the front door you could smell the fetid air. There were no windows, and the only light sources were the front door and the standard-issue white candles which he lit at night. Peering into the gloom, I could see he had a small table, an old armchair, discarded fruit boxes and other junk he had accumulated. He cooked on the constantly burning open fire in the corner. Beside the fireplace was a makeshift bed piled with grey blankets. It was strangely mysterious.

Billy lived only a couple of hundred yards from our place, and every Sunday Beria dished him up a roast chicken midday dinner on a tin plate which I had to deliver. Curiously, in the twelve years Beria lived in Gwalia, she never once caught sight of him. Every week he bought a dozen eggs from her, for which she charged him two shillings and sixpence.

We sometimes played on the open flat area near his camp; it was also where we built our Guy Fawkes bonfire. Billy hated any noise and didn't like us being around. If we made too much noise he came to the door and glared, menacingly. I was not in the least bit scared, but it was enough to send some of the other kids scuttling away. Summer and winter, Billy Woof-Woof closed the door to his humpy at about half past four.

∞

The lease around the Sons of Gwalia mine was littered with rusting mining machinery, shallow contaminated running waterways, railway tracks, piles of fine black sand, and huge mounds of toxic tailings. There was a hand-operated kalamazoo. We climbed on, pumped like mad, and rode up and down the railway tracks. When it got too hard, we jumped off and walked home, leaving the kalamazoo for the men to find and collect.

The slimes, as they were known, were the residue of treated ore. The crushed dirt, still containing the gold, was treated in enormous stirring vats using a potent mix of water and chemicals. At the completion of the gold-extracting process, the residue was piped off and dumped. The slimes covered about a quarter of a square mile, stood about eight or ten feet high, and contained a high level of arsenic and cyanide. Once it had solidified, it remained moist and slippery, and we used it as a skating rink. Located on the edge of the town, it was not fenced off and was far enough away to be free from adults. It was a favoured meeting area. We removed our clothes, boys and girls, and skated naked on our bums and bellies up and down the mirror-smooth surface. Before getting dressed, we washed away the grey slime from our bodies in the contaminated water and chemical run-off.

Under sufferance, Nita and her girlfriend took me with them when they went to wander around the town. It was the last thing Beria said as we left: 'And you stay away from the slimes, you hear me?' Having promised, they ignored her instruction. When we got to the slimes, Nita said, 'Wait here, and don't follow us.' I was only four, and no sooner were they out of sight than I followed. I put one foot on the slimes, my legs slipped from under me and I landed on my back. When I managed to stand, I was covered from head to toe in the grey tailing. Nita was furious. In desperation she and her friend removed my clothes and tried to rinse them in the run-off water, which made them worse. There was no option. I had to run all the way home naked. Despite the seriousness of the situation, Nita and her friend couldn't stop laughing. When I ran into the house, Beria was furious at being disobeyed. Nita was grounded for a week and had to wash my clothes by hand.

∞

On the way down to the block there was a small bridge built from discarded railway sleepers which passed over trickling run-off from the mine. It smelt strongly of sulphur and chemicals. The stones over which the water flowed had turned bright yellow, and were coated with a treacherously slippery scum. We spent hours playing and splashing around in the water, and often swallowed mouthfuls which had an unmistakeably metallic taste. A few feet from the bridge was the narrow-gauge railway track, which ran for thirty miles into the bush. It was the wood line, and it supplied the Sons of Gwalia mine with the 30,000 tons of sandalwood and mulga it burnt each year to produce gas which generated electricity. The line's small steam engine, Ken, was built in 1934, in the railway yards of Midland Junction, Perth.

The area covered by the wood line was approximately 800 square miles, involving 4000 miles of twenty-inch track. It was said to be the largest such line in the world, although only sufficient track was maintained to operate a few spur lines at one time. As an area became exhausted, the track was lifted in sections (complete with mulga log sleepers), transported, and re-laid in another area. The spur lines were laid two miles apart so that woodcutters were always within a mile of the track.

My father worked for a couple of years on the wood line, hauling the carts loaded with mulga logs. Boozy Miller was the engine driver. On wood-line days he left home at half past four in the morning and returned late in the evening.

The cutters working on the wood line were mostly Italians and Slavs. A number of families, including children, lived in one- and two-roomed portable huts made from hessian and attached to a light frame so they could be lifted and transported by train to the next area. The cutters built bough sheds for additional room and established vegetable gardens. Water was a precious commodity, transported on the train, which also brought regular supplies of meat, fruit and vegetables and tins of canned food by the gross. The cutters bought their axes by the case and the remains of camp sites along the line were littered with Kelly axe-heads. When the men returned to Italy to marry, they brought their new brides back to Australia and took them to live on the wood line. It was a tough and lonely existence. Some lived out there for years, only occasionally coming into town, usually to see the doctor. There were so many children on the wood line the Education Department provided a teacher, who also moved with the camp.

At the end of a day's hauling and shunting, the engine dumped its hot coals at the side of the track. The ashes weren't fenced, and there were no warning signs. As the coals cooled down the powder-fine surface ash turned greyish white and it was impossible, without testing, to guess the temperature of the residue.

Kay Quarti burnt her feet, as did Diane Gray, who was four years old, suffering second and third degree burns. She was running at a pace and landed in the middle of the ashes before realising the coals beneath the surface were red hot. Part of the flesh on her feet was cooked, and the skin lifted. Her older brother, Dennis, ran home, screaming. Harry and Joan Gray were our nearest neighbours at the time and Beria went racing to assist Joan. Diane was taken to Kalgoorlie by the Royal Flying Doctor Service, and later transferred to the Princess Margaret Hospital for children in Perth for a series of skin graft operations.

Several years later, Diane was run over by her father as he backed the truck out of the yard. He felt a bump and, on checking, found Diane. She was taken to the hospital but seemed to be suffering no ill effects.

By the 1950s the Sons of Gwalia mine was in decline, and about a month prior to Christmas of 1955 a rumour swept the town that the mine was about to shut down. There were always rumours, but this time we took it more seriously. Everyone was anxious, the kids as well as the adults. Steve, concerned that in the mass exodus he might miss out on a job in one of the other goldmining towns, decided to move to Kalgoorlie. 'We'll be going straight after Christmas,' Beria told me. 'I haven't told your father yet, but I'm going to take you with me.'

It was the last thing I was expecting, and in the weeks leading up to Christmas I thought about nothing else. I'd been to Kalgoorlie twice, once with Beria and once with my father, and I was excited at the prospect of living in a big town but I was a bit nervous about the Olympic pool. It was a quiet Christmas, and I didn't think anything when Lewie, Jean and their one-year-old son, Trevor, came to visit on Boxing Day. Just as they were about to leave, without any warning, Beria turned to me: 'Lewie and Jean are going to take you to stay with them in Leonora for the time being. I'll send for you in a couple of weeks when we get settled in Kalgoorlie.'

My stomach dropped. I had no inkling I was being left behind, and tears welled up in my eyes and rolled down my cheeks at the thought of being separated from her. Lewie was fourteen years older, and while I loved him I didn't want to live with him and Jean. He teased me for fun, and called me a sissy when I didn't want to be part of what he reckoned was normal for boys, and he made fun of me when I cried.

I followed Beria to my bedroom and watched silently as she bundled my clothes into a suitcase. Then, without any fuss, she walked me to the front gate where Lewie's Bedford truck was parked. She kissed me goodbye and was back inside the house before we'd gone. I was in a daze and didn't speak on the two-mile journey to Leonora. My father lived with Lewie and Jean, and he was waiting when we arrived. He gave me a hug and a kiss and we walked down to the milk bar in the main street. He didn't mention my mother, or anything about me going to live in Kalgoorlie.

By the time I got up the following morning my father and Lewie had already gone to work. I was desperate to see Beria, and asked Jean if I could take the taxi bus, as I had done so many times, and go to Gwalia. She reckoned Beria would be too busy packing and getting the furniture to the station. I thought about Beria all day.

The Kalgoorlie train departed from Gwalia on Wednesday and Friday mornings at nine o'clock. I was awake early, and I pleaded with Jean to take me to the station to say goodbye. 'I can't,' she said. 'I don't have any clean clothes.' As time passed I became more frantic. In desperation, I suggested she wear her wedding dress and stay in the car. At nine o'clock I watched as the kitchen clock ticked over. I had been separated from Beria many times, but in the back of my mind I always knew she was still living at Grinning Joe's house, and sooner or later I would be going home again; however, this time it was more painful. Kalgoorlie was a long way away and I had no idea when I'd be seeing her again.

Beria promised to write, so every Wednesday and Friday morning I called at the post office. Sometimes I was there, waiting, before the doors opened. 'Anything in the name Rocchiccioli?' After a couple of weeks the postmaster, sensing my disappointment, told me not to worry and explained Beria's letter had probably been lost in the mail. I never stopped hoping and I went to the post office twice a week for months, but Beria's letter never arrived.

My father was hospitalised in the second half of the previous year when his big toe was crushed while he was working underground. Every second or third day Lewie collected me after work and took me to see him and a couple of times I went during the day with Beria. He had a metal cradle in the foot of the bed to keep the weight of the blankets away from the toe. Soon after this he caught a serious chest infection and was away from work for a week before Lewie heard he was sick. On his way home Lewie called in and was surprised to find he was so sick he couldn't look after himself. Lewie took him back to their place straight away and Jean nursed him back to health. He was on compo for a month or so. He accepted when Lewie suggested he become a permanent boarder, and Lewie went and packed up his house.

Now I was living with them as well. My father and Lewie were gone all day and I stayed with Jean and the baby. I liked Jean. She'd always been good to me. She helped me colour in a picture which I submitted to a school competition and won. But I wanted to be with my mother; nothing else mattered, and the longer the separation continued the more irrational I became. It was a mistake sending me to live with Lewie and Jean. She was twenty-two and taking care of a one-year-old baby, as well as Lewie, my father and me, whose behaviour deteriorated with each passing day. She was also recovering from a complicated first pregnancy. Jean was a petite woman and it was a miracle Trevor survived the difficult forceps birth. Beria was dismissive of her condition. 'The way Jean carries on about it, you'd think she was the first woman ever to have a baby.'

Trevor was at the mashed vegetable stage, and the daily preparation of his food was a protracted carry-on. On the stroke of midday he was strapped into his high chair and fed a bowl of pumpkin, carrot and potato, mashed with butter and powdered milk – a combination which had taken the best part of the morning to prepare. To encourage him to eat Jean played aeroplanes, whizzing the spoonful of food around his face to make him laugh and then popping it into his mouth. He spat as much as swallowed.

I was prone to a squeamish stomach and easily put off my food. When Beria cooked me an egg on toast she took a mouthful, always. The thought of eating off the same fork as her turned my stomach, but I wasn't game enough to ask for a clean one. I had an aversion to Beria's garlic breath and sometimes it made me heave when she kissed me. The sight on my plate of the slimy viscous blob attached to the yolk of the egg made me heave and push it away. If it accidentally ended up in my mouth, I spat the food back onto the plate. Several times I brought up what I had already eaten.

With Beria, I was accustomed to coming and going in the house as I pleased, but my behaviour was so bad Jean bolted the flywire kitchen door to keep me out. When she did allow me into the kitchen at feeding time I felt sick watching her scoop the mashed vegetables from the bowl with a teaspoon, then rounding it off in her mouth before feeding it to the baby. When Trevor wouldn't eat she was heard to say, 'If you don't eat your food, I'll cut your whistle off'. Lewie overheard, and after a terse spat between them the threat disappeared from feeding time.

I was fed my lunch after Trevor. Sometimes it was half past one, even two o'clock, before Jean finished clearing the kitchen, by which time I was ravenous and agitated. I grew more obstreperous by the minute and turned into a ranting monster, shouting and screaming, demanding to be fed. I became irrational. Jean shouted and abused me, threatening to tell Lewie. She never hit me; however, once she grabbed me by the shoulders and shook me, forcefully. She had a habit of putting her tongue between her teeth when doing anything which involved physical exertion. I retaliated. 'Mum said before you got married you drank gin and went with all the blokes.' Jean was deeply offended, not realising I had invented the story.

What little remained of Jean's day after the washing, ironing, cooking and cleaning was devoted to bathing, powdering and mollycoddling the baby, and checking to see whether he was awake or asleep, in need of a feed or a nappy change, or a bottle of freshly squeezed orange juice. Jean was obsessed with germs and cleanliness, and the sterilising of Trevor's feeding bottles was meticulous. She washed everything twice and slung off about Beria's housework, and her carelessness with food storage. Beria thought nothing of leaving stew overnight in an aluminium saucepan and reheating it the following day, serving it on toast for midday dinner. When Beria's grand-daughter Karen asked her if she was 'keeping her house clean these days', Beria was ropeable. Not surprisingly, she blamed Jean. 'Where else would she have heard that? It could only have come from Jean. The bloody cheek of it. And anyway, if she doesn't think my house is clean enough, she doesn't have to come here.'

The series of floor-to-ceiling flywire doors and windows on the enclosed side verandah were sheltered from the sun by a dense copse of oleander trees. After lunch Trevor was put to sleep there, and no matter how quiet I was, Jean blamed me if he woke up. He became the bane of my life. With his blond hair flicked back in an exaggerated wave at the front, he was propped up in his pram like a prize piglet. To keep him amused I had to take him for a walk, wheeling him back and forth along the dirt footpath beside the side fence. I clenched my teeth and squeezed the handle of the pram so tightly my knuckles turned white. When I purposely jolted the pram, throwing him backwards, he screamed, which brought Jean running to check. At other times I had to sit with him on a rug in the shade of the huge pepper tree which grew beside the gate. Lewie had cemented the small sheltered area at the front of the house and on the hottest days Jean wet the cement, left the hose trickling nearby, and sat Trevor in the running water.

On the day I turned nine in February 1956 I started school in Leonora. My father stayed home from work and took me to enrol. It was a two-minute walk to the school and I was so unhappy I cried when he left me. It was a hot summer and I suffered constant nose bleeds. Without warning, blood would drip from the end of my nose and splatter on the white page of my exercise book. I spent the best part of some days lying on the wooden bench outside the classroom, with an ice-pack on my nose, and spitting blood as it ran down the back of my throat.

When I sat on the oiled timber floor in the third classroom used for folk dancing, it stained the seat of my shorts. 'You tell the teacher I said you're not allowed to sit on the floor,' an infuriated Jean used to tell me. 'She doesn't have to do your washing. I do.' Each week I faced the same dilemma, knowing Jean would rouse on me when I arrived home. Finally, I stood rooted to the spot, dropped my head and refused to sit down. When I burst into tears the teacher took me outside and I told her what Jean said. From that day I was seated on a chair at the back of the class while the other kids sat on the floor.

The woodheap was around the side of the house adjacent to my father's bedroom. A nearby patch of twenty giant sunflowers gave a dazzling splash of colour as they turned their yellow heads, the size of dinner plates, to follow the sun. After tea my father and I would sit in the dark on a couple of planks and talk. He listened silently to my never-ending litany of grumbles about maltreatment; of being made to polish the front verandah as a punishment; of being forced to wait for my food; and of being locked out of the house. During the day Jean bullied me into repeating our conversations, pretending she already knew: 'We came and listened at the window, and Lewie knows what you said.' Every night, before Jean let me get into bed, she made a song and dance out of pulling back and shaking the top sheet and blankets, checking for centipedes and scorpions. I watched, terrified. I was nervous of being on my own in the house. Jean was sometimes away for two or three hours at a time, going to see the doctor or calling in to see her mother.

When Jean left me one day I became so agitated I repeatedly slammed the door between the kitchen and the lounge room. The reverberation caused one of the china bookends on the mantelpiece in the lounge room to fall and smash. The ornament, a dog sitting on a book, was a present from Beria. When Jean returned I told her what I'd done. She didn't believe me, and accused me of 'fishing around' on the mantelpiece.

In a fit of pique, Jean called Beria a thief. She reckoned Beria had come into the house when they weren't there and pinched a bundle of Lewie's furniture receipts, which were kept on top of the kitchenette in a small Mills and Ware's cardboard school case. Beria scoffed in disbelief when I told her. 'What a lot of bunkum. How the bloody hell would I know where she keeps her receipts? And anyway, when would I have been there on my own? You can tell her from me she's romancing.'

My collection of books, toys, cards and games vanished when Beria moved to Kalgoorlie. Even the Swansea bicycle my father had given me the previous Christmas disappeared. I was now riding a battered, unpainted frame with no mudguards, a hard leather seat and a slipping chain.

While Beria shopped every day and rarely sent me to the shops, it was the opposite with Jean. Most days I was sent to collect the greengroceries from her mother's shop. The house was on the edge of the town, close to Tank Hill, and it was a hot trip in the middle of the day. I fell one day when the chain on my bicycle slipped. Unable to control my rage I lay on the ground, crying and shouting abuse, kicking at the bicycle until the mother of a friend came to my aid, gathering me up and taking me inside her house, the living room of which was cooled by a large water fan. It was the only one in the town. She sat me down with a cold drink, stopped my crying, and listened to my tale of torment. She sent me on my way after I made a promise to never again use such 'unpleasant language'.

Sometimes Lewie came home at midday. One day, just after he'd gone, Jean and I became embroiled in a screaming match which continued until Lewie reappeared. Jean gloated. 'See? You didn't believe me. I told you what he was like.' Lewie grabbed me firmly by the ear, almost lifting me off the ground, and gave me a couple of firm clips under the ear and a proper telling-off. I wasn't scared of him but I was cautious, which was made worse by Jean saying I'd be better off if Beria gave me to Lewie for good. When I told Beria, she was wild. 'What's she talking about? Tell her not to be so bloody ridiculous. I've never heard anything like it. I wouldn't dream of giving you away to Lewie.'

One afternoon I attempted to mend a puncture in my bicycle tyre, something which I had done often. When it failed several times I started swearing and crying and threw the puncture kit. It was Saturday afternoon and my father was nearby, watching. He came to my assistance and settled me down. For the rest of the school holidays my father took me to work with him on the mine, leaving a little before seven in the morning and returning at half past four. We rode our bicycles to a nearby house and joined a group of men who travelled to the mine on the back of an old utility. Huddled in the corner, I sat next to my father, watching the men and not saying a word.

I spent the first part of the morning watching him work, and at ten o'clock I went to the pool. At midday we sat together and ate our cheese sandwiches. For the couple of hours until the pool opened again I walked the short distance down the hill to Grinning Joe's house. It was still unoccupied. I stood outside the front gate and stared, hoping Beria might have come back and forgotten to send for me. I wanted to be with my mother and for the time being the empty house was as close as I could get to her. A couple of times I knocked on Joan Gray's door to see if she had heard from Beria.

One day when Jean came back from a visit to the doctor she announced he'd ordered a holiday for her and the baby. 'Doctor's orders,' she told anyone who would listen. 'It's my nerves, you know. They can't stand it.' Jean talked about her nerves all the time and made no secret of the fact she thought I was partly responsible for her condition. While they were on a two-week holiday I went to stay with Lewie's mother-in-law, whom I called Auntie Mary, and her equally agreeable husband, Uncle George. I adored her, and I think she liked me.

Auntie Mary provided me with a balance of love and discipline. From the moment she took control, all my problems disappeared. The transformation was instantaneous. On Saturday morning she took me to the shop and kept me occupied with chores. She baked the most delicious pumpkin cake and scones. When Nita was away at boarding school my father sent her food parcels, which always included one of Auntie Mary's famous pumpkin cakes. Her teenage daughter, Pam, was friendly and vivacious and took me along with her school friends wherever they went. Auntie Mary was a straight shooter, always saying what she meant and it didn't matter who was there. She would shout from the kitchen to Pam in the bathroom: 'And don't forget to wash your fanny!'

The piano was the real joy of staying with Auntie Mary and I tinkled for hours. She taught me the opening bars of the march tune, 'Napoleon's Last Charge', which I played over and again. It was all short-lived. When Lewie and Jean returned from their holiday I went back to live with them.

Jean was an excellent cook and prepared a hot tea every night with lots of vegetables. She baked Swiss rolls, sponge cakes, and Anzac biscuits, which were stored in a pantry on the front verandah. The green-trimmed cream enamel container was a wedding present. It had 'biscuits' painted on the front. I was allowed two biscuits for school playlunch, which I collected as I left. They were my favourite, and I always took one extra.

Lewie and Jean kept the phone on when they moved into their rented house. Their number was Leonora 73, and one night, without warning, Beria phoned Lewie to say they were on their way back to Gwalia. When he heard, my father didn't make any comment. Beria and Steve arrived on the Tuesday night train, and Lewie took me to meet her. She'd been gone four months. I held her hand from the moment she stepped onto the platform. Without telling my father, Beria decided I was going back to Gwalia to live with her. On the Saturday morning Nita, who was in town from the sheep station where she worked, telephoned to say she was coming to collect me that afternoon. She arrived at about one o'clock, by which time Jean had packed my case.

Lewie drove us back to Gwalia and I couldn't contain my excitement at the thought of once again living with Beria. While they were away on holiday, Lewie and Jean bought me a couple of shirts and several pairs of shorts. When Beria unpacked my case the new clothing was missing. I didn't care. I was happy to be home again.

Steve's days of earning big money on the mine were past, and although there were still difficult times he didn't seem to hit Beria so often. His focus of attention was his daughter, Joan. Beria called her the apple of his eye.

In about the middle of 1956 we moved from the post office street to a house at the bottom end of Tower Street. It was the last in the main block on the way to Leonora, and was owned by old Mrs Stewart, one of the town's eccentrics. It was identical to most other houses in the town – a kitchen, two bedrooms, a lounge room with an open tin fireplace, and a bathroom located on the end of the back verandah. I had the smaller bedroom opening off the kitchen. The front verandah was closed in with chocolate brown wooden slat blinds. The exterior, the shed and the pigeon loft were all painted with flat burgundy.

The front was hidden behind thick jade, a sturdy succulent which required little water. Beria planted a small patch of buffalo grass at the base of the huge gum tree in the corner, which soon became a nesting ground for hundreds of vicious purple bull ants. Armed with a can of deadly Dieldrin dust, Beria went into battle. Even on the windiest of days, she wandered around the yard looking for ants, disappearing in a cloud of the Dieldrin dust. Jean was convinced it was dangerous. Beria didn't take any notice: 'What are you talking about? Mazza wouldn't be allowed to sell it if it was dangerous.'

Despite Steve's lack of interest, Beria planted herself a small flower garden at the back of the house next to the rain tank. She even made him dig the ground for her. She grew large bushes of her favourite egg and bacon – a miniature snapdragon – and statice – a small purple and white flower which grows on an angular stalk. At the side of the house, directly underneath my bedroom window, was Steve's vegetable garden. He did the watering, pulled out the weeds and threw them on the ground for Beria to cart away.

The huge pepper tree in the corner of the chookhouse shaded a large area. On the hottest of days Beria would hose down under the tree, then leave Joan in her pram to enjoy the cool while she went to the shop. People were astonished when they asked, and she told them: 'I've left her locked in the chookhouse under the pepper tree. It's the coolest place in the house.' I took care of the thirty or so pigeons which were housed in a loft built from disused rainwater tanks. Every morning they were set free to fly around the town, and at sunset they returned. When the need arose it was my job to catch them, wring their necks, and pluck and clean them. Beria made a delicious stew which we ate with polenta. My father taught her and she had his magic touch.

When Lewie and Jean shifted to a house down near the Leonora oval my father went with them; however, my weekend visits became less frequent and more difficult. Lewie and Jean had a bitter falling-out with Beria which went on for some months. As usual, it was Lewie who made the peace. He and Jean drove me home from Leonora and following some discussion outside the house he convinced Jean, for the sake of peace, to bury the hatchet. As far as I could make out, Beria and Jean were as bad as each other. They asked me constantly: 'What did she say about me?' I hated them being bad friends, and found their relentless interrogating for incriminating particulars from imagined conversations unbearable. It was a great relief when they started talking again. To break the ice Lewie said when he saw Beria: 'How are you, you bad-tempered old bitch?' Beria didn't even smile at him.

It was summer school holidays of 1956 and an especially hot day. I had gone to visit a friend who lived nearby. She was about fourteen, but looked much older, and was physically well-endowed. The girl's mother had been taken ill and sent away for several months, leaving behind my friend, her father and a younger sister. I never met the mother and her condition was never discussed. The father was an agreeable man who worked on the mine while my friend attended to all the domestic duties and helped look after her younger sister.

My friend was having a flirtation with Tony, one of three young Italians living next door. She often slipped behind their washhouse to meet him and, hidden from sight, engaged in some serious kissing and fondling. I was with her when her father called her away in the middle of a passionate session. He was inside the house, unaware of his daughter's sexual tomfoolery.

Eventually the activity moved from behind the washhouse to inside the house. My friend's father worked mostly afternoon shifts, which provided Tony with the perfect opportunity.

It was early evening and we were sitting and chatting under the grapevine-covered shelter, which protected the rear of the house, when Tony appeared. He was in his late teens, possibly twenty, and the only body-builder in the town. He used a bullworker which he purchased by mail order from *Man* magazine. Tony wore jeans and tight black T-shirts, through which you could see his muscular chest. He and my friend were sitting on the bench under the vines and I was on the lawn a few feet away. They soon started kissing and cuddling and the next thing Tony suggested they go inside. She agreed, and I followed. They went through to the bed on the front verandah and he didn't waste any time getting down to business. I was standing at the door watching. She was on her back and he was lying on top, kissing her. Tony helped her remove her shorts then stood up, undid his fly, pulled down his jeans and got back on top. He seemed in no hurry and took a little while to complete the task. When it was all over they chatted and joked for a bit, and he left. Tony visited repeatedly, coercing my friend into sex. She claimed to not enjoy his visits, but didn't know how to stop him. My friend didn't realise the fourteen-year-old girl who lived across the road was visiting Tony next door, and doing the same thing.

In January 1957 Beria and Steve went to Perth for a fortnight on his annual holiday. Taking me wasn't even a consideration. Naturally, they took Joan. I was sent to stay with the butcher, Harry Gray, and his wife Joan, which I didn't enjoy very much. There were four kids who tended to run riot in the house. One of the boys, nicknamed Bully, was the worst. He had a glass eye which he popped out at every given chance. 'Do you want to see my eye?' he would ask, and have it in his hand before you could reply.

With an eight-year age difference between me and both of my sisters, I had lived for the most part as an only child. I found staying with the Grays an unsettling experience, especially since they were so boisterous. I was amazed when Beria and Steve returned home from their holiday with a gleaming black Holden Special car; more importantly, my present from Beria was a pair of brown scuffs. They were stylish – a leather sole and two wide brown straps across the front. I wore them constantly, sometimes with shorts and iridescent green or day-glo pink socks.

The Holden Special was Steve's second car. The first was an Oldsmobile, with a tartan interior and a back seat the size of a double bed, and was so deep I couldn't see out of the rear passenger window. For no apparent reason, Steve announced to Beria he was going to paint the Oldsmobile and bought two large tins of Dulux apple green high gloss paint from the Co-Op store. The car was parked on the gravel road at the front of the house. With no preparation, he proceeded to apply a single coat of paint using a two-inch brush. He was unperturbed when several strong gusts of the hot north wind deposited a fine layer of gravel on the wet paint, reducing the sheen and leaving the surface as rough as coarse sandpaper. He sold the Oldsmobile when he needed some cash.

According to Beria, Steve was the worst driver in Gwalia, if not Australia. He was legally blind, could barely see two inches in front of his nose, and wore thick glasses which were always dirty. A car ride with him was a nightmare. He drove on the wrong side of the road, causing oncoming cars to swerve and pass on the inside. According to him, they were in the wrong. Fortunately, he lost too much money on the horses and sold the Holden. Beria was delighted: 'I don't care if he kills himself, but not somebody else.'

Bluey and Dot Mathews were the parents of my friend Brian – or Pinky as he was known. They managed the State Hotel and Pinky was allowed to invite me to stay. We slept upstairs on the side verandah behind a partition. Mrs Mathews let me stay for three or four days at a time, during which I hardly went home. It was a novelty to have running hot water in the bathroom and a pull-the-chain lavatory.

I had my meals with the family in the hotel dining room, with its pressed tin ceiling, large overhead fans and tables set with starched white damask tablecloths and napkins. It was my first experience of a three-course meal ordered from a menu. I was ten years old and somewhat overwhelmed by the procedure on such a grand scale. Nita, who had recently returned to Gwalia, was employed as housemaid and waitress. I didn't know what she meant when she asked if I wanted an entrée. To avoid embarrassment I said, 'Yes, please.' But I wasn't a big eater, and after entrée, main meal, and pudding – tinned apricots with a huge dollop of tinned cream – I was full to bursting.

The cook, Josie Breda, had five children by four men. She was an unusually short, solidly built, unprepossessing woman. Her dark hair was cropped, pulled back off her face and sat flat to her head. Josie lived in Tower Street with her mother, Norna Franchina, and her daughters Joyce and Dorothy, who were my friends. She kept to herself, and her reticence bordered on the anti-social. I saw Josie at the State Hotel and passed her numerous times in the street, but we never exchanged a word. At the end of her shift in the kitchen Josie trudged her way home carrying a couple of bottles of beer. Norna and Josie enjoyed a drink, and after dinner in the summer they sat outside the front of their house, drinking. Norna was tough and vicious, and free with her language. She didn't put up with anyone's nonsense and most kids were scared of her.

A lot of men were drinkers, but at the turn of the twentieth century it was illegal for anyone to construct a licensed premises on a mine site. Consequently, the sly grog trade was rife in Gwalia. The first Labor government in Western Australia tackled the problem, and in 1902 allocated £6000 for 'the building and furnishings of a state owned hotel'. It proved so popular, and took so much money, that within two years they added another main bar. For those men living in the boarding houses, the State Hotel was their only meeting place for a game of darts or snooker, which they played for money, always. The billiard table was a gift from the inland explorer, Sir John Forrest.

The barmen worked hard. The men were paid fortnightly, and on a pay day an eighteen-gallon keg lasted twenty minutes. The hotelier claimed the tap was never turned off. Using sheer brute force, the barmen hoisted full steel kegs of beer into the main bar using a 'handy billy' – a simple pulley and tackle. A beer tap, attached to a steel rod, was inserted into the keg and tapped into place using a wooden hammer. The keg sat on the counter, and to keep it cold it was covered with a heavy purpose-made quilted blanket.

The state-owned hotels in remote country areas were authorised to operate six days a week from 9 am until 11 pm and on Sunday for two frantic sessions: ten to noon, and three to five. It was illegal for ladies to drink in the public bar; instead, they were accommodated in the front parlour with padded leather chairs, tables and a piano, or outside in the beer garden, which was shaded by an enormous verandah and a copse of giant gums, and was cooled by the yardman constantly hosing down the cement paving and the nearby buffalo grass. Beria worked in the laundry and it was stifling. While she was washing and ironing, I'd go and sit on one of the wooden benches in the cool, or walk barefoot on the wet cement, splashing in the puddles which pooled in the uneven cement. When the barman spotted me he gave me a glass of icy cold raspberry lemonade. The lawn area looked onto three red clay tennis courts, hand-built by the locals, who carted and crushed dozens of giant red ochre white-ant nests. The far court shared a fence with the hotel's turkey pen. The birds were wild, caught in the bush where they lived in large flocks. One magnificent-looking male who wandered around the beer garden had taken an aggressive dislike to kids and flew at us – feathers ruffled and gobbling ferociously – if we ventured too close. The turkeys, like the ducks in the yard, were destined for the hotel dining room. Beria was partial to a feed of wild turkey. 'When I was living with Sergio, we went to stay for a couple of nights in Kathleen Valley, just outside of Agnew. The next morning, when I looked out onto the flat, there were hundreds of wild turkeys warming themselves in the sun. Sergio shot one and cooked it the same way they did back in the old country. It melted in your mouth.'

Josie Breda had Sunday evening off from the hotel, and the menu in the dining room was soup, cold meat and salad, and tinned fruit and cream. Everything was left in readiness and Nita had only to serve and clean up. When she arrived at five o'clock one Sunday, Mrs Mathews was drinking with friends in the beer garden and had forgotten to light the kitchen stove. Nita muddled through in an agitated state, and when she got home and complained, Beria hit the roof. The next morning she went to the hotel and confronted Mrs Mathews. The pair exchanged harsh words, and in typical Beria fashion, she told Mrs Mathews to make up Nita's pay. On the spot.

※

Being old enough to take a nightly shower in the underground change rooms on the Sons of Gwalia mine was as meaningful as your first holy communion, and marked a significant turning point in your life. It was the day on which you became a link in a chain of local tradition – the transition from a bath at home supervised by mum to being part of a man's world. It also had a practical application. It rid the house of the boys and freed the basic bathroom for the girls. I waited several years to join in and felt so grown-up to be part of the group who made their way up the hill between half past five and six o'clock every afternoon in the winter months. In the summer you didn't need a shower – you went to the pool every day.

Often, I had stood outside the change room waiting for my father, but today Billy Garbellini was taking me and his younger brother, Nat, for the first time. Mimicking the men, and the older initiated boys whom we had watched with such envy, we set off with our towels wrapped round our necks, carrying our cake of

Palmolive soap in a plastic container. The expectation as we entered through the green door of the underground workers' change room was palpable. We followed Billy into the cavernous gloom and took our first tentative steps into a man's world. It was nothing like I imagined. The combined pong of the acrid carbide from the miners' lamps and the damp ore-coated working clothes, suspended fifteen feet in the air on the rope-and-pulley hangers, assaulted my senses. There was something threatening about the sight of dozens of men's trouser legs dangling lifeless in mid-air – cavorting like demented ghosts on the ceiling. The cement floor was damp and the room stifling from the large steam pipes which dried out the men's working clothes for the following shift. The hot air was difficult to breathe and burnt my lungs. There were rows of slat benches where each man had his own spot. The open showers were against the wall.

Following Billy's lead I placed my towel on the bench, shyly removed my clothes and walked naked to the showers, my hands covering my modesty. I was uncertain; this was the first time I had taken a shower, except under the garden hose. Three young miners were already under the shower, talking and laughing over the sound of the water splashing onto the cement floor. They were facing the wall. It was the first time I saw a naked adult man. When they turned to get out I was taken aback by the size of their cocks and the mat of surrounding hair.

In the early part of 1958 my father moved from Leonora to live in Gwalia. For a couple of weeks before he moved into the mine mess, he shared with his longstanding friend, Macka Mackay, living in a small, pink three-roomed camp on the edge of the mine, near Grinning Joe's house. The mine mess was a modern, well-maintained boarding house which provided meals and accommodation for single men. He furnished the single room with his own furniture. I enjoyed having him live nearby and visited regularly. He kept a supply of his favourite Mills and Ware's coconut macaroons and Ritz light fruitcake, a couple of slices of which made a visit even more pleasurable. He threw all his coins into a large Sunshine milk tin and always let me dive in for a handful as I was leaving.

It was around the same time Nita and her boyfriend, Italo, unexpectedly returned from working on a sheep station outside of Leonora. Nita was employed as a live-in housemaid and nanny, and Italo worked as a station hand. Their return was surrounded by some mystery and, from what I overheard, a note of controversy. I half heard a conversation and was told to mind my own business when I tried to butt in. They moved into Beria and Steve's house. With four adults and two children in a four-room house, it was a bit crowded. Italo took over my bedroom while Nita and I were relegated to sharing the closed-in front verandah, which was bitterly cold on the frosty winter nights. Beria made me a horse blanket using a single thickness of washed sugarbags which she covered on one side with blue tartan and on the other with a brushed cotton winceyette. It was so heavy I hardly stirred in the night.

Most of the tension in the house could be traced back to the constant squabbling between Nita and me, and the standard of the meals Beria was providing. Beria had no interest in cooking and the menu was uninspired. Steve was a fussy eater, living on a diet of rump steak or lamp chops with potatoes and cabbage or silver beet. Beria always bought him the best cuts of meat and complained to the butcher if the quality wasn't to her satisfaction. The menu for the rest of us wasn't deemed a priority, even though Beria was collecting £6 a week in board – more than enough to feed everyone. Nita and Italo resented being served sausages and stews night after night while Steve sat eating rump steak. It got to the stage where they weren't bothering with the evening meal, living instead on bags of mixed picnic biscuits from Mazza's shop, which they bought and consumed on the short walk home. Beria was totally unaware of their festering grievance. Nita discussed it with my father and between the pair of them decided he would rent a house and have Nita, me and Italo live with him. He made the decision without talking with my mother, something he never usually did and which was out of character for him.

As it happened, I was happy living with Beria. I kept out of Steve's way and he seemed more resigned to my presence, so there was no reason for me to move. While I would have preferred to stay with Beria, there was nothing to suggest living with my father and Nita would be anything other than harmonious. However, I soon discovered it was a quantum leap out of the frying pan into Dante's roaring inferno. For Beria, our departure marked a return to the bad times. Without the additional board money coming in each week, Steve had less money to drink and gamble, and became more aggressive. It was a dark period.

The three of us, and Italo, moved into a small two-roomed house – a kitchen and a bedroom – in one of the back streets. Nita had the bedroom, Italo slept in a partitioned area on the back verandah, and my father and I shared a double bed on the front verandah.

Our next-door neighbour, Dimitri Christoff, was a short, middle-aged belligerent Pole, who hated animals. He owned a .22 rifle and shot other people's dogs if he thought they came too close to his chooks. He wandered alone around the vast flat behind his house, with the loaded gun slung over his shoulder, guarding his free-ranging chooks and searching for a potential target. When he fired in the general direction of our dogs we remonstrated with him, and he threatened to shoot us too. The policeman arrived regularly to deal with Christoff's intransigence. It made no difference. He had no regard for the law or other people, and responded with a load of gibberish, arguing it was all a Communist plot. Christoff was obsessed with his chookhouse. The substantial wire and iron pipe structure was covered in lush morning glory and was the coolest and the cleanest in the town. His de facto, Margarethe Kromek, was a gentle smiling woman who tried to teach me to speak Polish and sang to me in German. Her favourite song was 'South of the Border'.

Neta Togni lived directly opposite in a dilapidated house which seemed to be sinking into the ground. Neta walked with a pronounced limp, the result of being kicked by a horse. There were whispers of scandal and it seemed she was unmarried, but I never asked and it was never mentioned. She was a kind woman who didn't have a mean bone in her body, but there was an air of sadness to her. Many days during the school holidays I had either dinner or tea with Neta and her daughter Ann, who was about my age. Ann and I soon became friends, and when Neta was out of sight Ann and I would lie on the bed on the front verandah practising kissing endlessly.

∞

The one-bedroom house proved too small for three adults and a growing child, and I was delighted when my father announced he had bought a four-roomed house in Tower Street, one door away from Beria. Now I had immediate access to both parents.

The previous owner had been something of a handyman and fitted out the interior using recycled pine gelignite boxes to build cupboards and benches. Unfortunately, the pine swelled and buckled and most of the surfaces were uneven. On the back verandah he had cut a circular hole into the top of the bench to accommodate a standard tin washing-up dish. The kitchen floor was polished cement, and the flywired verandah windows were fitted with home-made blinds, cut and shaped from sheets of raw galvanised iron. They were fitted with ropes and pulleys, and effectively blocked out both the summer heat and the winter cold.

Although my father and I had seen a great deal each over the years, we had never lived together and this was, for both of us, a period of discovery which was sometimes contaminated by the feisty relationship between Nita and me. I discovered my father was taciturn and humourless. I can't remember the two of us having a conversation or sharing a joke. He rarely smiled and he never laughed. He watered the grapevines, grew watermelons and rockmelons in the disused chookhouse, and used rainwater for his magnificent clump of Sturt peas, which grew wild in the frontyard. When the Governor of Western Australia, Sir Charles Gairdner, and Lady Gairdner, paid an official visit to the school, I presented him with a sizeable bunch of Dad's Sturt's peas carefully wrapped in greaseproof paper.

My father was a keen gardener, and as the grapes began to ripen on the vine at the back door he wrapped each bunch in a brown paper bag to protect it from the birds. He went berserk if you picked and ate the grapes from the still-ripening bunches. He also planted a flowerbed for Nita, and it was made clear to me I wasn't allowed to have any part of it. One day, fed up with her churlishness and my father's support of her troublemaking, I pulled out a number of plants and then lied. They suspected my involvement but couldn't prove it.

I made my own bed, kept my room spotless, helped polish the linoleum floors, set the table, and wiped the dishes every night – in silence. Nita and I never had a conversation. However, she decided I wasn't doing enough and I now had to get up early each morning and do the watering. Before he went to bed that night I asked my father to wake me at five-thirty. He was puzzled when I went outside and started watering the black muscatels because it was something he did every morning. 'Why are you doing the watering?' he asked. When I told him what Nita had said, he sighed audibly, as he often did, and sent me back to bed, telling me not take any notice. 'She's not your mother, and she is not to tell you what to do. That's my job.' Nita was livid when I gleefully repeated Dad's words. She barely spoke to me for weeks.

Nita and Italo went to the pictures on both Wednesday and Saturday nights, mostly in Gwalia, but sometimes they took the taxi bus into Leonora. From time to time on Saturday night they took me along with them, although I was happy at home with my father. I also walked a few paces behind them, and one particular night it was obvious they were arguing, quietly but angrily.

Over the months Italo had paid for my ticket on a number of occasions, but this time when we arrived at the ticket box he said, loud enough for me to hear, 'He's not my kid. Why do I always have to pay for him?' I was shocked. I looked first at Nita and then at Italo, who had always been pleasant – except when he took Nita's side in an argument. Although we lived under the same roof for about a year, we never had a conversation about anything, and I had never been cheeky to him. I didn't know what to make of it. My eyes filled with tears, and for the first time in my life I think Nita felt sorry for me. She spoke quietly, explaining she had no money, and sent me to ask Beria for two shillings. Beria was upset by what Italo had said but didn't have the money so she went to her next-door neighbour and borrowed it. By the time she returned I had lost interest and Beria told me to stay the night. From then on, I only went to the pictures if I had the money for my ticket.

Nita's job was to stay at home and keep house for my father and me. It was an arrangement recognised by the Australian government and which provided a tax deduction for my father.

My sister and I formed what was, at best, an uneasy alliance and managed to survive – more or less. Inevitably there were fracas, some of which were more serious than others. Regardless of fairness, my father was given to taking Nita's side and rarely listened to me. Beria told me to ignore it all. Besides, Nita was totally involved with Italo and we all assumed she would marry him, and soon. Italo Cher was a good-looking, stylish northern Italian with light brown wavy hair. He was devoted to Nita and my father thought it a good match; and so did Beria.

In the winter of 1958, Italo went to visit his family in Italy. There was some suggestion Nita would go with him, and even talk of a proxy marriage while he was in Italy to prevent him from being called up for national service. Several months before his departure they sent me to Beria on a debt-collecting mission. Steve had borrowed £100 from Italo, who wanted it repaid before he left for Italy. It was a hot day and Beria was on her hands and knees polishing the floor. The perspiration was streaming down her face. When I delivered the message she reacted defensively, then began to cry. 'If they want their money, tell them to bloody well come and ask themselves. And tell them I said they're not to send you to do their dirty work.'

The sight of Beria crying always upset me. I ached to the pit of my stomach and wanted to comfort her. I raced back to the house, delivered the message, then took one shilling out of my moneybox, jumped onto my bike and rode to Mazza's to buy Beria an icy pole. It was so hot it was the only thing I could think would make her happy.

Only a matter of months after Italo left for Italy, Nita met Frank Mafrici. Things developed at a pace, and Nita wrote and told Italo of her new relationship. He was shattered by the news and wrote her to that effect. Italo's blue aerogramme letter arrived around Christmas. After reading it, Nita was clearly upset, and when she was out of the house I went snooping and found the letter on her dressing table. I read it but never mentioned it to anyone, not even Beria. One phrase stuck in my mind: 'I never imagine you would forget me so quick.'

On one side of Tower Street, running half the length of the town, was a raised footpath. The other side of the road was wide enough for the Italian contingent of soccer fanatics to practise their skills. In the late afternoon or the cool of the evening, with minimal traffic to disrupt them, they got together outside Mrs Patroni's to kick the ball around for an hour or so. They were a good-natured group of lads who made a lot of harmless noise, wolf-whistling and cat-calling when a single young female passed within sight.

Beria noticed Frank Mafrici, a short Italian with black hair, a big nose and swarthy skin, ogling Nita. She chipped him: 'Hey, you.'

Frank looked around. 'Who? Me?'

'Yes, you. Just keep your bloody eyes off her.'

As fate would have it, Nita ended up marrying him.

When Frank started going out with Nita he had a 250cc BSA motorbike which he sold to Max Gistinger. At the same time Max sold Frank an old cadet rifle. A couple of weeks later Frank returned the rifle, complaining it wasn't powerful enough. According to him the bullets dribbled out of the end of the barrel. Max was rather perplexed by Frank's claim: 'Really?' he said. 'They didn't do that when I used it,' and suggested they put it to the test. 'Why don't you stand over there in front of me and we'll fire the gun and see what happens. If the bullets dribble out, then you won't have anything to worry about, and if they don't, you won't know.'

Max Gistinger came from Heidelberg in Germany and worked in the lamp room on the mine, servicing between 100 and 150 battery-operated helmet lamps every day. He was a proud, good-looking, muscular man who wore satin elastic bathers without a modesty skirt, causing something of a stir the first time he appeared at the pool.

Around the town Max was known as Mr Fix-It; he could repair any broken household item. A linguist who wrote and spoke excellent English, he was also something of a bush lawyer for the Italian and Slav miners, filling out their mandatory sick-claim forms, which they lodged with Doug Quarti, the timekeeper. Max listed one man 'as suffering from rigor mortis'. Doug was never quite sure if it was meant as a joke or a test of his attention to detail. After reading it he said to the claimant: 'I think you could be a bit stiff in getting paid for this one.'

When he couldn't find a wife in Gwalia, Max advertised in a German newspaper. The first bride-to-be accepted the money for the airfare and disappeared. The second one, Erica, arrived and they were married in the Leonora Registry Office. Erica was an electronics technician and she and Max had three daughters.

Weddings in Gwalia were regarded by everyone as a major social occasion. Regardless of being invited, most women in the town gathered outside the church to look at the bride and throw confetti. Kids joined in as well. Barefoot and scruffy, they milled around in the background, staring intently. Eleven-year-old Nat Garbellini, shirtless and with his hair standing on end, was in the background of several of Valma Giovanazzi and Ron Sanfead's wedding photos. I was mesmerised by weddings, especially the organ music. I wanted to know every detail of the services. I searched and found the Latin Nuptial Mass in my missal.

I had a Spirax sketchbook and designed wedding dresses, often strapless and sometimes one-shouldered. Noreen Tagliaferri was my first real bride and my eyes nearly popped out of my head. She was a floating vision of fine white lace and tulle, with a large bow at the back, and deep layers of ruffles around the bottom half of the full skirt. Her long tulle veil was held in place by a fitted satin and lace cap. Once I went to the house of a newly married couple and knocked on the door: 'Would you show me your wedding dress, please?'

The ornately decorated wedding cake, with the icing sugar bride and groom sitting on the top, fired my imagination. Baffled by the process, I went and asked Mrs Chamberlain if I could have a look at her icing gun and the nozzle attachments. The wedding cake was always put on display at the breakfast, sometimes on a small lace-draped table but usually in the centre of the opened presents, all laid out on a trestle table on the side wall.

Tuesday and Thursday were popular wedding days, allowing the couple to set off by train the following morning. While they were away on their honeymoon it was the job of the bride's mother to cut up the cake and send guests and friends a slice through the post. It arrived a couple of days after the wedding in a tin container, usually with two wedding bells or a church steeple embossed on the lid. I waited outside the post office, and when I saw someone holding a little silver tin I didn't hesitate. 'Excuse me, if you're not going to eat the wedding cake, could I have it, please?'

In 1955, a mumps epidemic swept through Gwalia. I was one of the first casualties and spent three weeks in bed. Just weeks before Mary Bendotti married Mervyn Ross Sullivan, she fell victim. After a final check-up the doctor considered the contagious stage past but insisted the infected area be kept warm. Mary's mother, Carolina, made her dress and added a headdress of cotton wool concealed behind a lace wimple. Mary wouldn't allow any photographs to be taken.

Mrs Bendotti's husband, Pietro, was killed on the mine, leaving her with two children, Agnes and Mary. Pietro Bendotti and Andrea Fassanini were working underground on the Sons of Gwalia when they were overcome by fumes. They entered the bottom of a shaft area too soon after an explosion and the deadly heavier vapours had not cleared. Fassanini collapsed after he went to help Bendotti. By the time they were missed and the alarm raised, both men were dead.

⁂

Quirino Ferrari arrived in town and it didn't take him long to notice Ollie and Curly Garbellini's daughter Peggy working in the confectionary and newsagency section of Mazza's shop. The prettiest girl in town, Peggy was tall and a naturally gifted athlete, but she was also a bully. She bashed us all and gave the hardest arm-cork and the most painful Chinese burn of almost any other kid in the town, boy or girl. She had hammer toes which she used as a weapon. 'If you don't do what I tell you, I'll get you with my hammer toe.' We were terrified of it. Even the boys knew she was serious when she threatened to knock you out.

Quirino was handsome with dark hair, and he drove a big pink and black Pontiac. One day he asked me to take her a message: '*Vorrei lei bacio mi balli*,' which means, 'I want you to kiss my balls'. I didn't understand what he meant but when I told Peggy she laughed.

One night in the winter of 1956, Peggy threw the town into turmoil. She was about thirteen and went missing following a lunchtime disagreement with her mother. She was a popular girl and the word spread. The entire adult male population was galvanised and out searching. Peggy's grandmother, Mrs Robinson, lived a couple of doors down from us, and after Ollie had been to see her, she came on to Beria. They were huddled together at the front gate waiting for news. I was only a few feet away in the shadow of the jade, listening to every word. Peggy was like a sister. I was frightened by the news reports of the recent triple sundown murders and my imagination was racing. The train departed that morning and I wondered if she had stowed away and was now in Kalgoorlie, or maybe she had been kidnapped by a man. I even thought she might be dead. Straight ahead from our house, down by the railway line and obscured by the huge pepper trees, were several disintegrating railway huts. I was convinced Peggy was there.

By the time Beria packed me off to bed I was in a state. When I got home from school the next day, Beria explained Peggy had been found under the bridge over near the state school and was in hospital: 'She lost her memory. Ollie said she'll be home in a couple of days.'

When I saw Peggy she told me the whole story. She and Ollie had a fight at lunchtime and Ollie slapped her face. To teach her mother a lesson she took off, planning to come home when everyone was asleep. When it got dark she hid under the bridge. When she heard the men walking around she realised they were looking for her. She was spotted by Ian Watson who called out, and the men came running. Peggy laughed about the loss of memory: 'When the doctor started asking questions it was the first thing that came into my head. I think he guessed what had happened.'

∞

Every day I thought about learning to play the piano. I knew every house in Gwalia which had one and I couldn't walk past a piano without lifting the lid and touching the keys. If I wasn't allowed to touch, I stood and stared. The fact that I couldn't play a note didn't dampen my enthusiasm for it. After school, a couple of times a week, I would set off, carrying a bundle of Nita's old sheet music from her days at boarding school, and walk the two miles to Auntie Mary in Leonora so I could tinkle for half an hour. When I had satisfied my need, I walked home.

My friend Jan Quarti was being taken to the convent for lessons, which only intensified my passion. I was so envious. Mrs Quarti drove a white Zephyr with a blue stripe, and many times she and Jan, oblivious to my obsession, passed me on the main road as I was walking home. When I saw the car approaching I would quickly move away from the side of road into the surrounding scrub and squat with my back turned, pretending to be looking at something on the ground.

When I asked my father he agreed to pay for piano lessons, and every day I pestered Beria to ask the Dominican sisters if they would teach me. It was several months before she relented and went to see them at the Gwalia convent. Beria was gone for about half an hour, but as she came closer after the meeting I guessed the answer from the look on her face. 'I'm sorry,' she said, 'but she said no. They won't teach you to play the piano unless you go to the convent, and there is no way I am sending you back there again.' I dropped my head in disappointment. 'Sweetheart, I'm sorry, there's nothing I can do. You know I would if I could, but I can't. You'll just have to forget about it, alright?' Beria gave me a big hug. I cried for days, at the same time trying to think of a solution. It was Sister Mary Saint Anne who said no – the same one who had clashed with Nita in Dongara – and I never forgave her.

I was determined to find a way to have piano lessons. When Kay Quarti came home from Methodist Ladies' College in Perth, where she had been a boarder, I was struck by an idea. Kay was a pianist of some talent and once a week she came to school to provide the accompaniment for folk dancing classes. It was one of my favourite times in school.

Dark-haired, with an hourglass figure, Kay was a glamorous and vivacious personality, and popular with the young men. I watched her intently and never passed up an opportunity to be near her. She joked about how, before she went away to boarding school, her sister Jan and I would at every opportunity be kissing and hugging in the playground during recess.

I didn't know what Beria would say, so I kept quiet until I figured out exactly how I might bring my idea to fruition. I'd been to Mrs Quarti's house many times. They had a huge mulberry tree in their yard which she allowed us to climb during summer to pick the ripe juicy berries. The main branches of the tree hung over the corner of the house, and I climbed up and sat on the roof for hours, talking with Jan and eating mulberries. Sometimes, uninvited, I went and talked to Mrs Quarti while she did the washing.

It took me a week to summon the courage, and when I knocked on the door my heart was thumping so hard I thought it would leap out of my chest. Overwhelmed by the importance of her reply, I blurted out: 'Miss Quarti, the nuns said no, so my mum said please, would you teach me to play the piano?' There wasn't a moment of hesitation. 'Of course I will. Come back after school tomorrow and we'll start.' I was so overcome I burst into tears. It was the happiest moment of my life. After so much waiting, I was finally going to learn to play. I had taught myself to read music – 'Every Good Boy Deserves Fruit' – so she started me at grade one. Kay had a supply of sheet music and the first piece from *Jumbo Notes* was Bizet's 'Toreador's Song' from *Carmen*, arranged in F major, which I played with great gusto. I never missed a lesson, and for the year before Kay moved to Perth I went once a week, school holidays included. Kay was a patient teacher, and each lesson went for about an hour. I practised at every opportunity and made rapid progress. By the time she moved away I was already playing grade two pieces.

In truth, Gwalia boasted a number of musicians who played a variety of instruments. Some of the Italian men played the button and piano accordions. Food and music were important to them, keeping them in touch with home. Around the town in the summer evenings, you could hear the Neapolitan and Sicilian folk songs – 'Santa Lucia' and 'Torna a Surriento'. One of them played the bowl-backed Neapolitan mandolin.

Lucy Tognali was thirteen when she took over as organist at the Catholic church, replacing Sue Major, who went to Perth for her nursing training. Lucy played for benediction, and at the weddings of girlfriends who had been classmates: 'While Chris Stokes was signing the register, she asked me to play "Believe Me if All Those Endearing Young Charms", which was played at her mother's wedding.' Unaware of the church's ban, Lucy always played Mendelssohn's Wedding March. I was besotted with Lucy. She was ten years older than me, tall with dark curly hair and a good figure. She was always pleasant, imbued with self-confidence, and worked in the haberdashery section of Mazza's store. Her mother, Lizzie, made all her clothes and she was always fashionably dressed. The most I ever said to her was, 'Hello, Lucy.' She wore strapless one-piece bathers, and when she came to the pool I stared, loitering in the hope she would notice, and mostly I was not disappointed.

For a few months I went to the Church of England Sunday school. Melda Mazza was the organist and we sang 'Hear the Pennies Dropping' and 'All Things Bright and Beautiful'.

During the Second World War, pianist Laurette Chamberlain and her husband Harold played with various big bands. Nita always referred to her as 'Mrs 1-2-3'. If I walked past her house and heard her practising I knocked on the door and asked if I could come inside and listen. I was mesmerised by the sound, and by the sight of her hands skimming the keyboard. Mrs Chamberlain was part of a trio. Her husband, Harold, a fitter on the mine, played saxophone, and Hughie MacKay, the butcher, and then Norm Watson, played drums.

The Chamberlains and their adopted son Eric arrived in Gwalia in 1947 from Mount Sir Samuel, where they ran the hotel. Mrs Chamberlain had employed an elderly Aboriginal woman, Kitty, to do the washing and ironing. When the goldmining town closed down, Kitty and the few Aborigines still living there got a lift on the mail truck to Leonora and went to live on the native reserve a couple of miles out of town on the way to Station Creek. From time to time Kitty would walk the four miles to Gwalia to see Mrs Chamberlain. She never went inside the house. She sat under the giant pepper tree in the backyard, eating the food which Mrs Chamberlain provided. Having Kitty in her backyard was a breach of the law.

Pianist Melda Mazza was part of a quintet – clarinet, saxophone, drums and trumpet – which provided music for the winter ball seasons of the 1950s. When the latest 78 rpm records arrived at their shop, Melda Mazza lent them to one of the musicians to prepare the band charts. They rehearsed regularly, and always played the latest hits.

I was frightened by the chorus from the hit song 'How Much Is That Doggy in the Window?', sung by Patti Page:

> *I read in the papers there are robbers,*
> *with flashlights that shine in the dark.*

It was enough to set my nerves jangling. Without saying a word, I would leave the room rather than listen on the wireless to police and crime serials involving murder, eerie sound effects, people screaming in fright, or evocative musical themes. They sent me checking for intruders.

Most evenings, when I was living with my father in the Tower Street house, I went to Harry 'Baldy' Taylor's house for an hour of piano practice. A widower, Mr Taylor was the winder driver on the mine, and also did the books at the butcher shop. Despite his rather dour appearance, he was an agreeable man. He always wore a beret, and rode a bicycle, wearing metal trouser clips around his ankles to prevent his cuffs catching in the unprotected chain. Beria called him 'Happy'.

The piano was in the front room, which opened from the closed-in front verandah, and ran the width of the house. It had altered little since the sad death of his wife Lucy four years earlier. It was well furnished with a three-piece cut-velvet lounge suite, several small wooden tables, on which he displayed his extensive stamp collection, and a china cabinet. The floor was covered in patterned linoleum. Tucked tight in the corner was a walnut upright piano, the top of which was covered with framed, hand-tinted pictures of his family. The storage space under the stool was crammed with Mrs Taylor's sheet music, which had not been disturbed since she died and was the chief source of the room's mustiness.

Even though Mr Taylor was always in the kitchen, some nights I was inexplicably unsettled. Often, I was certain there was a presence in the room. Many times it felt as if someone were standing behind me, watching me play. It frightened me so much I was too scared to turn and look. It only happened in that room, and only at the piano. Several times I was so unnerved I leapt to my feet, packed my music and ran. We lived less than a two-minute walk away, but I sprinted down the middle of the deserted road, terrified someone would leap from the shadows or from behind a lamppost and chase me. My fear of the dark never abated.

Most nights, especially during winter, my father was already in bed by the time I returned from practice. I'd put more wood on the fire, make myself a steaming cup of Milo, open the oven door and sit close, warming my feet, daydreaming and staring vacantly at the blue and yellow flames as they leapt from the spitting log before they disappeared into exhausted nothingness.

There were so many cats and dogs in Gwalia they almost outnumbered the people. The dogs came in all varieties: kangaroo dogs, cocker spaniels, corgis, cattle and sheep dogs, blue and red heelers, and lots of mongrels. We knew the names and the owners of nearly all of them.

Beria's neighbours, Mr and Mrs Grudniski, inherited two kangaroo dogs from Mr Januzkiewcz when he went to live in Kalgoorlie. Bobby, the smaller, was black, and Rexie was a huge golden-brown animal. Mr Januzkiewcz's treatment had made them vicious and they needed to be muzzled when they were off the chain. One day, they managed to escape from their yard unmuzzled and charged Beria, who had the good sense to stand still. They barked and ran around her for a time before Rexie ripped through her skirt and gave her a decent nip on the rump before retreating back inside.

Early one Saturday morning a couple of weeks later Mrs Grudniski came rushing into the house. She was crying hysterically and the front of her dressing gown was covered in blood. The two dogs had fought inside the house. She had managed to push Bobby into a broom cupboard and dragged Rexie outside and chained him up. She asked Steve to bring his gun and shoot Rexie. Steve's eyesight was so poor his first shot only wounded Rexie and he went mad, snarling ferociously and trying to leap at Steve. The second shot killed him.

Over the years we had dogs, cats, goats, sheep, a piglet, pigeons, bantams, cockies, chooks and roosters, joeys, lizards, and tadpoles which grew into frogs.

Billy, the black goat, was my first pet and we were inseparable, playing together all day. I was eighteen months old and he was about six months. When I became tired of walking, I climbed up and rode on his back. One day Billy found his way into Beria's bedroom and chewed the bottom of her petticoat, which was hanging on the wardrobe door. That was it as far as Beria was concerned and she gave Billy to the McMeekens, who ate him.

We always had a dog – sometimes two – and there were four during the time I lived in Gwalia: Woolly, Patchy, Puppy and Tippy. There was no veterinary surgeon in the town so if they became ill, or were involved in a serious accident, it sometimes involved home surgery. Ollie Garbellini came to the rescue of a dog badly ripped during a fight. She gently pushed the dog's gizzards back in place, and with her daughter Ann holding its head she sutured the wound using a domestic needle and thread. Ollie was no seamstress, but the dog survived without infection. If they didn't recover of their own accord, they were shot.

Woolly was a beautiful, gentle dog with a soft pale brown and white coat. He felt like an Angora rabbit. It was a winter Monday morning and we were living in Grinning Joe's house. As I did first thing in the morning I went outside to find my Woolly. I called and then went searching. As I rounded the corner I was confronted by Woolly lying on his right side and facing me. He was wet from the overnight frost, totally stiff, and his tongue was lolling out of his mouth. I couldn't stop crying. Beria wouldn't tell me but I later found out it was Steve's fault. He hated other people's pets, and when he saw someone else's cat wandering through our yard he laced a tin of sardines with cyanide stolen from the mine. As with Patchy, they wrapped Woolly in a sugarbag and threw him into the mine's furnace.

Puppy was a big dog, and a glorious looking animal. Golden with a touch of black and a huge square head, he was strong and obedient. He knocked things over when he wagged his tail. Beria trained him well, and during the chicken-rearing months there could be as many as twenty chirping yellow chicks standing on Puppy's back and head as he lay basking in the sun outside his kennel. Pointing and wagging her finger, Beria warned him, with equal emphasis on every word: 'Pupp-yyyyy.... don't you touch those chickens!' He seemed to understand, and never did – not once.

Although he belonged to Beria, for some reason Puppy took a shine to Nita and came to live with us. Beria didn't want to give him away and tried everything to keep him home, even resorting to chaining him, in the hope he would understand where he lived. The moment she set him free, he bolted across town and went to Nita. In the end Beria was forced to admit defeat.

I already had my dog, Tippy, and he and Puppy became great mates. Although neither of them had been desexed, they lived happily together and rarely fought. With a dog chained at both the front and back door, the place was impregnable. Unfortunately the family of Aboriginal children living next door teased him constantly. Nita was friends with the wife – a big woman – and a couple of times when the husband came home drunk and started to hit his missus she came running for protection. My sister let her sleep in the spare bed on the verandah. But no matter how much Nita threatened, the kids wouldn't stop teasing Puppy, poking at him with sticks through the fence, which drove him to distraction. One day he leapt the fence, gave chase and cornered them. He wasn't a vicious dog, but he gave one of them a nip. The policeman got involved, and Puppy vanished. Nita didn't offer any explanation about his disappearance, but I suspected Frank was involved because I knew he wasn't a dog lover.

A couple of days later, I was walking around the base of Mount Leonora in an area I rarely went to because it was where they emptied the night-cart pans. Quite by chance, I stumbled across Puppy's decomposing body tied to a tree. He had been shot through the head and was still wearing his collar made from Nita's old dog collar belt. I ran across town to tell Beria. She was ropeable, since she still considered Puppy to be her dog.

Goats, sheep and pigs came and went. One day you'd be out walking with them, the next you'd be sitting at the table eating them. All the goats were called Billy and all the lambs were called Mary. One Mary was so sickly when she arrived she didn't have the strength to stand. Beria nursed her day and night. We bottle-fed her and Billy on warm Sunshine powdered milk, which they drank from a beer bottle fitted with a baby's teat. Billy and Mary bonded and seemed to think Beria was their mother. They followed her everywhere, even to the post office. When she walked across the flat they trotted along behind her and wouldn't be turned back. Beria had only to stand at the front door and call their names and they came charging. They grazed happily on the wild tomato bush which grew out on the flat, but only so long as Beria stayed with them. If she slipped away, leaving them on their own, they galloped home like frightened children, baaing in unison. We loved Billy and Mary so much even Steve couldn't bring himself to kill them. He asked a friend to cut their throats. Steve cooked them on the spit, but I wasn't the slightest bit hungry that day.

The piglet came to us from the slaughter yards after the sow rejected him. The runt of the litter, he would have died but for Beria's care. He was friendly and we fed him a sloppy mixture of pollard, bran, milk and vegetables. One day he escaped from the chookhouse, where he lived peacefully with his feathered companions, and went tearing down Tower Street, followed by Nita and Italo. They were laughing so much they had trouble catching him. Beria said it was like something out of a Ma and Pa Kettle film. The pig didn't have a name and ended up on a Sunday spit.

It was my last year in Gwalia and early one morning when I went out into the backyard to feed Joey the kangaroo, he went for me, trying to seize me in a clinch and lifting his foot to claw at my stomach. Beria warned me it would happen and I knew it was time to let him go. I opened the back gate and off he went – hopping away in the direction of Mount Leonora.

The Bonaminis' kid goat kept coming in and eating the bowl of wheat in Beria's chookhouse. Steve went mad when he arrived home in a temper one Saturday afternoon, having lost all his money at the betting shop, and spotted the goat with its head in the dish. Swearing and cursing, he rushed into the house, grabbed Lewie's gun, took aim at the goat and fired. As it happened he only grazed its snout. The goat leapt in the air, then turned and headed for home, bleeding and bleating. Minutes later Mr Bonamini came knocking on the door, shouting abuse. Steve was so belligerent Mr Bonamini reported him to the police and had him charged. Steve's imminent court appearance was the talk of town, and he was such a braggart he skited about it. The mine manager, Reg Barden, who played cards with Steve, told him to plead guilty, which proved costly. The Magistrate, Mr Brown, fined Steve a hefty £10 – almost a fortnight's basic wage. It would've been much more if he'd known Steve didn't have a gun licence.

I couldn't stop listening when Beria told Joan Tagliaferri the story about Steve and his mate Jacky Prince. They were three-parts shickered when they decided to go out to the slaughter yards to pinch a pig. 'They tried to shoot one of the piglets but missed and shot the mother. They brought it back and there we were, at three o'clock in the morning, in the bathroom, with the bath heater going, trying to shave the pig with Steve's hand razor. We kept one half, and Jacky and his wife Lena took the other half. Jacky and Lena decided to give Jacky's parents one of the legs of pork. The only problem was Jacky's parents had a boarder, Franklin Biggs, who worked at the butcher shop where they pinched the pig. In the end Jacky's parents had to bury the leg of pork in their backyard!'

In February 1957 I turned ten and, after years of pleading, Beria finally agreed to ask Steve if I could have a birthday party. To her surprise, he agreed. I was overjoyed. For the first time I was allowed to invite six boys into the house. I chose the list carefully, writing and hand-delivering the invitations. A friend of Beria's, Joy Millar, helped organise the after-school party. We sat down at the table on the back verandah to demolish a birthday spread of cakes, sandwiches, soft drinks and a small roast chook, which, divided between seven boys, didn't go far. By four o'clock all the food was gone. I had a wonderful time with lots of presents, and I felt special.

When Steve arrived home from work at about a quarter past four the party turned sour. On discovering Beria hadn't saved him any chicken, he went berserk. The boys scattered in all directions and the party came to an end. I walked down to the nearby railway line, sat on the bluestone chips surrounding the sleepers and had a cry. Once again I was the cause of friction in Beria's life. I waited until the sun was about to set and, knowing I had to be home before dark, I walked back to the house.

In the spring of 1958 two missionary oblates of Mary Immaculate from St Patrick's Basilica in Fremantle arrived in Leonora and Gwalia, prompting a flurry of religious activity. As part of their goldfields missionary tour, they said the rosary and benediction every night. My father had no interest in the church, although the arrival of the missionaries prompted him to light the copper for extra baths. Dressed in my best clothes, every night for a week I took myself off to benediction, listening as the young priests told stories of their glamorous lives, and of their joy and love in the service of Jesus Christ. I was smitten, and spent the week in a state of grace, ransacking the house for religious artefacts. Each night, like the three kings bringing gifts for the infant Jesus, I carried to the altar holy pictures, rosary beads, various medals and anything else which I thought appropriate for a blessing.

Nita and her boyfriend Frank attended on the last night and Frank bought me a framed picture of the Virgin Mary which, together with all the other religious objects I owned, was placed on a small altar in my bedroom where I knelt to pray.

When the oblates of Mary Immaculate left at the end of the week I felt a sense of loss. The Nazarene himself couldn't have made a deeper and more lasting impression. Their nightly sermons had transported me and, in what Beria always called my vivid imagination, provided another glimpse of the world which lay way beyond Gwalia.

A couple of weeks later, as we were walking home one night after the pictures, Nita rebuked me harshly when I attempted to join the conversation. Frank took her side, making a comment which I didn't like. When they stopped at Clara Paravicini's gate to talk I continued on home, collected the picture of the Virgin Mary, went back to where they were talking and threw it at them, sprinting home before they realised what I had done.

As I grew older I was happy to be on my own, sketching and reading, or playing the piano. I didn't spend much time with the other kids in my final year at primary school; I was last to arrive in the morning and I went home at midday. And I preferred the company of girls. Susan Mazza and I were playing on the footpath outside the Scolaris' house. Not realising Beria was watching from her front gate, Roma Scolari appeared from out of the grapevines and started to have a go at me. Beria let fly, giving Roma both barrels. 'Hey, who the bloody hell do you think you're talking to?' she roared. 'He's not doing you any harm so just leave him alone. You and your bloody lah-di-dah ways; you think your shit doesn't stink. Well, it does; and if you're not careful I'll come over there and give you a bit of hurry-up, and see how much you like it. Now mind your own business and get inside.'

Roma didn't say a word and retreated back into the grapevines. Beria didn't have a kind word to say about Roma and this incident only made things worse. Except for when she had to serve me in the chemist shop, Roma never spoke a word to me, and was one of two people in Gwalia I didn't like. The other was a friend of Beria's. When we visited, I had to sit outside on the lawn and wait.

Steve had a jaundiced view of the world. With his heavy accent and poor command of spoken English I understood less than half of what he said – and most of it didn't make any sense anyway. I never really talked to him but Beria understood him, and when he wasn't drunk they seemed to talk quite amicably. Sometimes I even heard them laugh. Often, when listening to the news on the wireless, particularly items concerning Yugoslavia or the Communist leaders, he became agitated and ranted, fanatically. He jabbered about Marshall Tito and Joseph Stalin, both of whom he hated. I assumed from the tone of his voice they were personal acquaintances he left behind in Yugoslavia. Steve's cousin Vladimir Petar Salinovich lived in Kalgoorlie, and Steve hated him, branding him a German collaborator during the war.

Steve told Beria she was stupid when she disagreed with him, which always set them on a collision course. Steve believed in the might of the gun and was always threatening to shoot somebody or slit their throats. Drunk or sober, he argued major events were engineered by the Communists in an effort to seize world power. He dismissed the 1954 Petrov affair as Communist propaganda, offering a keg of beer to anyone who could prove him wrong. The front-page newspaper photograph of Mrs Petrov, surrounded by a contingent of Australian media and a large crowd of angry protesters, disturbed me. Wearing only one shoe, Mrs Petrov was being half carried, half dragged across the tarmac by two Russian security 'gorillas' to a waiting plane, bound for the Soviet Union. The men in the photograph reminded me of Steve when he was drunk. Since the only time I ever saw Beria cry was when Steve hit her, I assumed Mrs Petrov was crying because they had given her a belting.

The Dominican sisters living in the Leonora convent were a constant source of fascination. I had an insatiable desire to know every detail about their lives. Several times I managed to make it as far as the front gate, peering into the shadows with a burning nosiness, imagining, and itching to be invited inside. Nita told salacious tales from her schooldays in Dongara of inquisitive girls crawling through the sand dunes and spying on the sisters swimming at the back beach. I was agog at Nita's description of them laughing and frolicking in the water and wearing satin elastic bathers, the latest in fashion swimwear. Nita told Beria some of the sisters had good figures.

In the classroom, in a rare moment of relaxation, Sister Mary Bruno provided answers to the burning questions. She assured us, without demonstrating, she did have legs and hair. She somehow managed to remain patient when someone asked: 'Sister, was your mum surprised when she got a little nun baby?'

However, about her name she was less indulgent. 'Do you think if I got to choose my own name I would be called Sister Mary Bruno? Now get on with your work, you silly boy.'

Catholic children lived in fear of divine retribution, and prayed regularly throughout the day. Religious items were considered a tangible reminder of God in our lives and provided a source of inspiration. When she came from Italy Mrs Paravicini brought a framed oil on canvas of the Sacred Heart of Jesus, which hung on her bedroom wall. Mrs Pallotta, a neighbour who spoke no English and whom I visited regularly, also had the Sacred Heart of Mary and a portrait of the holy family. In my bedroom I kept holy water in a miniature white plastic crucifix and font, and converted a small two-shelf bookcase into an altar. At the centre of my daily devotions was a china statue of Our Lady of the Immaculate Conception, flanked by two tin-framed holy pictures – the Sacred Heart of Jesus and the children of Fatima. My collection of holy cards depicted Jesus, a Palestinian Jew, as fair-skinned, blue-eyed, with shoulder-length light brown wavy hair, surrounded by a golden halo of light. I assumed he spoke Italian and English. Beside my bed I kept a carved plastic figure of the crucified Christ, which glowed in the dark.

No part of our Roman Catholic life was deemed too mundane for apostolic elucidation. Papal encyclicals were studied and followed to the letter, more zealously by some priests than others. The purification movement was at its zenith. The Catholic Legion of Decency was buoyed and supported by the Holy Father. In a never-ending crusade against filth and depravity, the Legion annually published a comprehensive list of films and books to be banned by the Roman Catholic Church, which included the *True Confessions* and *True Romance* magazines which Beria and Nita read. At Sunday Mass on the Feast of the Immaculate Conception members not only promised to boycott any morally offensive film, but also swore never to patronise any cinema which had screened such a film.

When Our Lady of Fatima appeared in 1917 to the three shepherd children in Portugal, her message was unambiguous. If her requests were heeded, Russia would be converted, and there would be world peace. However, if the world failed to hear her voice: 'Russia would spread her evil; there would be wars and persecution of the Church; the good would be martyred; the Holy Father would suffer; and nations would be annihilated.' We prayed for the conversion of Russia, for the perfidious Jews, seeking God's intervention: 'Hear their prayers for the blindness of these people, that acknowledging the truth, they may be pulled out of their darkness.'

We knew Roman Catholicism created a social division, and like the saints and martyrs we were expected to face the trials and tribulations which followed from being a member of the one true 'Holy, Catholic and Apostolic Church'. It wasn't unusual for employers to discriminate in their advertisements: 'Catholics and Jews need not apply'. Catholic applicants concealed, even denied, their faith. For the unsuspecting, the Lord's Prayer was the litmus test. If, unthinkingly, you failed to rattle off the Protestant version, you were shown the door. In Sunday sermons, priests, instructed by their bishops under the guidance of Cardinal Gilroy, told parishioners to vote Labor. In turn, the Menzies government denied children attending Catholic schools free-issue facilities, books and stationery, which forced many cash-strapped families to enrol their children at state schools.

We believed in the infallibility of the Holy Father, Pope Pius XII, who in 1950 declared, as a dogma revealed by God and an article of faith, the Assumption of Mary. Sister explained: 'It means Mary was transported into heaven with her body and soul united.' No detail was spared: 'She was wearing little gold earrings.'

Weekly, we confessed and accused ourselves of venial and mortal sins, promising to abstain from any further form of self-pollution. 'God killed Onan for spilling his seed on the ground.' We accepted our penance with a sincere intention, and questioned each other as we emerged from the confessional: 'What did he give you?' It was a competition. The greater the penance, the higher the esteem.

It was a mortal sin to enter or attend a service in a 'heretical' church. Parents of a Catholic marrying outside the faith were forced to watch proceedings through an open door, while a practising Catholic acting as a bridesmaid at a Protestant wedding waited outside the church door during the service. Brides left their bouquets at the front door during Lent, and a mixed marriage was solemnised in the sacristy behind the altar, out of sight of the congregation. A papal encyclical on mixed marriages demanded the Catholic partner do everything within their power to convert the heretic.

Sex was a stumbling block. When one of her former students announced her engagement, Reverend Mother felt duty bound to offer her advice. Sexual intercourse was to be endured and would be made bearable if the woman said the rosary while submitting to her duty. For a young man setting out on married life, the first-night advice in the Roman Catholic sex education handbook was unambiguous: 'Be a man, not an animal.'

The goldfields attracted their share of eccentrics and Gwalia was no exception. No one cared, providing they didn't make a nuisance of themselves.

Bob Pini and his wife kept everyone amused for months. She was as short and dumpy as he was tall and thin. In the middle of summer she went to the pictures wearing a full-length fur coat. She looked like a monkey as he sat next to her, shelling and feeding her peanuts. For a short time they lived in a house at Halfway Creek. Newlyweds Jacky and Lena Prince were next-door neighbours, and whenever Beria saw Jacky he regaled her with stories of the Pinis' shenanigans.

One afternoon Jacky heard laughing and squealing coming from next door and went to the kitchen window to check. Jacky, who according to Lena loved sex and wanted it three times a day, couldn't believe what he was seeing. He called Lena to come and have a look. Lena was an attractive but naive woman and was embarrassed by the sight of a naked Bob Pini chasing his equally naked wife around the yard. Looking at him it was obvious what he had in mind.

The Pinis moved to a fully furnished house owned by Mrs Stewart in the centre of the town. Mrs Pini complained the pan lavatory against the back fence was too far away; furthermore, there was a constant queue of men loitering in the lane and pestering her for sexual favours. To cut off any potential competition at the pass, Bob Pini moved the pan onto the back verandah. The town was aghast. The pans were only emptied twice a week.

When his wife complained the double bed was too high, Bob Pini sawed off the legs. When they had a serious falling-out and went for a time without speaking to each other, he said she wasn't good enough to eat at the same table as him or sleep with him, so he cut both the kitchen table and the bed in half. When they refused to pay Mrs Stewart for the damage, she took them to court and won.

In a town bereft of formal entertainment the Pinis were as good as a three-ring circus, and everyone was in on the joke. However, one day we woke up and they were gone. That's how it was in Gwalia.

I didn't clean my teeth until I was ten, and I never once saw Beria clean hers. I'm not sure she owned a toothbrush. However, when I was about seven the State Health Department sent a government dentist to examine the teeth of all the children in the remote goldfields.

This was my first encounter with a dentist and I had no idea what to expect. However, I wasn't too keen on the idea after I overheard some of the big kids talking. They made a visit to the dentist sound painful. When we arrived at school on Monday the dentist's caravan was parked in the schoolyard. After a brief explanation, he set about conducting preliminary examinations. At the end of the day I was given a note for Beria, explaining I needed a filling and seeking her permission. Since it was a free service, and there was no dentist in the town, Beria willingly signed.

The next morning the treatment began in earnest, and he didn't waste time. While one kid was in the chair being treated, another was loitering nervously at the door. As soon as you arrived back in the classroom the next kid was sent out to wait on the verandah. It was hot, and with nervous perspiration running down the back of my neck I started to panic when the kid before me emerged from the caravan, unsmiling. Suddenly it was my turn. 'Come in, young man,' the dentist called.

I climbed the two steps and was inside the surgery. He pointed to what looked like a barber's chair. I sat down and watched as he went about preparing. It was stifling inside the small caravan and the dentist kept mopping his brow with a small white towel. He was a solid man with a beard, and it was difficult to tell whether he was young or old. Unlike the local doctor, who always wore a white coat, the dentist was wearing an open-neck shirt, and shorts with long socks. 'You need a filling, so I have to drill a hole in your tooth,' he said. 'Open wide.'

He pulled the drill arm into position and placed his foot on a pedal at the base of the apparatus. The moving part of the drill was driven by a leather belt, and staring up from the chair it reminded me of Beria's Singer sewing machine. I was rigid with fear, unable to move as the dentist began drilling my live tooth. The smell of burning caught in my nose, and the heat from the drill intensified as tiny bits of enamel flew around my mouth and lodged in the back of my throat. The pain was blinding. I thought it would never end. Finally it was over and he sent me back to the classroom with a temporary filling. Two days later I went, reluctantly, to receive the permanent filling.

Up until then, Beria had been my dentist, removing my milk teeth using a length of strong cotton. It was painless and never failed. She attached one end of the cotton to the loose tooth and the other to the knob of the open kitchen door. With one hand on my chest to keep me from falling forward, she slammed the door, ripping the tooth out of my head. Other times she tied the tooth with cotton, braced me against the wall with one hand, and yanked with other. I rinsed my mouth with warm salty water until the bleeding stopped and put the tooth in a glass of water for the fairy to collect.

The Point Peron Camp School was designed for children from the far inland of Western Australia for whom seaside holidays were normally impossible. The Education Department had commandeered and transported disused Air Force buildings from the Pearce airbase and established this special school on a headland at the southern end of Cockburn Sound, with protected beaches, limestone cliffs, reefs and panoramic views. In the latter half of 1956, the Education Department sent out details of a camp school to be held there for two weeks in February.

I had no doubt it would be an adventure. I knew everything about seaside holidays, having taken so many of them with the Famous Five, the main characters in the Enid Blyton children's adventure series. I had the entire set, and after much deliberation I concluded it would be exactly like *Five Go Down to the Sea*. I was eager to attend.

However, ten days at Point Peron cost £20, which was a lot of money and, as I thought, more than Beria could afford. 'I'm sorry, sweetheart, but I don't have the money. If you want to go, you'll have to ask your father to pay for it.' I thought about it for several days and went to visit him at the mine mess where he was then living. 'If that's what you want, of course you can go,' he told me. I ran home to Beria, overjoyed at the prospect of my first seaside holiday. Lying in bed at night, my head was filled with romantic notions. I tried to imagine how it might be. But as the time drew closer, my serious self-doubt caused me to hesitate and question my ability to compete as an equal with other kids. I spent much of my childhood suffering from embarrassment and imagining I was the butt of peoples' jokes. My sister-in-law Jean made it worse by calling me Sad Sack – a pathetic comic-strip character who was tall, thin and ugly.

I had visited Perth only once in my life, in 1954, but this was different. From the school we could see across to the Garden Island naval base and Penguin Island, just half a mile away. A couple of times, when the tide was out, the teachers walked us along the sandbar to and from Penguin Island, to see the colony of fairy penguins; other times, closer to the shore, we foraged and watched the tiny crabs and other sea creatures sitting in the warm ponds.

We were looked after by a group of student teachers and volunteer parents who travelled with the group. The place was run like a junior army camp. We slept in the barracks, ate in the mess, and showered in the ablutions block. It was the first time I said grace before a meal. We were expected to help wash and dry the dishes, make our beds and clean the dormitory. For an anxious and insecure child who never wanted to stray too far from home, this was my initiation into communal living and was the most exciting adventure in my life. I loved it and wasn't homesick. I enjoyed the daily routine and the regular meals and they took me to Mass on Sunday.

Although I knew all about the wild roar of the sea from the Famous Five books, nothing had prepared me for the vastness of the ocean. I was bursting with anticipation. After lunch we set out for the beach. In single file we followed the narrow path, trudging through the thick undergrowth of tea trees. The hot steep sand dunes were covered by the brightly coloured flowering succulents, red pigface and magenta portulaca. I could smell the salt spume in the air. When we came over the top of the dunes I beheld, for the first time, the sun sparkling on the Indian Ocean. The water was the colour of lapis lazuli. I stopped and stared at the expanse, slack-jawed; it was like a giant millpond for as far as the eye could see, and under an endless azure sky. As the other kids began running and sliding down the sand dune, I hesitated, stunned by the seascape. The trainee teachers following up the rear moved me along and I made my way down to the water's edge, to splash in the shallows.

We were taken on several excursions, including a visit to the Watsonia meat works to watch pigs being electrocuted and turned into legs of ham and rashers of bacon. Inside the works, the dark shadow of death lingered around every corner and the stench of the charnel house hung heavy in the air. I watched in horror, barely able to move, as a distressed and squealing pig was dragged and secured by a burly slaughterman. The electric shock pads were placed on the temple of the powerless animal and the pig's final squeal was sickening as it keeled over and lay lifeless on the cement floor. I turned and ran outside to the waiting bus, sick to the pit of my stomach. One of the teachers followed after me. I was defiant and wouldn't be persuaded to go back inside: 'No,' I said sharply as tears welled in my eyes. 'It's cruel and I don't want to see it.' I stayed on the bus and didn't say a word for the rest of the excursion.

Nita and I were two incompatible children; we squabbled about everything. We were never close, nor did we share a joke or a sibling secret. I was inclined to my mother's forthright personality – given to arguing and having the last say. Nita – who was not without a sense of humour except when it came to me – seemed to have more of the peevish traits of my father. Time did nothing to bring us any closer. When we lived with our father he was exasperated by our constant bickering. The spats almost always happened in front of him, and as a consequence I was often the object of his anger and frustration.

As a girl, and a teenager, if things didn't proceed exactly to Nita's plan she would take the huff, and stomp to her bedroom and sulk, lying on the bed for extended periods, ignoring any attempts at cajoling her, sometimes to her own detriment.

When Beria came back from the Co-Op one day in the high summer of 1953 bringing an ice-cream for both of us, Nita, in a fit of pique, wouldn't eat it. 'Eat it, or I'll shove it down your throat,' Beria warned. I thought it was a joke and laughed, while Nita, who was fourteen, thought Beria's threat way beyond her capabilities and said, 'I don't want it.' Beria saw red and without warning, grabbed Nita with one hand, pushed her to the floor, and shoved the ice-cream into her mouth. I thought it was a game until Nita burst into tears. 'Next time, do as I bloody well tell you,' Beria warned as she left her lying on the floor, crying, her face covered with ice-cream. I was gone from the front verandah before Beria could bark, 'Ronnie, go and collect the eggs.'

Left alone, I was a quiet child and Beria rarely had cause to raise her voice, let alone hit me. When it was just Beria and me, I spent the evening reading Arthur Mee's *The Children's Encyclopaedia*, which Beria gave me as a Christmas present in 1953. They cost £55 on time payment. Beria commented: 'I honestly can't remember Ronnie ever being naughty.'

Only once did I try Beria's patience beyond endurance. It was the winter of 1957. I was ten, and Nita was about eighteen. The three of us were sitting together in front of the open fire one night playing cards. It had been a bad week of bickering between Nita and me, and Beria was starting to get fed up. She chipped us constantly. 'Will you two stop your arguing? You're getting on my nerves. Now Ronnie, go and read a book or find something else to do before I take to you.'

When the squabbling continued, Beria snapped. She jumped up, grabbed me by the arm, hauled me off the lounge and took to me. Her rage had been building up, and having lost control she couldn't stop. Using her open hand she hit me repeatedly around the legs and the back while I screamed and tried to break free. Finally she released her grip and I raced into the kitchen to where Steve was standing and sheltered behind him for protection. Beria followed. I was crying and she was screaming at me: 'I am sick and bloody tired of you two arguing all the time. Now get to bed before I take to you again. And I don't want to hear another peep out of you.' Heartbroken, I did as I was told. Beria didn't mention it again, and Nita and I gave each other a wide berth for a time.

In the summer of 1958 when I was living with my father and Nita, I came home from school at lunchtime and Nita was there with her new boyfriend, Frank Mafrici. Our squabbling was out of control and I shouted at her: 'I am going to tell Dad what you're doing!' Whereupon Nita grabbed the strap and started belting me. I was sitting on a chair in the kitchen and when I attempted to get away she pushed me back. She was a solid and physically strong girl. Frank stood watching as she hit me repeatedly about the legs. 'What are you going to tell him?' she shouted over and again. 'What are you going to tell him?'

When she stopped I jumped onto my bike and rode to Beria's house. I was sobbing and could barely see the road for the tears streaming down my face. Beria was getting Steve's midday dinner when I burst in. She listened to what I had to say, checked the marks on my legs, and then sent me outside to calm down. I sat on the green wooden bench at the side of the house near the vegetable garden, in the cool shade of the passionfruit and grapevines. While I went back to school Beria paid Nita a visit. 'I'm telling you, Nita. You keep your bloody hands to yourself. Because if you don't, I'll take the strap to you, and I'll give you a hiding you won't forget in a long time.' I didn't tell my father but things between the pair of us were frosty for a couple of weeks. However, the strap disappeared, and Nita never hit me again.

Obviously I had pricked her guilty conscience. When she married Frank in March of the following year, she was three months pregnant.

On Friday, 15 August 1958, my sister was one of eight debutantes presented in Leonora. After my father talked it over with Nita, he said I could go along to the ball, but I had to behave myself and do as I was told. I agreed, but I would have danced with the devil to be allowed to attend. The ball was held in the Federal Hall and the girls were being presented to the State Minister for Health and Justice, Mr Emil Nulsen, and his wife, Constance. A former hotelier and store keeper, Mr Nulsen was the local Labor Member for Eyre, and in his youth he roved the area as a bicycle rider, horseman and amateur boxer.

This was to be my first ball and it all sounded so exciting. It was mid-winter, and I watched enviously as Nita went to weekly evening rehearsals. The constant talk of deep court curtsies, long white gloves, delicate bouquets of white and pink crepe paper roses sprinkled with lily of the valley set my mind spinning. I hankered for more information and I yearned to be involved. I asked as many questions as I dared, but Nita wasn't interested. My father bought her a dress from Mazza's shop in Leonora. Made from white flock nylon, with a full circular skirt, and a ruche yoke neckline which formed tiny puff sleeves, it cost £25.

When the day of the ball finally arrived I was so excited it was all I thought about at school that day. As soon as my father arrived from work at four o'clock he lit the copper and Nita and I had a bath, in the same water. I wore my best long-sleeved brushed-cotton pale pink and grey tartan shirt, short trousers, and shoes and short socks.

The inside of the hall and the stage had been decorated with multicoloured crepe paper roses and fern. In the centre of the hall were festoons of balloons and streamers. The group of young men and women waited nervously in an anteroom, laughing and talking. They all seemed so grown-up and sophisticated as they posed for photographs. I had never seen so many beautiful dresses in one room. The young men looked dashing in dinner jackets; some were hired from Kalgoorlie, others were borrowed from their fathers.

The presentation of the debutantes took place at half past nine. I sat alone on a bench at the side of the hall and watched. Each girl was announced by Mr Doug Quarti, and the boys were lined up on either side of the hall. After her name was announced, each girl walked slowly down the maroon carpet, dropped a deep curtsey, then moved away to join her partner.

I was so proud when it came time for Nita to be presented. She went red with embarrassment when her name was called, and was so nervous her bouquet was visibly shaking. It was the first time I could remember her having her hair set. At the end of the presentation they danced a Pride of Erin waltz. Lost in my own little world, I mentally noted every detail of the beautiful young girls in long white dresses and the debonair young men in dinner jackets as they swirled across the dance floor.

Bernice Quarti was one of the organisers of the ball. Together with her sister-in-law, Melda Mazza, who played the piano, they had spent weeks rehearsing the couples for the night. Mrs Quarti looked so beautiful in a cocktail-length, pale blue brocade princess line dress. Her daughter Kay was one of the debutantes. Mrs Quarti was a stylish woman and during the rehearsal period talked with the girls about their dresses, suggesting the décolletage should be modest. On the night, it was Kay's dress which was the most revealing, an irony not lost on her mother. 'It was totally unintentional,' Bernice explained. 'When the dress arrived and Kay tried it on, she disappeared in all the tulle around the neckline. I had no alternative but to alter it in the way I did.'

I had been to several weddings, but this night was different. I wanted it to last forever. Just as supper was about to be served, Nita sent me home in the taxi bus. This was my first brush with glamour and it sounded a chord deep in my psyche. It was a little after half past ten when I arrived home. My father had gone to bed. It was cold and the fire in the kitchen had gone out. I changed into my pyjamas, turned out the light, climbed into bed and pulled the blankets over my head for warmth. As I lay in the darkness I relived every single detail of the evening, but in my excitement I'd failed to notice the short swarthy Italian paying so much attention to my sister. When, finally, I fell asleep my mind was a kaleidoscopic wash of images which I had never previously dared to dream existed for someone like me.

※

I used to hear people saying to Beria: 'He's got the gift.' She said music was in my blood. Beria was blessed with a better than average singing voice, my Aunt Edith played the piano, and my great-aunt Nell's daughter, Dulcie Weiring, was a piano teacher in Kalgoorlie. Nita learned to play at boarding school but wouldn't practise. According to my great-aunt Gladys, my great-grandfather had a fine tenor voice and needed only a few beers to be coaxed into performing his favourite Scottish airs.

When Beria worked as a housemaid at the State Hotel, I went with her to work. There was a piano in the upstairs parlour and before I had lessons I tinkled, meaninglessly, using both hands and pretending to play. One day I picked out, with one finger, the first four bars of the Bridal March from *Lohengrin*. 'Here comes the bride.' It is only two notes – middle C and F. When Beria heard, she stopped polishing the brown linoleum in the hallway and came into the parlour. 'Who taught you to play that?' she asked. I wasn't sure if she was cross with me. 'I worked it out for myself,' I told her. She didn't seem surprised. Even when I couldn't read a note, I constantly carried around a pile of music which I studied. If we went visiting and there was a piano, I had to play. I was so keen to own a piano, I cut and saved advertisements from newspapers while trying to work out a scheme. I discovered there was an organ on the front verandah of Old Mrs White's empty house. If I put my hand through the broken and decaying latticework and pushed aside the heavy canvas cover I could touch several of the bass keys. The contact with the dusty and buckling ivory was enough to momentarily satisfy my passion.

By the time I was eleven years old, after one year of music lessons from Kay Quarti, I was able to provide the musical accompaniment for the folk dancing classes at primary school. In class I provided the accompaniment for singing lessons, playing the melody on a grey plastic tonette – a precursor to the woodwind instruments. It cost seven shillings and sixpence. Later I progressed to the recorder, which my father bought for me. Housed in a black leather box, it cost thirty shillings and was my most prized possession.

Every recess, while the other kids were running around playing games I went into the hall and practised. Most days after school I played for about an hour. Some nights, after my father had gone to bed, I balanced the music against the large tin of powdered milk and, facing the long side of the kitchen table, I imagined it to be the keyboard and I played every single note.

Lois Stevens, whose father was a well-known piano tuner in the goldfields, taught for a year at the Gwalia state school and lived at the State Hotel. She was a pianist of outstanding ability. There was a piano in the upstairs parlour on which Lois practised, and from underneath the balcony you could hear her playing. I sat on the bench outside the men's billiard parlour and listened. Lois didn't know, but sometimes I sneaked upstairs and sat on the hotel balcony. I knew better than to ask, but when it came to my music I didn't care.

My father never once heard me play, and he never talked with me about my music. Apart from Beria, no one paid any attention to it.

For Christmas Beria bought Joan a three-octave piano, which I sorely coveted but never managed to acquire. It was never played since Joan had not the slightest interest or modicum of musical talent. Eventually she broke several of the keys and hid it under the spare bed to avoid Beria's wrath.

I couldn't wait to be old enough to attend the sung midnight Mass at the Gwalia's St Francis of Assisi Church. Lucy Tognali was the organist, and Mesdames Scolari, Paravicini, Bendotti, Giovanazzi and Tagliaferri – the last of whom had an exceptional voice – sang the full 'Mass of the Angels' in Latin. In time, Mrs Bendotti was joined by her daughters Agnes and Mary. It took the choir a couple of months to learn the Mass, practising weekly in two-hour blocks. This sung Mass, in a small tin church, in an unknown and remote corner of Western Australia, with a group of women from the other side of the world, was my first exposure to the rich mellifluous sound of the brass and reed organ, and simple unison choral singing. It touched my soul, making a deep and lasting impression.

Sometimes, when I felt like it, I rode my bicycle to the cemetery, which was a couple of miles out of town along a graded dirt road. It was an isolated spot in the middle of a bush clearing, fenced around with wire, and a short distance from the base of Mount Leonora. I liked being alone in the ancient silence. The trees were stunted and sparse and there was hardly a blade of grass. It had a small lychgate and was divided into Catholic, Anglican, Methodist and Presbyterian sections. I wandered through the headstones looking at the names, especially of those men who had died on the mine. Many were familiar and some of their children still lived in Gwalia. The eight-inch diameter glass domes filled with porcelain flowers and a single white dove, all suspended on wire stems and tinted in the palest of sun-bleached hues, were in varying states of disrepair. A couple had been broken by vandals. Some of the Italian headstones were fitted with faded photographs of the deceased. These migrant men and women, who came and called this country home, were buried in the hot red ochre of an ancient landscape, light years removed from their homelands. It was the antithesis of all they had known and loved. Even the stars were different. But it was a peaceful and eternal silence in which they slept.

In September 1958 Lewie and Jean's second child was due. Like the first, it was a complicated pregnancy and a forceps birth. Jean was in hospital for several months beforehand and I went to see her a few times.

When Lewie came to see Beria, and he cried, I knew there was something wrong. I didn't say a word and tried to listen, but Beria was in no mood for me to be hanging around and I was told in no uncertain terms to scram. After Lewie left, Beria explained the baby was stillborn and was going to be buried the next day. There was no mention of me attending the funeral, which took place after the day shift on the mine. It was late evening before Beria and Steve arrived home. She didn't have any flowers but removed a red silk rose from the topcoat she was wearing and placed it in the coffin with her infant grandson.

Beria cried, which was unusual. 'He was the most beautiful baby,' she said. 'Not a mark on him, and he looked as though he was asleep.' I wanted to know more but I recognised the set of her jaw and the note of finality in the tone of her voice. It was a warning to shut up. The baby was never mentioned. He was named Luigi after his father and he sleeps in an unmarked grave in the Roman Catholic section of the cemetery.

The following year, my friend's sister, Jacqueline Bond, drowned. She was three and a half. The Bonds lived in Tower Street and had several children, including a daughter with whom I sometimes played. Jacqueline was the baby. During a flash flood the gully and the stormwater drain by the side of the house filled with water and were running at a pace. Somehow Jacqueline was caught up and swept away by the force of the current. I went to see my friend but she was unhappy and I didn't know what to say. The family placed a death notice in the *Kalgoorlie Miner*:

God wanted an Angel Queen,
That's why he took our Jacqueline. 24th April 1959.

Soon after the tragedy the Bond family packed up and left town. I had no idea they were planning to leave and when I went to visit the place was deserted. I walked through the empty rooms, wondering.

In January 1959, just four months after the death of their baby, Lewie's best friend drowned. One Saturday, Lewie and his mate

Armando Antonio Giovanni Spadanuda – Sputnik as he was known – went out for a day of shooting in the bush. To cool off on the way home they stopped at Malcolm Dam. Lewie never learned to swim but Sputnik dived in and swam around for a bit before disappearing without a sound. The policeman, Tom Clews, and one of his colleagues from Leonora made a raft out of petrol drums and spent Sunday dragging the dam without success. Lewie came to visit Beria several times during the time of the search. He was distraught and I reeled at their speculation about Sputnik's body being stuck under a ledge. At daylight on Monday a couple of volunteers threw the hook over the side and found him, first try. They said he died from cramp caused by the extreme cold water. I listened in horror to the talk of his bloated body. Spadanuda was twenty-three. His body was later exhumed and buried in Perth's Karrakatta cemetery.

The two months leading up to my sister's wedding were packed with an equal share of family drama and anticipation. My father took me to Steve the tailor for my first single-breasted suit. I chose a black wool fabric with a fine dark green fleck. It was my first pair of long trousers, and on the day I felt uncomfortable and self-conscious. Nita gave me a wax orange blossom for my buttonhole.

My father was puzzled by Nita's sudden resolve to rush headlong into this marriage. He made it obvious he disapproved of the engagement and pleaded with her to reconsider. When he was unable to sway Nita he employed his own tactics, and without warning or justification he refused to sign the official marriage papers. Since Nita was only nineteen, she couldn't marry without his permission. His lack of cooperation made life very difficult.

Frank Mafrici didn't attempt to discuss his and Nita's plans with my father, choosing to leave the dispute to her. One night while we were having tea Nita tried to talk to him again. My father was so annoyed he grabbed his plate and cutlery and threw them onto the nearby bench. The knife flew in the air and bounced off Nita's shoulder. He was most apologetic, which gave Nita the upper hand for the moment. He blamed me.

Realising my father was not about to give in, Nita went to see Beria. Unaware of my father's opposition and the ongoing tension, she signed the papers, believing it to be a mere formality. When my father and Beria discussed the situation he was upset by Nita's duplicitous behaviour and threatened a boycott of the wedding, going so far as to say he wouldn't give her away. In my naivety, I offered to take his place, which was not what she wanted to hear. Finally, at the eleventh hour, he relented in time to race his daughter down the aisle.

In an oversight, Lewie and Jean weren't sent an invitation, and were most offended. Nita assumed, given their childhood closeness, that Lewie would be there anyway, with or without an invitation. In the event, a stand-off developed and showed all the signs of it developing into an ugly, full-blown family row. There was a lot of blustering, and the stand-off continued while Lewie's and Nita's degrees of hurt were hotly debated. In the end, Nita and Frank went to visit and the invitation squabble was resolved.

I went to Mass for three consecutive weeks to hear Father Tobin read the wedding bans. Nita and I sat separately. The sombre season of Lent fell in March and their wedding date was considered an unusual choice. The priest wore violet vestments, the altar was stripped, statues and holy pictures were draped in black, and flowers were not permitted in the church. The more pedantic priests insisted bridal bouquets be left at the door. In my enthusiasm I sought Father Tobin's permission to allow flowers in the church and was so delighted when he agreed I rushed home to share the good news with Nita, who was none too pleased. 'It's none of your business,' was her ill-natured reaction. I was crushed by the ferocity of her surliness, which over the years had been a major contributing factor to our enmity.

On the day before the wedding I decorated the communion rails with fern, and several dozen hand-made crepe paper roses which I borrowed from Mrs Bendotti.

Nita Lillian Rocchecioli married Franco Mafrici at five o'clock on Thursday, 5 March 1959, in the Gwalia Catholic Church of St Francis of Assisi. The temperature was 105 degrees and the inside of the tin church was like an inferno. It had twelve rows of wooden pews, a side lady altar with a statue of Our Lady of the Immaculate Conception, and the stations of the cross hung in brown wooden frames. Two rows from the back, under a grey sailcloth cover, was a pedal harmonium stacked with dog-eared albums of Allan's Melodious Voluntaries for American Organ, and musty novena hymnals. The baptismal font was in the porch, above which was a framed portrait of Pope John XXIII.

It was a white wedding and my sister wore the same dress she had worn for the debutante ball, but with a long machine-embroidered tulle veil held in place by a small flat hat of white satin. It was too hot for fresh flowers, besides which there was no florist in the town, and she carried a bouquet of pale pink and white waxed-paper roses. The bridesmaids had a matching smaller version, and Mrs Bendotti made their dresses. After the wedding I asked Nita if I could keep the bouquet but she ended up throwing it in the bin. Gino Passeri was the best man. 'Pity he's not the groom,' Beria commented.

Beria lived near the church, and walked there with my sister Joan. Steve was working and saw no reason to take the day off. After the service, Beria went home to meet him and together they came to the breakfast and reception. Beria wore a pale pink and white, rose-patterned flock-nylon dress with a deep square neckline, a ruche insert, puffed sleeves and a full circle skirt. She didn't wear a hat, gloves or stockings. Joan wore her pink silk organza party dress, with black patent leather shoes and white socks.

From the moment Nita arrived at the church and throughout the entire service I cried, uncontrollably. My father tried to console me but I couldn't be comforted. The sonorous tone of the organ only made me feel worse. Before the wedding I bought several yards of white satin ribbon and lace at Mazza's store and, alone in the evening, I sat at the kitchen table, cutting and binding a cardboard horseshoe before affixing various ribbons and appropriate hand-made decorations which I copied from a bridal book. As the newlyweds were leaving the church, Joan and I each gave Nita a satin horseshoe. As she took it from me I realised she would be gone from the house forever, and as much as we fought I hated the idea and began to sob once more. Clearly taken aback by my level of distress, Nita hugged me for the first and only time in her life.

At about six-thirty the bridal party arrived for the wedding breakfast at my father's house in Tower Street. The front room, which was usually empty of furniture, had been set up with a couple of kitchen tables and chairs and set with cutlery and china, some of which was borrowed from friends. Alma Mazza and Shirley Dwyer, the wife of the Leonora policeman, served the wedding breakfast of chicken and salad and wine trifle. Mrs Chamberlain made and decorated the traditional wedding fruitcake. Even though Beria and Nita saw each other most days, Beria did nothing to assist with the preparation, not even on the day. And she made it clear when she learned Nita was having a baby: 'I'm telling you now, don't come and ask me to babysit for you, because I won't.' Nita never asked, and Beria never offered.

Nita and Frank paid for everything, including the reception for forty or so people in the Leonora Hall. It was a traditional country wedding, with dancing and supper. Frank ordered from Kalgoorlie four large boxes of small mixed cakes, pies and sausage rolls. It was the first time I tasted a Napoleon slice. Beria spent much of the night circulating in the hall, pouring beer from a glass jug. When the beer supply ran out, Frank organised another keg. It all came to an end at around eleven o'clock.

Despite my father's constant reassurance, I sensed my circumstances were about to alter, and not necessarily for the better. For almost two years I had known real security, but over the years there had been countless broken promises and I learned it was safer to wait and see. My intuition was right. A few months after the wedding my father sold his house to Lewie and Jean. It was a repeat of the old story. They had a child, Trevor, and as they moved in I was moved out. In about June, and without discussion I was sent to live nearby with Nita and Frank. It was where I stayed until I went away to boarding school in the following January.

∞

The food was good in Gwalia, and there was no shortage of excellent cooks and caterers. Alma Mazza, Eileen Major, Shirley Dwyer and Doreen Clough accepted paying jobs. Lucy Taylor, renowned for the quality and taste of her food, cooked out of the goodness of her heart. You provided the ingredients and she provided the labour. When Lena Beccaria married Jacky Prince, Lena's mother, Rose, had walked out on the family, and with no one to help her Lena had no idea what to do. When Mrs Taylor heard about it she took over, arranging the whole thing. On the night before her wedding Lena and her father plucked and cleaned five chooks which they took around to Mrs Taylor to cook for the wedding breakfast. Lena had no idea Mrs Taylor was ill, and only a few months after the wedding she died from cancer. Often when I went to the cemetery I read her headstone: 'God's finger touched her and she slept.'

Dot Mathews and Lesley Bowden not only baked, but they also decorated square, round and heart-shaped fruitcakes. They worked in the cool throughout the night to prevent the icing sugar setting in their hands, moulding and creating clusters of pastel roses and yellow-centred violets which cascaded across the top and down the side of the cake. They used an eyedropper to measure the food colouring into the icing. The fine-piped filigree and rosettes were crowned with silver cashews. The cake was brushed with raw egg white and spread thick with hand-made marzipan icing, on top of which the royal icing, made from a mixture of powdered icing sugar, lemon juice and raw egg whites, dried to a smooth, hard, matte finish. They created delicate rosebuds on the ends of toothpicks, which they pushed into the cake. The two- and three-tier elaborately decorated works of art stood on white icing-sugar columns.

When Pearl Hay married Gino Passeri, Shirley Dwyer made and decorated the three-tier cake. It was sitting in the lounge room at Mrs Hay's house when a red dust storm went through, leaving the white icing with a pale pink tinge.

In the summer the catering was hot, arduous work and apart from the pies, pasties and sausage rolls, nothing was cooked in advance. The facilities in the three Leonora and Gwalia halls were basic. Water was boiled in a copper and the domestic range of black English Aga stoves were small. Despite the limitations, the cooking was done while the dance or wedding reception was in progress. The mountain of food went from the stove to the table. The kitchen sent out bowls and platters of savouries, salmon mornay, roast chicken, curried eggs, cheese straws, sandwiches with fillings of every description, sponge cakes filled with tinned cream and apricot or plum jam and topped with cream and crushed jelly, passionfruit sponge fingers, rich moist fruitcake and my favourite – traditional wine trifle made from slices of Swiss roll, thick custard, tinned peaches, sliced banana, desiccated coconut and a liberal splash of muscat. When Jack Bell, the owner of Clover Downs sheep station, married for the second time he had crayfish flown in from Geraldton, 200 miles away.

The halls had a separate room for the kegs of beer and bottles of soft drink. There were no fridges and bottles were kept in tin tubs or 44-gallon drums filled with water and ice. The barman filled the glass jugs and a couple of people wandered around topping up everyone's glass. Beria always drank a shandy. Two was about her limit, and only once did I see her tiddly. Lewie, Beria and Steve went to the State Hotel for a Sunday afternoon session. Later, back home, Beria tried to fry us some eggs for tea but was so confused she put the shells in the pan and threw the eggs into the fire. I was sitting at the kitchen table with Lewie, who was watching Beria and trying to work out why she was digging around in the hot coals with the egg slice. When he asked, she was giggling so much she couldn't get the words out. Laughing, he pushed her out of the way and took over the cooking.

∞

I taught myself to cook on a wood stove after Nita got married and I was living with my father. I was eleven and baked a moist date cake from a recipe of my own invention. I used a round tin with a royal crown pressed into the base which could be filled with jam and tinned cream when the cake was turned-out. There is something about the taste of food cooked in the oven of a wood-burning stove and I learned quickly how to work the fire and control the temperature. My father was an exceptional cook and was proud of his European heritage. 'If the Italians hadn't come here and showed the Poms good food, they'd be running around naked, eating lizards.' His Sunday lunch rigatoni was 'fantastico'. He cooked the sauce in a battered heavy aluminium saucepan, using a pound of medium chopped rump steak, two brown onions and a small bottle of Rosella tomato sauce. The sauce was dark and thick, and when it simmered the bubbles were so heavy it looked like a mud pool. He served it with lots of freshly grated Romano cheese, which melted in the heat of the pasta and dripped down your chin.

Every day after school I began the preparations for our evening meal. I lit the fire using petrol-doused cotton waste, filled the kettle and put it on to boil for my father's pot of tea, then peeled the potatoes and shelled the peas or strung the beans. As I became more confident in the kitchen I began to experiment. I'd watched my father prepare the meat sauce many times but I was uncertain about cooking the spaghetti. The first time was a disaster. The pasta had been boiling for an hour when he arrived home from work. My father never wasted food and was annoyed when he peered into the bubbling saucepan, filled to capacity with stewed spaghetti. We ate it in stony silence and I was hurt by my father's surliness.

When Nita and Frank moved house, they had a clean-out and I lost all my primary school books, dozens of beautifully illustrated Italian holy cards, an irreplaceable pile of sheet music, school reports and various certificates from the Gould Bird League and the Boy Scouts. The greatest loss was my suitcase of used Christmas cards, which Beria and I had collected for five years. A number of ladies in the town knew about my hobby and in the second or third week in January I was inundated with cards. Mrs Bailey gave me a pile of cards which smelled strongly of cloves. It was a smell which I didn't know but which added to the cards' beauty and forever reminded me of her.

Many of the elaborately decorated Christmas cards were imported from England and featured northern hemisphere images of the Christian festival. The European snow scenes were often heavily encrusted with layers of silver glass-glitter and tied with watermarked silk or satin ribbons. I had cards with almond-eyed Persian kittens and Scottish terrier puppies wearing tartan ribbons popping cutely out of wicker baskets; superbly laid Victorian dining tables, glowing by candlelight and groaning under the weight of a Dickensian Christmas feast; thick, hand-cut and folded watermarked parchment protecting elaborately designed pop-up views of nativity scenes; and ornate baskets filled to brimming with delicate pansies, roses, carnations and lily of the valley. Others were cut into pop-up shapes of silver Christmas bells, bluebirds and robin redbreasts, candles and even a steaming, round plum pudding topped with a sprig of holly. Some were protected by double sheets of gossamer tissue paper.

My collection of about a thousand cards was lovingly stored in a battered, fabric-covered overnight suitcase, and stacked in perfect piles according to size and type. In the darkest moments I retreated into my own little world. Alone, I spent hours sitting on my bedroom floor, sorting through and savouring the beauty. I never tired of them. They brought me great comfort and abiding happiness; they calmed my soul in moments of profound misery, and were my simple initiation to the exciting and fascinating world of art.

The small park with playground equipment between the State Hotel and the railway station was a welcome refuge, offering both shade and cool. It was built specially for the kids, and apart from the beer garden at the State Hotel was the only grassed public meeting place in the town. We spent hours hanging upside down from the monkey bars and watching each other's faces turn red, or sitting on the seesaw, talking and trying to bump each other off. In the early evening it became the meeting place for the older boys and girls, and for romance to blossom. The fluorescent blue light on top of the centre pole was turned out at nine o'clock. The older kids knew that Mollie Nye, who lived opposite, spied on them from her front verandah, and then told tales.

A couple of weeks before Christmas, a working party of men transformed the park into a wonderland which became the focal point for all the kids in the town except the Aborigines – they were excluded. The putting-up of the tree and the hanging of the lights took several days. The annual ritual hardly altered. A working party went into the nearby bush and felled a suitable tree. The sight of Ike Nye's old utility arriving with a tree on the back brought the kids running. I stared in awe as they strapped the native pine tree to the light pole and decorated it with coloured 75-watt globes. Four overhead strings of coloured lights ran from the gold star at the top of the tree to the corners of the park. After the street arches in Perth erected for the Queen's visit, it was the most thrilling thing I had seen, ever. In the two weeks leading up to Christmas the coloured lights were turned on every night at sunset, and the park was filled with kids. The oasis of twinkling lights in the park shone as dazzlingly as the star of Bethlehem at the first Christmas. It never failed to warm my heart.

Christmas Eve in the park was a night for the children, with as much Peter's ice-cream and ginger beer as we could consume. Kids, their faces scrubbed to shining, arrived with their parents. The excitement was palpable. A stampede followed when the word went out: 'Father Christmas is coming!'

We all pushed forward to the cyclone-wire double gates of the park as the fire engine, with its brass bell ringing, pulled up at the side entrance. As he climbed down off the truck Father Christmas was swamped. Once order was restored, we waited our turn for the distribution of presents; the anticipation was almost too great to bear. Grouped by age, we passed along in front of Father Christmas, seated on a throne behind a rope barrier and distributing his largesse with a lot of good-will and much ho-ho-ho-ing. Magically, he knew the name of every kid. My curiosity was pricked when a pillow fell out from underneath his red coat and was hastily retrieved and shoved back into position.

The night was organised through the mine, and paid for with donations from the men. Every year Beria threatened to boycott the evening, complaining at length how the value of the gift I received was far less than the one pound contribution Steve made on my behalf. My father also paid for me but never attended.

I said nothing to Beria, but came to realise there was no Father Christmas when Steve, with a couple of drinks under his belt, recognised one of his gambling mates hidden behind the wig and cottonwool beard, and started shouting out to him. Even with his heavy Slavic accent and broken English, he revealed to everyone within earshot the identity of the man behind the faded and battered costume.

By Christmas of 1957 I was living with my father and Nita. Christmas Eve came and went without mention, and the Christmas tree in the park became a thing of the past. Beria and Steve still took Joan, but I wasn't included.

One afternoon in 1958 I was riding my bike with Joan sitting on the crossbar, something I did often. Blink, her dog, was running beside us when he jumped at Joan, causing me to swerve and lose control. Joan fell into the dirt and skidded, hitting her head against a large rock sheltering a water meter. The next-door neighbour, Mrs Grudniski, was a nurse and came running when she heard our screaming. She cleaned the wound, and although she knew it wasn't serious she had her husband drive Beria and Joan to the hospital, leaving me behind to wait with Blink. Joan was only three and I was convinced she was going to die.

I was sick with fear at what Steve would say. When he arrived home from work, Joan was waiting. With her head swathed in a crepe bandage, which exaggerated the injury, she ran to him. 'It wasn't Ronnie's fault, Dad,' she reassured him. 'Blink did it.' Steve listened to Beria without saying a word, all the while eyeing me threateningly.

※

Depending on how many she killed and ate, Beria always had about forty chooks – a mix of First Cross, Black Orpington, Rhode Island Red and Plymouth Rock, and always one, occasionally two, contented roosters. Invariably she'd kill and eat one of the roosters: 'It's too much trouble having two roosters in the chookhouse. They're always fighting and picking at each other's combs until they bleed. I had a couple of them fight to the death once.'

While I lived with Beria much of our time was spent feeding the chooks with a mixture of shell grit and laying pellets, pollard and bran in the morning, scattering their wheat at night, collecting the eggs, changing their water, and letting them out in the morning and locking them in at sunset. They wandered around the flat, scratched in the hops and weeds, and took regular sand baths. At the first sign of danger they'd come squawking through the hole into the chookhouse.

The favourites were given names. Polly the pet bantam hen lived well into old age and followed Beria around the yard, standing just inches away while she pegged out the washing. Oscar, the part dingo dog, who suffered from eczema on his snout, hated the chooks running free in the yard. Beria trained him to round them up, issuing him commands like a sheep handler. She could spot an ailing chook from a hundred yards. 'No, don't touch that one,' she called to Oscar, 'it's sick.' Oscar understood everything and would leave the ailing hen standing in the middle of the yard, alone and looking forlorn.

Beria didn't care if the work was dirty, and used her bare hands for everything. Every second day she raked and collected the manure for the vegetable garden. The chooks' main water container was a large camp oven which she bought new for the kitchen but it turned rusty. The water was laced with a tablespoon of Condy's crystals, a natural disinfectant which turned the water pale purple. Chooks feel the heat, and in the hot weather she filled a four-foot square tray with three or four inches of water so they could cool their feet and splash around. They had four or five laying nests which Beria lined with old jumpers and chaff bags and cleaned out each week. She kept a marble egg in each nest, which discouraged them from finding new laying spots. Apart from wheat, and the warm mixture of pollard and bran, Beria fed them all the household scraps. A pale yolk always got the same reaction: 'These chooks haven't been getting enough greens!'

Every month Beria examined the hens and checked the chookhouse for ticks and lice. It was a joint effort and we had great fun. The chooks made a hell of a racket, squawking and flapping as I chased and caught them. Beria did nothing by half-measures, vigorously rubbing under their wings with her home-made mixture of dripping and kerosene, killing any blood-sucking parasites. Beria's father-in-law, Mirko, gave her a heavily infested bantam hen. In a matter of days the ticks wiped out part of her run. Boy, did she give him a telling-off! If she came across an infested bird she quarantined it and nursed it back to health. She poured boiling water along the iron and wooden roosting perches and tied a kerosene-soaked rag at either end to stop the ticks from moving around.

Only once in all those years did Beria forget to lock up the chookhouse at sunset. The foxes came during the night. Steve had been on the afternoon shift but said he was too tired to check when he heard the noise. When she went out next morning Beria was greeted by the sight of forty dead Rhode Island Reds scattered around the yard and across the flat. The foxes killed and drank the blood but left the carcasses. She tried cooking one but it was tasteless so she burned the lot. It was a huge financial loss for her.

Beria was always running an eye around the chookhouse: 'Catch that one for me,' she would say impatiently, pointing. 'No, not that one, the other one. Bring it here; it's constipated.' I had to hold its beak open while she poured a dose of castor oil down its throat. A day later the chook would be running around in perfect health. On Sunday morning she would choose the chook for midday dinner. 'That one there,' she'd say, pointing. 'She's egg-bound.' Sure enough, when Beria put in her hand and pulled out the gizzards: 'See? What did I tell you?' When it came to chooks, Beria was never wrong.

Occasionally, and mostly for my benefit, Beria agreed to set a clucky hen. One of the regular nests would be prepared, usually an old drum, and the hen would be set on a dozen eggs, all carefully dated with an indelible pencil which you wet with the end of your tongue before writing. For two weeks we watched and waited as the bad-tempered sitter turned her eggs, and pecked at us when we attempted to check on her clutch. The sight of the skinny, blood-covered chicks breaking their way out of the shell was magical. Within seconds they staggered to their feet and within the hour were transformed into chirping balls of yellow fluff. It was a dangerous time, and you had to watch the mother didn't sit on them. Beria helped any newborns which had trouble breaking free from the shell. She was skilled and gentle when it came to the hatching of chickens. When the umbilical cord stuck to the mucous membrane inside the shell it required a delicate and dangerous procedure. If you pulled too hard they bled to death. The following day was my favourite: the sight of the hen with her brood all following behind, chirping nervously.

Once a year Beria took delivery of one hundred week-old chicks. We spent several days building the makeshift incubator, constructed from two small rainwater tank halves pushed together and lined with jumpers, blankets and dozens of two-inch strips of flannel undershirt. The strips, which reached to the floor and trapped the heat, were tied to pieces of dowelling placed at intervals across the top. A kerosene hurricane lamp sat in the centre of the incubator and burned day and night.

The chicks came by train from Kalgoorlie in specially made cardboard boxes divided into sections packed with fine straw. The sound of a hundred chirping chicks in cardboard boxes is deafening. Unpacking them, one at a time, Beria inspected and then placed them inside the incubator. I always hoped for a sickly one. Beria carefully wrapped it in a jumper and settled it in a shoe box, which she placed on the open oven door for warmth. I checked every five minutes to make sure it was still alive. Beria kept the fire going all night and rarely did they die. 'Ronnie, will you leave that chicken alone?' she said repeatedly. 'How many times do I have to tell you? You're going to kill the bloody thing with kindness.'

The first time the three-month-old chicks were allowed to run free was chaotic as they discovered the joys of scratching in the dirt. They escaped into the paddock through fence holes we didn't know existed. Trying to catch them was great fun and we both laughed a lot. The little yellow bundles of fluff twisted and turned, making it nigh on impossible to grab a hold. As you held the terrified chick in your cupped hand, peering into their beady eyes, you could feel their tiny hearts thumping like bass drums: bah-boom, bah-boom.

For Beria, the birds weren't only food, they were also a means of earning money which, unfortunately, Steve always took from her. She fed them four or five times a day on a diet of finely chopped hard-boiled eggs, lettuce and cooked meat. She checked on them at all hours of the day and night. Not even the freezing night temperatures stopped her. Wearing only her nightie, she would climb out of bed and head outside to the garage. If there was a problem she might be there for an hour, and of the hundred chicks only one, at worst two, died. About 80 per cent of the chooks would be fattened, killed and dressed, and sold at Christmas for £1 each. Roosters make for better eating and one year Beria raised a hundred of them. Beria's chooks were the most popular and best tasting in the town. There was no question: What Beria didn't know about chooks wasn't worth knowing.

It was never talked about, but everyone, even the kids, accepted that sometimes men on the mine got killed. Giuseppe Scolari was a huge bear of a man who never failed to make a fuss of me, and I never passed up an opportunity to seek out his company. He had a sedan car, and if I saw him working on it I went to stand and watch, and chat.

In December 1958, only a week from Christmas, Mr Scolari was injured. He and Andy Fassanini were working together out at Two-Mile Wells, the water storage area for the mine. Mr Scolari was working at the bottom of the well, while Fassanini was lowering a supply of nine by two foot solid jarrah beams. It is thought the timber snagged on the wall of the shaft, the rope slipped, and the beam fell away. Trying to warn him, Fassanini called to Mr Scolari, who popped his head out from his protective shelter and was struck full force by the falling beam. It smashed through his helmet and opened his skull. I was paralysed with horror at the talk of being able to see his brain.

His son Peter was an eighteen-year-old apprentice on the mine. Each day the apprentices would gather outside the office of the mine engineer, Bill Jordan, in anticipation of the midday whistle, waiting to leap onto their bikes for the ride home. It was Eric

Omodei who, in the minutes before the whistle, broke the news to Peter: 'Your dad's had an accident.'

Peter spoke first to Bill Jordan, who had no information, and then rode home to tell his mother, Rina. They drove to the Leonora hospital and were surprised to find them still waiting for the patient to arrive. When Peter and Mrs Scolari arrived back at Two-Mile Wells, somewhere between thirty and forty-five minutes after the accident, they were still bringing Mr Scolari to the surface on a stretcher. Peter was held back from the scene by the mine staff, who considered his father's head injuries so horrendous he should not see them.

Eric Omodei, who helped with the recovery of Mr Scolari's body, was climbing the ladder and keeping pace with the stretcher as they hauled him to the surface. Several times the injured man reached and grabbed onto a rung of the ladder, and Eric was unable to break his grip. Mr Scolari came from Albino, a village in Lombardy, and in a moment of desperation Eric began talking with him in his guttural Bergamasque dialect. Miraculously, Mr Scolari responded, releasing his hold.

In the ambulance on the way to Kalgoorlie, Mr Scolari was attended by Dr Peter Halley and his wife, who was also a doctor. Lewie drove and he covered the 147 miles over the unsealed corrugated road in less than two hours. Peter, his mother and two sisters, Roma and Enis, followed in the family car. Giuseppe Scolari died and was buried in Kalgoorlie.

The inquest was held in Leonora. There was a special procedure set down for mining deaths. It was a first experience for policeman Tom Clews.

When being questioned, he said: 'The piece of timber probably slipped through the rope.'

The coroner chastised him.

'You can't say that. You're not an expert.'

In 1957 I joined the children's branch of the United Ancient Order of Druids, run by old man Leaney and Eric Omodei. We met every Thursday night at a hall in Tower Street, Leonora, next door to Mrs Ansley's house where I was once sent to live. The Gwalia contingent of members gathered at the designated meeting point from where we were collected in Bob Howard's Volkswagen Kombi van taxi bus. The Lodge, with all its surrounding paraphernalia, was a mystery but I loved the theatrics. We marched around, sang songs and conducted a meeting with a strict running order and rigid protocol. At the end of the night we played a form of carpet bowls, using a full complement of snooker balls.

The Leonora chapter of the Druids was a Fun Branch of the Order for boys and girls. It was non–denominational, and we learned the symbolism of the colours, the Equality of the daffodil, the principle virtues of Equity, Integrity and Obedience, and the Seven Precepts of Merlin, which led you to lead a happy and fulfilled life. Through duty to God, country, family and oneself, and strict Obedience – the password of our chapter – you became a good neighbour.

As part of the rigmarole, the office bearers wore specific broad collars which wrapped around the nape of their necks and hung on their chests like the ears of a cocker spaniel. These padded decorative collars were made from burgundy velvet, elaborately embroidered with gold and silver thread and fastened with a gold plaited chest cord and a French knot.

I was appointed Door Keeper, whose responsibility was to check all members leaving and arriving. If a member arrived late they had to satisfy me they were bona fide and, most importantly, knew the password. A knock at the door had me calling loudly to the chair:

'An alarm at the door, Worthy Arch.' Whereupon he commanded me: 'See who knocks, Brother Rocchiccioli.' It was my job to slide open the hatch, peer into the face of the latecomer, demand their name, slam the hatch shut in their face, and report back: 'Brother Smith knocks, Worthy Arch.' Once more I was commanded: 'Check for the password, Brother Rocchiccioli.' Again I would slide open the hatch and demand of them the password. 'Obedience,' would come the frantic reply. Again the hatch would slam shut and everyone waited as I turned to face the chair: 'Password correct, Worthy Arch.' Then the final command from the chair: 'Brother Rocchiccioli, admit Brother Smith.'

I went to and from these Druid meetings with a girl who lived opposite and was several years older. She was pretty and dark-haired, with large breasts, all of which made her popular with the young men. She wasn't unaware of her physical attributes, or of their potential to attract attention. One night as we were walking home she seemed unusually excited as we approached the turn-off a short distance from home. 'I have to go and meet someone,' she said. 'Come with me.' We walked a short distance to the entrance of a deserted back lane used only by the night cart. It was about nine o'clock on a cold winter night, and most houses were already in darkness. Lurking in the shadows was a young man I recognised and knew to be her boyfriend. He was about sixteen, shortish with a solid physique, and an apprentice on the mine. 'Wait here,' she whispered, and went to meet him. They started a lot of eager kissing and cuddling and then crouched down on the ground. In the moonlight I could see clearly what was happening. They were only feet away from the lavatory. She sat on the ground and lay back against the galvanised iron and wire fence of the chookhouse with her legs apart and her skirt up around her chest. He unzipped his fly and pulled down his trousers and underpants, neither of which he removed. He had done this before, mostly in the back row at the picture theatre, surrounded by his mates. There was a bit of manoeuvring between her legs and some anxious whispering before he got himself into position and bounced up and down for a time. It all came to a quick and dramatic finale with an erratic and extended groan. In a few seconds he was on his feet, pulled up his trousers, zipped his fly and disappeared into the night. As we made our way home she seemed a little upset by the whole incident. I promised never to tell.

The young man who lived in the house on the side of the hill on the way to the pool fancied himself as something of a stud. His silver and black Gold Flash 650cc motorbike was the pride of his existence. He had lived in Gwalia for a couple of years and was one of the ringleaders of the harmless local mafiosi, all of whom worked and socialised together and went for meals at Mrs Patroni's boarding house, a short walk away. Each Saturday night he and his mates could be found at the pictures. Wearing the stylish Italian suits they brought with them when they arrived, they were the best dressed guys in the town and were always circling, in search of vulnerable prey.

A little after three o'clock on a scorching Saturday afternoon, the mercury was hovering at about 105 degrees in the shade. The house had no fence and he was out the front tinkering with his bike when he saw my fifteen-year-old friend on the other side of the road, heading for the pool. She was wearing a skirt and her bathers and it was hard to miss her breasts bursting out over the top of her swimsuit. As she drew level he called her over. She walked across the road, and when he invited her inside she accepted.

After a short while she left, and five minutes later arrived at the pool in a highly distressed state. Through tears, she regaled Peggy Garbellini and two older girlfriends with a detailed description of the encounter, claiming to have been raped. They sympathised and offered their support. Her grief passed and within half an hour she was in the water laughing, shouting and having an enjoyable time. The alleged rape was never reported to the police and she and the alleged rapist remained on the most friendly of terms.

Mad Mullocker's camp in the main street was set a distance back from the road, next door to old Mrs Varischetti, who was a friend of Beria's we often visited.

Mad Mullocker was unconventional, to say the least. He once painted everything green, including his cutlery and the tree trunks. At Mazza's shop he bought whatever they offered him. His dilapidated front fence was made from scrap rusting tin and wire and protected an abundance of glistening bright green and white striped watermelons and perfectly rounded pale-skinned rockmelons. Freshly watered, they could be smelt from yards away, and while they were visible from the street they remained out of arm's reach. Every season it was the same pantomime. At all hours of the day and night young lads tried to pinch them. It became a summer challenge, something to help pass the time. Rarely were the melon bandits successful. Mad Mullocker guarded his crop ferociously and kept a handy supply of pelting-rocks.

When Mad Mullocker moved on, Giovanni Longa eventually moved into the camp. Longa was instantly recognisable from his bowed legs. After years of working in cramped and wet underground conditions, his knees had locked into position, causing him a most peculiar gait. Rather unfortunately, his eyes weren't aligned either and seemed to lead lives independent of each other.

I was a healthy kid, but in the second half of 1956 I suffered a severely ulcerated mouth and, after a week of not being able to eat, Beria sent me to present myself at the hospital surgery. The doctor took one look inside my mouth, called for Matron Corner, prescribed a six-hourly course of intra-muscular penicillin injections and admitted me. He examined me thoroughly and later told my father the ulcers were caused by stress and a sustained lack of nutrition. I was the only patient in the children's ward and the doctor or the matron checked my mouth every six hours for three or four days.

My stay in hospital coincided with a shortage of qualified nursing staff in the goldfields, and Matron Corner was allowed to train several nursing aides, including Pamela Le Feuvre, to administer injections. The white liquid penicillin was given with a glass syringe fitted with a steel needle, which was sterilised and re-used. It looked frightening resting in a white enamel kidney bowl. Pamela and my sister-in-law Jean were sisters. I had known Pamela for much of my life and having her look after me and give the injections was reassuring.

I was hospitalised for ten days. My father and Lewie and Jean came to see me but Beria didn't, and no arrangements had been made to collect me. It was hot. I walked along the bike track through Halfway Creek, shortening the distance to Gwalia, and arrived home exhausted. It was midday. Steve was at the pub for the Sunday morning session and Beria was at the stove cooking risotto. She turned around as I walked into the kitchen. 'Oh hello,' she said. 'You're home then.'

∽

I wasn't a fussy eater, and although I never went hungry I suffered from malnutrition. Jean was the only one who prepared a balanced diet daily. Beria served mostly meat and potatoes.

In late November 1959, my immune system collapsed from a vitamin deficiency and I broke out in debilitating boils and carbuncles. Again, the doctor prescribed a course of penicillin. I was living with Nita and my diet was poor. For months I had eaten no vegetables and was surviving on packets of Maggi chicken-noodle soup with bread and butter, tomato and white onion sandwiches, pasta with meat and tomatoes, potatoes, some fruit, and Weetbix. For the second time in my life, I was acutely malnourished.

The flow of bodily poison from the cluster of four boils on the outside of my right wrist was so severe I couldn't stand without vomiting and the doctor was forced to strap my arm against my body in a sling. The moment it was removed from the sling and allowed to hang by my side I felt nauseous and needed to lie down. Despite the seriousness, I wasn't left to recover in bed. Nita played weekend softball and a match was scheduled in Leonora. I went with her to look after her baby boy, walking the two miles to and from Leonora, with Nita pushing the pram. My head ached and I barely survived the afternoon.

Twice daily Nita bathed the four pustules on my arm and the one on my right leg in warm salt water. It was weeks before they showed any sign of clearing. The abscesses were grossly distended, and squeezing and bursting them was excruciating. I screamed at the slightest pressure. The painful carbuncle on my leg caused me to walk with a limp. When it burst, the oozing pus and blood were putrid, and it continued to suppurate for several days after the core detached. It healed, leaving a circular scar the size of a sixpenny piece.

I was so ill I missed school and my father became concerned about the state of my health. Jean had long felt my care and diet were inadequate. When the doctor told my father I needed more vegetables and nourishing food, it was Jean who insisted I join them for the evening meal. She was an excellent cook, and every night I ate a nutritious meal with a variety of fresh vegetables. I flourished, and ate like a horse.

∞

Christmas Day 1958 was a real scorcher – up to 112 degrees. The night before, Beria and Steve, together with Lewie and Jean, took Joan and Trevor to the Christmas tree in the park. Joan was nearly four years old and Beria bought her a pink silk-organza dress from Garratt's in Leonora. It was made in England and cost £8. Trevor, who was the same age as Joan, took one look at her in the party dress, grabbed her by the hand and said, seriously: 'Don't worry, Joan. I won't let them laugh at you!'

On Christmas morning, while Beria was cooking the chook for midday dinner, Steve nicked off to see his mate, Ron Harris. He was the train driver on the wood line and married to Beria's friend, Audrey, who taught at the state school. Between them they drank a bottle of Scotch whisky with milk. When Steve staggered back at around midday he could hardly stand up. Beria had never seen him so drunk. He was helpless. He tried to lie down on the double bed on the front verandah but kept falling off onto the cement floor. Twice she picked him up, the third time she left him, lying in his own vomit. 'Bloody well stay there.' When Steve sobered up he turned nasty and gave Beria one hell of a hiding. She was still black and blue a month later. It's the only time the extensive bruising was clearly visible.

On Christmas afternoon I went with Lewie and Jean to see Beria and to collect my present. Beria was in the kitchen when we arrived, crying. 'I can't put up with this anymore,' she told them. I went and sat in the sewing room, which had no door and was off the kitchen. When Beria came looking for me she realised I had been listening to every word they said. She gave me a hug.

'I hate him, Mum,' I said to her. 'And I just want to kill him.'

'So do I sweetheart,' she responded, trying to make it a joke, 'but like I always say, he's not worth hanging for.'

Slowly but surely my world was changing. I had one more year of primary school and already my father was talking about me 'going away to college'. A few weeks earlier, in October, His Holiness, Pope Pius XII, died. The news of the Holy Father's death filtered through to me some days later, when I was playing tennis with a friend on the dirt court at the state school. It was like a bolt from heaven. I didn't know what to think. Pius XII had been the pope for my entire life. I knew people died, but I had never considered the possibility he could die and there could be another pontiff. I had revered the portraits of the thin man in the embroidered papal robes, wearing little round steel-rimmed glasses, with his hand raised in a blessing. The next morning at Mass the priest wore black vestments, and the altar and statues were draped. Nita and I went together but I wasn't allowed to sit with her. Even when we walked to and from church she made a point of staying either in front of me or behind me. A month later it was announced we had another Pope, John XXIII. The priest hung his picture in the entrance to the church, and everything was normal again.

Come July 1959, Nita was seven months pregnant. Lewie and Jean had moved into the house with my father, and now I was living with Nita and Frank. My friend, Robert Guild, lived in Tower Street, and as I did most Sunday afternoons I called round to see him. I went round to the back of the house and found him sitting on the doorstep. We talked for a bit and when he got up I followed him into the kitchen. Mr Guild was standing near the fire watching as Robert's mother Anne struggled to prepare a family meal. I hardly recognised her. She didn't speak and barely acknowledged I was there. Her face was almost completely black, and her light red hair was matted with a combination of fresh and congealed blood.

On the previous night, in another one of his drunken rages, Mr Guild had given her a belting. Her skull was cracked open and she seemed to be having trouble moving. My stomach started churning in the same way it did when Steve bashed Beria. I stayed for only a short time and, desperate to help, I ran across the flat to Nita and begged her to visit. She was reluctant, but finally agreed to walk the short distance to their house.

Anne was a thin, fragile woman, who was battered regularly by her alcoholic husband. She suffered broken bones and ribs, facial cuts and abrasions, and seemingly permanent deep bruising to her face and body. During one beating he punched her so hard in the face he smashed her denture, part of which she swallowed. The couple had two children, a girl and my friend Robert. One day at school, a couple of years later, Robert broke down during recess. 'My mum's in the hospital, and I don't think I'm going to have her for much longer.'

In the following days came the news Anne was dead. She was thirty-five.

It was a foregone conclusion that, like Nita, I too would be sent away to boarding school. My father taught himself to read and write English and was determined I have a proper education. The idea of leaving Gwalia, and Beria, filled me with a mixture of fear and excitement. It was such a momentous prospect I thought of little else for most of 1959. When the boarding school proved slow in responding to the application, my father told me to send an urgently worded telegram. The mother of my school friend, Peter Walton, was most understanding, and after she stopped me from crying she wrote it out for me.

At the post office some days later, Neil Glossop handed Nita a large manila envelope. When I saw the return name and address I realised it was the tangible proof I was going away to boarding school. Nita wasn't about to indulge me, taking advantage of the situation. 'Just wait,' she said dismissively. 'I'll open it when I'm ready.' By chance we met Beria at Mazza's shop. I complained and Beria chipped her. 'Don't be so bloody selfish. He's the one who's going away, not you. Now open it and let him have a look at it.'

Nita's churlishness couldn't spoil the moment. Later that evening, my father and I sat at the kitchen table, and he watched proudly as I pored over the clothing and book lists and studied the black and white photographs of the dormitories and laboratories, and of the two-storey brick boarding houses surrounded by rose gardens and playing fields.

I said goodbye to the fifty primary school kids on 18 December 1959. At the final midday assembly in the shade of the tamarisk trees, the headmaster, Mr Reilly, and his assistant, Sylvia Conlon, made particular mention of me and my music. I don't know why I cried. Maybe I knew I was seeing some of them for the last time. Of the six of us in grade 7, three went away to school. Beria was proud. 'He's going away to college,' she told everyone. The others stayed on at primary school for a year of supervised correspondence – a formality before being old enough to leave school and join the workforce.

The four weeks of Christmas holiday were a preparation, and my excitement grew the more I read the prospectus and studied the photographs. After months of Jean's food I was healthy. I lay in bed at night consumed with anticipation, remembering Nita going to boarding school, and the sobbing and elation which surrounded her leaving and arriving each term. Our relationship was a prickly one, soured perhaps by Beria's strictness, but I loved my big sister.

The holidays were different from other years. The average temperature was 103 degrees but I had no interest in going to the pool, instead spending my days at the house with Beria, and sitting in the canvas wading pool on the front verandah with my sister Joan. There were no cherries on Christmas Day. Beria gave me a box of muscatels and almonds, and a pair of green reversible bathers. My father and I had Christmas lunch with Lewie and Jean – roast chicken and trifle. They gave me a beach towel which I saved for boarding school.

The time dragged, and then suddenly it was tomorrow.

It dawned clear on the morning of my departure and I was awake early. Beria and Nita packed my case several days earlier and everything was in readiness. I had been living with Nita and Frank for the best part of the year. Soon after eight o'clock my father, Lewie, Jean and Trevor arrived. Nita had a young baby and didn't come with us to the station, but Beria and Joan walked there and arrived at the same time we did. My father and I had a carriage to ourselves. I had butterflies in my stomach as I sat waiting for the steam train to depart. Saying goodbye to Beria was always difficult, but somehow, this time, it was easier.

My father was fifty-one years old, and he chatted constantly. He even showed me the wad of money he was carrying in his wallet. To pay for me to go to school he had sold his only asset, a house, to Lewie, who resisted paying for the property until the final days. He and Jean were determined the money should be used for my education.

Nine o'clock ticked over. The stationmaster, Mervyn Gee, a short, officious character, blew his whistle and it was time. We stood together at the window and waved as the train pulled out of the station, gathering momentum and a full head of steam. We moved down the track, passing the tennis courts at the back of the State Hotel, the Australian Workers' Hall which doubled as the picture theatre, the Catholic church, the empty Co-Op and the adjoining butcher shop. Behind us was the football oval, and then Beria and Steve's house, where I could see her chooks out on the flat, scratching around in their sand bath. At the sweep in the track we passed over the wood-line bridge where my father worked on the train, through what remained of the old block where Mrs Bailey lived, and past the slimes. I could hear Beria's voice, calling to me as I went out the front gate at Grinning Joe's house. It was always the same: 'You stay away from the slimes, and be home before dark.'

Finally we came to the far edge of the Sons of Gwalia, with its tall black chimney stack belching into the clear blue sky. In a matter of seconds the rise of the South Gwalia hill came between us, and, in an instant, the mine and the town disappeared from sight. My father and I settled back into our seats as Gwalia was left behind. I was nervous and filled with anticipation. I couldn't wait for boarding school. My father was relaxed and happy. Eight years previously, almost to the day, he had taken the same journey with Nita.

I was almost thirteen, and on the brink of starting a new life. Gwalia was home, and I had no clue as we snaked our way through the familiar scrub and mulga, stopping at the towns and sidings, that Friday, 30 January 1960, was to be the single most important day of my entire life. No other date since my birth would have such an impact. It was 115 degrees in Gwalia that day; the same as the day I was born.

ACKNOWLEDGEMENTS

Sometimes when I look back to my childhood, it seems like another life, in another land. I think, often, about the little white-haired boy I left behind in Gwalia. If he and I were to meet again, I feel certain I would recognise him, but I doubt he would recognise me.

My mother, Beria, died at our house in Melbourne, May 2007. She was ninety-six and furious she was not going to be 100. After a visit to her doctor, Bruce Ingram, she said, 'You took me to see Bruce with a hernia, and I came home with cancer.' Three months later, as she said she would, she 'flew away'. She was a woman of indubitable courage, and we talked and laughed often about our days in Gwalia. There was never any doubt about the title for my story. Still, I can hear her voice – 'And be home before dark' – the last thing she called as I went out through the front gate of Grinning Joe's house.

And Be Home Before Dark has been seven years in the writing, during which time Beria and I reminded, and surprised, each other with stories and incidents. Curiously, given the degree of awfulness for her, she thought Gwalia was the best place she ever lived, and hankered for a return to 'the good old days'.

Gwalia was a time and a place the likes of which Australia will never know again. To the best of my knowledge, and delight, this is the first childhood autobiography from the goldfields of Western Australia. However, it does not happen by osmosis, but with the help and support of many people.

It was Sandra Harris, the former ABC and BBC radio and television announcer and presenter, who introduced me to the CEO of Hardie Grant books, Sandy Grant. He saw me on stage in the play I wrote, 'Now You Can Eat Father Christmas', in which I played my mother and thirty other characters, and he read my original manuscript – a combination of stories and personal ramblings – and recognised a spark of potential.

I worked first with editor Rod Morrison, who helped me find the voice of the little boy. He called me one morning to talk about the shape and time frame of the manuscript. It was obvious he was dancing around my sensibilities. 'Are you saying it gets boring after I leave Gwalia and go away to boarding school, so we should cut that section?' I asked. He was taken aback, paused for a moment, and said, tentatively, 'Well, yes.' And he was right.

Nene King, the former editor-in-chief of the *Women's Weekly* and *Woman's Day*, read the first draft for me. I was very much relieved when she called and said, 'I can taste the red dust.'

After fifty years I was revisiting my childhood. The book has reunited me with so many people from those days. Some remembered me – some did not. All helped to blow new life into the dying embers of the fire: Lucy Tognali Detez, Clara Paravicini Nasuti, Valma Giovanazzi Sanfead, Mary Bendotti Sullivan, Lena Beccaria Prince, Noreen Tagliaferri, Beryl Demasson, Alma Mazza, Ann Garbellini, Louisa Fanetti, Bob Tagliaferri, Peter Scolari, Bernice Quarti and her daughters, Jan and Kay, Eric Chamberlain, Max Gistinger, Tom Clews, Robert 'Mr Bob' Primrose, Bob 'Tauber' Mazza, entertainment reporter Peter Ford, writer and television producer Jane Kennedy, and especially Eric Omodei, my father's closest friend.

Magistrate Pat O'Shane, for her considered assessment.

Actor and close friend Jennifer West, whose encouragement never wavered.

My sister, Joan Hoskin, and nephew, Trevor Roccheccioli.

Ed McGuire and Sam Newman.

And my darling Aunt Edith.

My editor, Carl Harrison-Ford, was a godsend. After being overwhelmed by the magnitude of the job, he sent me an edited version which made my heart sing and fired me with a new enthusiasm. We grew up on either side of the continent, but shared a common path.

With a story so personal, there is an inherent reluctance to relinquish power. From the outset, I considered this to be a story from a boy's perspective; however, I was wrong. The determination and willingness of senior editor Emma Schwarcz was inspiring. For one so young and, more importantly, so far removed from my experiences in the goldfields, she understood exactly the story of this little boy. In the end, I considered myself fortunate to have Emma working with me. She didn't hesitate to share her thoughts – though sometimes cautiously – and bravely pointed to the parts she considered less interesting, or repetitive.

One year after Beria's death, and eighty-two years after my father arrived in Fremantle, I have written my story. From the bottom of my heart, from the length of Beria's life, and from the depth of our combined experiences, I thank you.